TECHNICAL GRAPHICS

JOHN BEDFORD AND COLIN PYNE

BOOK ONE

John Murray

© John Bedford and Colin Pyne 1985

First published 1985
by John Murray (Publishers) Ltd
50 Albemarle Street, London W1X 4BD

All rights reserved
Unauthorised duplication
contravenes applicable laws

Typeset and printed in Great Britain
at The Pitman Press, Bath

British Library Cataloguing in Publication Data
Bedford, John R.
  Technical graphics.
  Bk. 1
  1. Engineering drawings
  I. Title   II. Pyne, C. A. W.
  604.2'4   T353

ISBN 0-7195-4097-6

Contents

Preface iv

1 Drawing Instruments and Materials 1

Drawing equipment, colour, stencils, set squares, setting out drawings, set square designs.

2 Introducing Graphics 12

Pictograms to warn, inform, direct, suggest motion and other practical applications. Presentation using colour, design and grid work.

3 Lines, Arcs and Angles 18

Bisectors, perpendiculars, parallels, angles and line division. Centre-lines applied to pictograms and worked examples.

4 Triangular Structures 26

Examples in design, properties of triangles.

5 Quadrilaterals and Polygons 35

Methods for construction. Uses in structures, objects and patterns.

6 Circles in Design 45

Properties and uses of circles, tangents, and arcs with graphic and geometric examples.

7 Inscribed and Circumscribed Figures 55

Practical examples in graphic design.

8 The Ellipse 61

Properties and techniques for construction. Logograms based on the circle and the ellipse.

9 Loci 68

Understanding loci. Problems applied to graphic motion.

10 Scale Drawing 74

Constructing scales for enlarging and reducing, determination of heights, introduction to building drawing—scales and presentation.

11 Areas 79

Understanding areas, graphic determination of areas.

12 Enlargement and Reduction 86

Methods of enlarging and reducing areas, Pythagorus explained, solving problems by graphic means.

Index 91

Preface

Technical Graphics presents in two books a continuous course on the subject area of drawing for the environment currently described as graphic communication. By gradual development it progresses from basic requirements to the levels required by students taking first examinations.

In this first book we have set out to cover, in a clear and simple way, the basic ideas and techniques needed to form a firm foundation on which to develop modern methods of communicating information. Allied to this we have tried to promote an awareness of problems, in both design and drawing techniques, and of the need to develop sound and logical methods for solving these and presenting the solution.

Basic draughting skills are essential for students wishing to explore the many facets of graphic communication. For this reason the essential plane geometry and drawing techniques are explored in some detail. Orthographic and isometric drawings together with photographs of components made from a variety of materials are given in both books to provide a stimulus for students to draw accurately and well. Planometric, perspective and exploded drawings are dealt with in some detail and illustrated by drawings and photographs of household items in everyday use. Many of these are used to provide drawing practice and revision exercises. Design and the imaginative use of colour, shading and texturing are detailed. The use of mechanical aids such as stencils, templates and dry transfer materials is illustrated and encouraged but only after appropriate skills without aids have been achieved. Advertising techniques and the representation of structures, charts, mechanisms and buildings all receive textual coverage in this book in preparation for the more advanced work in book two.

It is our hope that students following this course of study will not only achieve technical success but also go on to appreciate the essential creative elements of this vital subject area.

JRB & CAWP

1 Drawing Instruments and Materials

The Tee Square

The tee square lives on the left-hand side of the drawing board as shown in Fig. 1:1.

The stock must always be held firmly against the edge of the board. Using the little finger and thumb as shown gives accurate control in small movements of the blade. The tips of the first two fingers act as pivots.

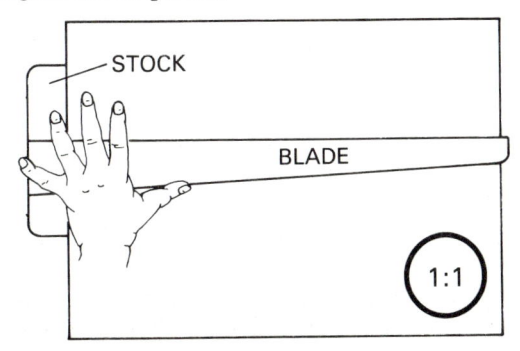

Set Squares

The set squares, both 30°/60° and 45°, may be used in either of the positions shown in Fig. 1:2, depending on whether you are right-handed or left-handed.

The set square bevel must always be on the top as shown in Fig. 1:3.

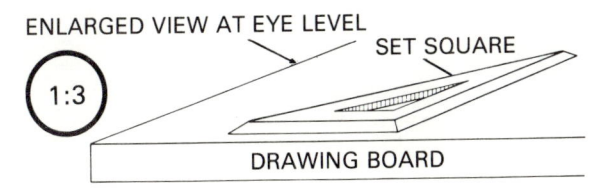

Right-handed students will find this the best position for the set square.

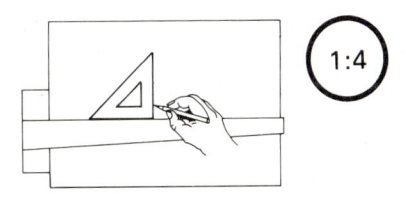

Left-handed students will find this the best position.

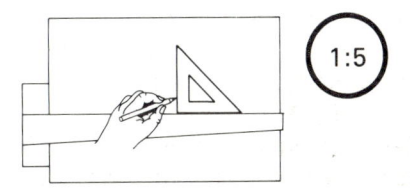

The pencil must always sit tightly in the bottom corner.

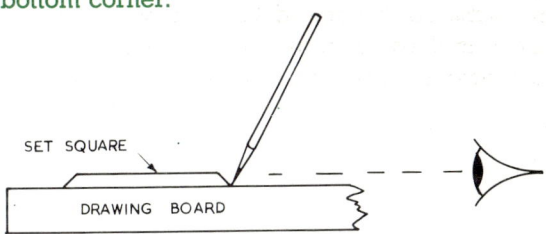

Pencils

A pencil is graded according to the hardness of its lead, from 7H (very hard) to 7B (very soft). As yet there is no definition of each degree of hardness; this may well vary slightly with different manufacturers. Therefore, once you have found pencils which suit your style it is as well to continue using that make. Uses of the most popular grades are given below:

Draughting	Notes	Art Work
4H 3H 2H	H HB B	2B 3B 4B

Some manufacturers produce an F grade, midway in hardness between H and HB.

1

Pencil Points

All pencil lines should be thin and clear. To obtain these the pencil point must be kept sharp.

Most people prefer the conical point (Fig. 1:6). Others prefer the chisel point (Fig. 1:7), especially for straight line work, as it remains sharp longer than the conical point.

A short stubby point makes accurate drawing difficult, so either use a pencil sharpener that produces a long tapering point or trim the wood with a knife. Finish shaping the lead on a smooth file or a piece of fine glasspaper. Hold the file stationary in your left hand, drawing the pencil towards you and at the same time revolving it against the direction of the downwards movement. The chisel point is produced by rubbing the lead forwards and backwards along the file.

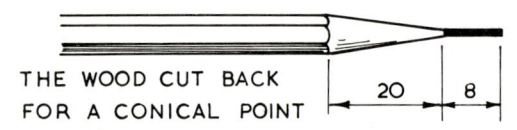

CONICAL POINT

CHISEL POINT

THE WOOD CUT BACK FOR A CONICAL POINT — 20 | 8

WOOD REMOVED FOR A CHISEL POINT

Ink Pens

These are used for final tracings of original pencil drawings. They can also be used by skilled draughtsmen to produce original drawings direct on to the tracing film. Most draughtsmen use ink on a plastic drawing film as this method tends to produce far better photocopies.

Parallel Motion Device

Many schools now use the parallel motion drawing board (shown right). This allows the straight edge to travel up and down the board maintaining a true horizontal edge from which the set squares may be used.

All horizontal lines are then drawn from the straight edge, vertical and angled lines being drawn from the set squares. These instruments are usually made from transparent plastic so that the whole of the drawing can be seen.

Universal Draughting Machine

This machine has sprung arms that allow the straight edges to move over the extent of the board. The straight edges can be locked at any angle with the magnitude of the angle being read off a calibrated scale on the central locking mechanism. Set squares would not be needed when using this equipment.

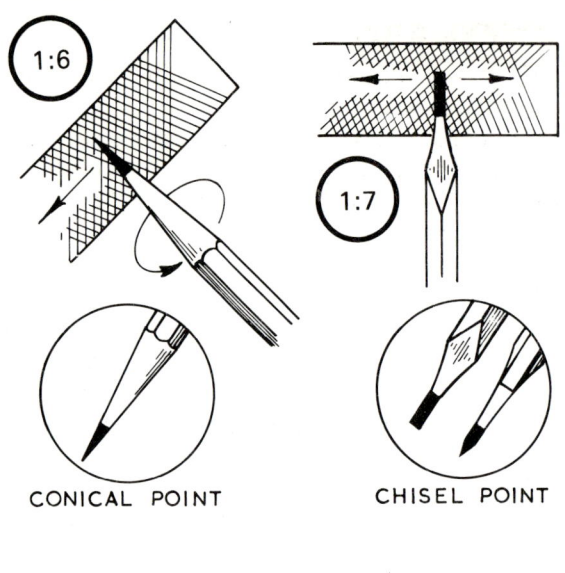

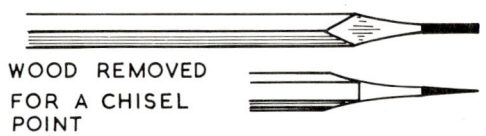

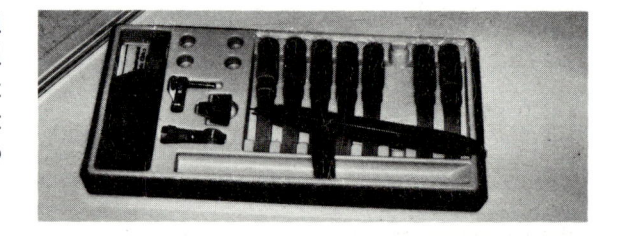

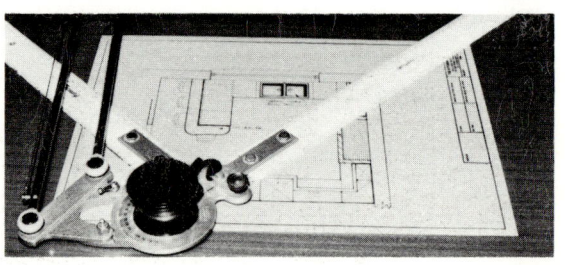

OTHER AIDS

Many other aids are required by the draughtsman to reduce the drawing time and to improve on the appearance of drawings, especially when drawing in ink. Common aids include the following:

Adjustable set square   These solve the problem of manoeuvring two set squares to obtain the correct angle.

Radius and circle templates   These are particularly useful when small circles or part circles have to be drawn. The centres provided on the templates allow the correct position to be easily found by placing a compass point through the centre. They are often made in a transparent plastic sheet material; some may be coloured.

Ellipse templates   Although it is necessary to know how to construct such a shape, constant repetition is avoided with use of the templates now available, including the ellipse on axes set at various angles.

French curves   These are made in transparent plastic and in a variety of colours, shapes and sizes. Normally, a set of three would ease the drawing of most complex curves and enable the drawing of smooth, sharp outlines.

Flexi-curve   The flexi-curve (not shown) is a hard, rubber/plastic material with a flexible central core that allows its length to be bent to any desired curve or shape whilst remaining flat on the paper so that its outline may be traced. Once used, it may then be changed or left for further use.

Designer templates   The photograph shows a building template being used to draw the position of a chair at a table (below right); also on this template are accepted outlines and details of other fittings such as cookers, hobs and sinks.

Templates are available covering all types of specialist trades including engineering, electrical circuitry, plumbing and advertising.

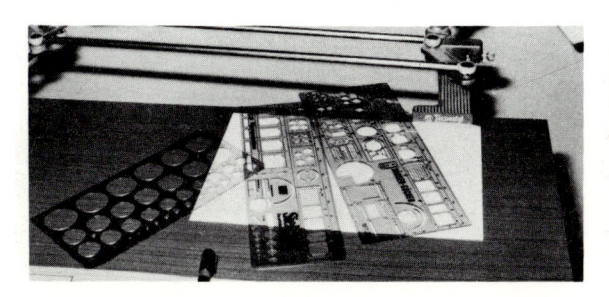

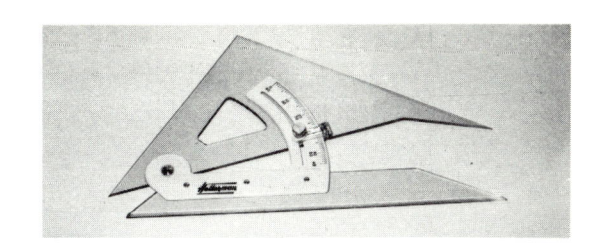

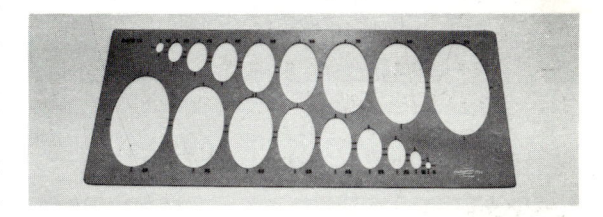

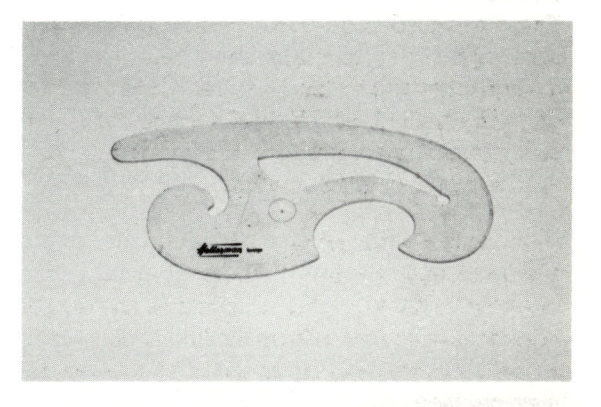

COLOUR WASH

Colour wash, inks, crayon and felt-tip watercolour pens are all used to improve the appearance and clarity of modern communication drawings whether they be building, engineering, electrical or any other type that comes under the general heading of Technical Graphics.

In all cases it is wise to consider well whether the drawing needs colour at all in order to improve it, as the misuse of colour might make the drawing confusing:

1 Use colour only where it will enhance the drawing.
2 Too much colour will distract and confuse the drawing, so use with care and thought.
3 Do not obscure lines by having any colours that are too intense.
4 Various materials lend themselves to a particular colour, e.g. metal (blue), wood (brown), brick (pale red), slate roof (grey). Choose colours carefully to indicate material used.
5 **When using cartridge,** use all colours thinned out as a colour wash:
   (a) Wet the paper with clean water.
   (b) Apply immediately a small amount of colour (with a size of brush suitable for the area to be coloured), and spread evenly over the area. **Do not over-wet the colouring area.**
6 **On tracing paper,** use colour inks. Thin out the colour first, then apply lightly and evenly.

PAPER

Placing the Paper

Set the paper near to the top of the left-hand edge of the drawing board. Make sure that its bottom edge is parallel with the tee square when this is firmly held against the edge of the board (Fig. 1:8). Fasten the paper in place using draughtsman's clips or adhesive tape. (Drawing pins spoil the board's surface.)

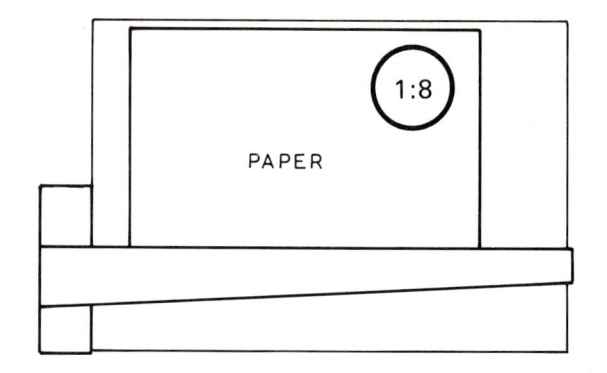

Paper Weight

Paper used in technical drawing and draughting varies, but the most popular in school use seems to be the medium weight cartridge drawing paper: A3 size with a weight of 118 g/m^2.

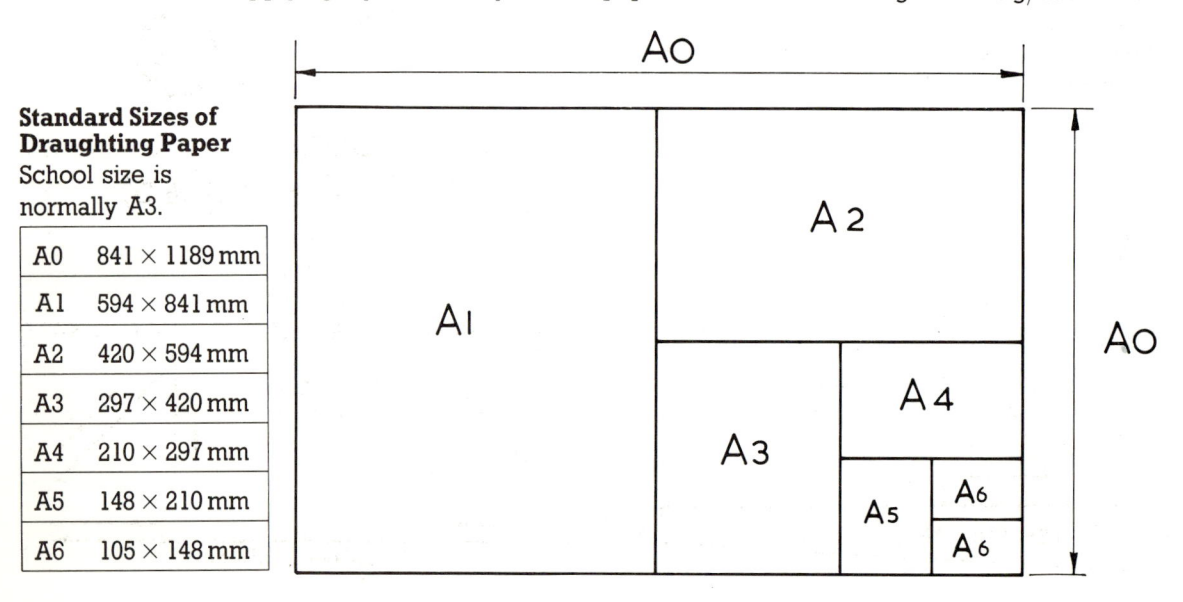

Standard Sizes of Draughting Paper
School size is normally A3.

A0	841 × 1189 mm
A1	594 × 841 mm
A2	420 × 594 mm
A3	297 × 420 mm
A4	210 × 297 mm
A5	148 × 210 mm
A6	105 × 148 mm

MEASURING

Before you can draw a construction line you must establish its position by measuring from the edge of the paper and marking in a dot or line. Measuring must always be done accurately. This is made easier by using a draughtsman's rule, as it has very thin edges that bring the graduations right down to touch the paper.

The ordinary school ruler has a much thicker edge and can easily lead to errors (Fig. 1:9). One way of overcoming this is to tilt the ruler and, holding the pencil vertical, slide its point down the appropriate graduation line on the ruler to mark in an accurately positioned dot on the paper. It will help towards accuracy if you sight downwards from above the pencil. Looking from the side of the pencil always causes errors.

A point or dot has an exact position but in theory it has no magnitude (size).

Golden Rules for Accuracy

Work always in this sequence:
1 Measure off the required distance carefully.
2 Mark in a tiny clear dot or a short thin line (Fig. 1:9).
3 Place your pencil point in the centre of the dot or line (Fig. 1:10).
4 Move up the tee square or the set square to just touch the pencil (Fig. 1:11).
5 Draw the line, moving the pencil in the direction shown below, always 'pulling' and never 'pushing' it (Fig. 1:12).

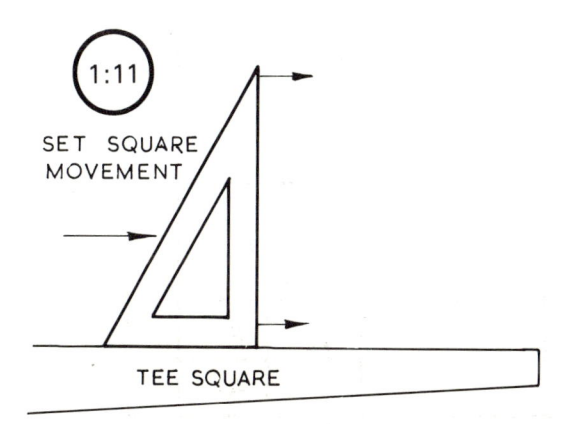

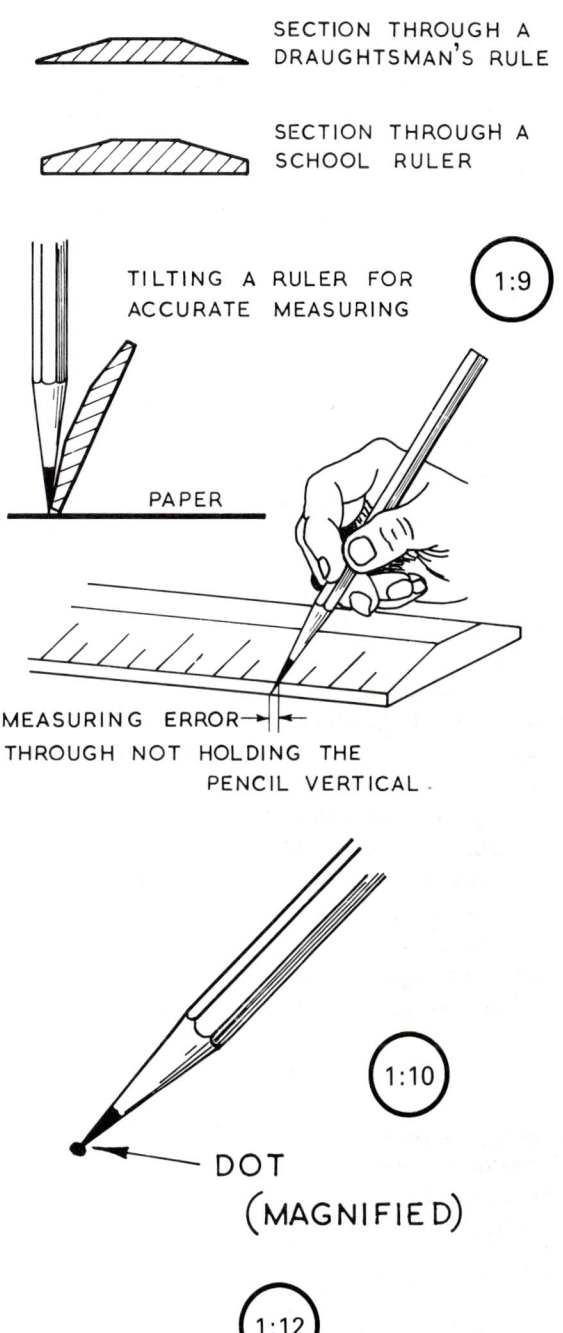

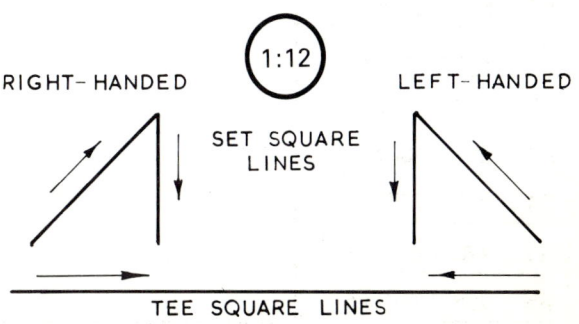

SECTION THROUGH A DRAUGHTSMAN'S RULE

SECTION THROUGH A SCHOOL RULER

TILTING A RULER FOR ACCURATE MEASURING 1:9

PAPER

MEASURING ERROR THROUGH NOT HOLDING THE PENCIL VERTICAL

1:10

DOT (MAGNIFIED)

1:11
SET SQUARE MOVEMENT
TEE SQUARE

1:12
RIGHT-HANDED   LEFT-HANDED
SET SQUARE LINES
TEE SQUARE LINES

5

PRESENTATION

Drawing the Border

1 Measure down the left-hand edge of the paper a distance of 10 mm and mark a dot (Fig. 1:13A).
2 Slide the tee square up to touch the dot and draw a line from it 10 mm in from each side of the paper (Fig. 1:13B).

You need only one dot as the tee square ensures that your line is parallel with the top edge of your paper.

3 Repeat the measurement, dot and line, 10 mm up from the bottom edge of the paper.
4 Mark a dot 10 mm in from the left-hand edge of the paper and slide the set square across to just touch it.
  Draw a vertical line to touch the horizontal line at the dot (Fig. 1:14). You will need to move the set square up or down to complete the line from the top to the bottom of your paper.
5 Repeat this on the right-hand side. You will now have a 10 mm margin drawn round your paper ready to act as a frame for your drawing.

Technical drawings are always framed within a border.

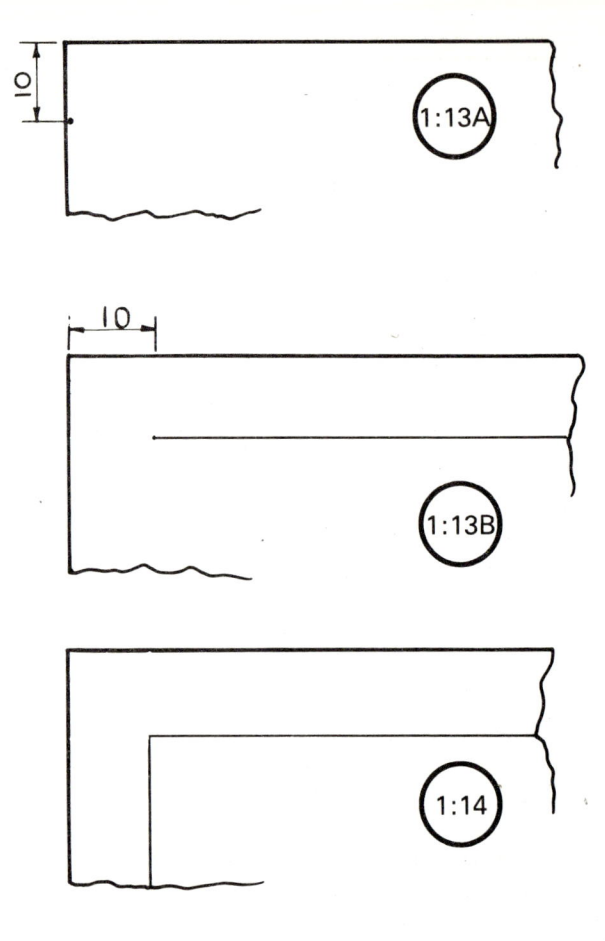

Setting Out the Title Block

There are many styles of title blocks in general use. The one shown in Fig. 1:15 is about the most widely acceptable for school use.

1 Mark a dot 15 mm above the bottom margin and draw a line from margin to margin thus enclosing the block space.
2 Similarly, mark in two dots 5 mm apart within this space and draw feint lines through them thus dividing the space into three equal strips.
3 All printing in the title block is done between the two feint lines and touching both of them.

Figure 1:16 shows an alternative system of title block commonly used on simple drawings in industry.

Figure 1:17 shows a more complicated style of title block used when the drawing is of an assembly which contains a number of parts.

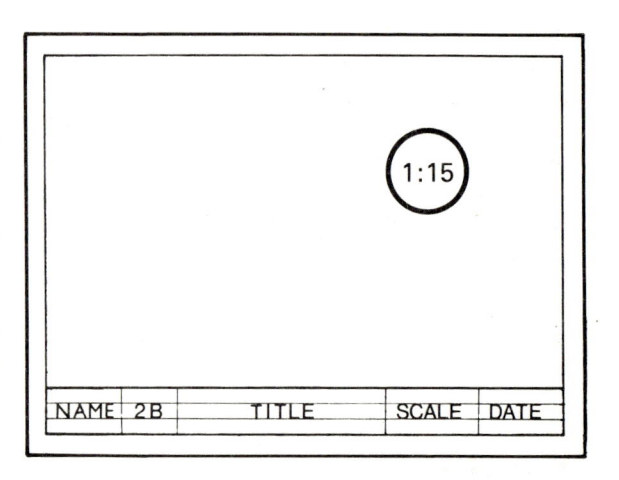

All three methods of title block layout shown are correct, as long as the information is clear and necessary.

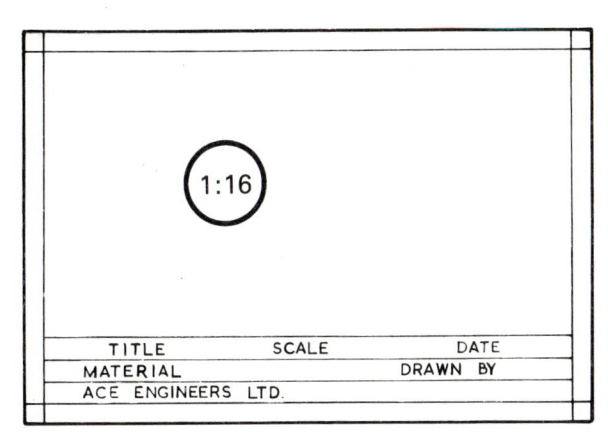

Lettering

Information on drawings is always given in **printed block capitals** as shown in *British Standards Publication BS 308.*

Good drawings are often spoilt by poor printing, so practise a good style.

Many different styles of letters and numerals have become accepted in modern times, the only firm rule being that the lettering is **plain, clear** and **easy to read**. The most commonly used modern style is that shown opposite. Note how the latters A C D G H K M N O Q W just about fill a square space (O and Q being made up from circles); the remainder (excepting I) fill from a half to two-thirds of a square. To give uniformity, spaces between words should be similar and about equal to the height of the lettering, and the distance between individual letters needs to be adjusted to give the appearance of uniformity. For example, when T follows L as in HIL T this creates too large a space. You should close up letters like these to preserve the balance.

Good lettering demands perfect parallels, and uniformity in height and weight of lines.

ABCDEFG
HIJKLMN
OPQRSTU
VWXYZ

1234567
890

Dry Transfers

Dry transfers are available as sheets containing letters or very complicated shapes ready to be transferred to the surface of the various suitable materials. They are easy to apply (after some practice) and effective, but expensive.

Letter Templates

Letter templates may be obtained in a variety of sizes and styles of lettering. They are mainly intended for use with ink draughting pens but others are available for use with black or colour pencils.

LINES

Draughtsmen make many different types of lines but for the moment we need to practise only three of them.

Construction Lines

These form the basis upon which we build up rectangular drawings; they must be drawn thin and feint but clear (Fig. 1:18).

Use no pressure on the pencil for construction lines; trail it by its own weight across the paper.

Centre-lines

These form the skeleton around which we develop the outlines of symmetrical or circular objects. They are a special type of construction line and should also be drawn feint (Fig. 1:19).

Centre-lines are never rubbed out. Note especially how centre-lines form a cross at the centre of a circle. Note also the conventional sign for 'centre-line' ℄.

Outlines

These should always be crisp and clear and darker than the construction lines (Fig. 1:20). They should all be of exactly the same darkness and—under a magnifying glass—of exactly the same width. Take special care to make the lines touch at all the corners, neither stopping short to leave a gap, nor going too far to show a projecting 'whisker'.

When you draw rectangular objects such as doors, gates and buildings, it is easier to start from a straight base-line or edge; but when you draw circular objects such as wheels or a clock face, you must always start with centre-lines. This is not only easier, it helps to make the drawing accurate.

Lines are named in three ways according to their positions as shown in Fig. 1:21.

A straight line is the shortest distance between two points (it has no thickness, only length).

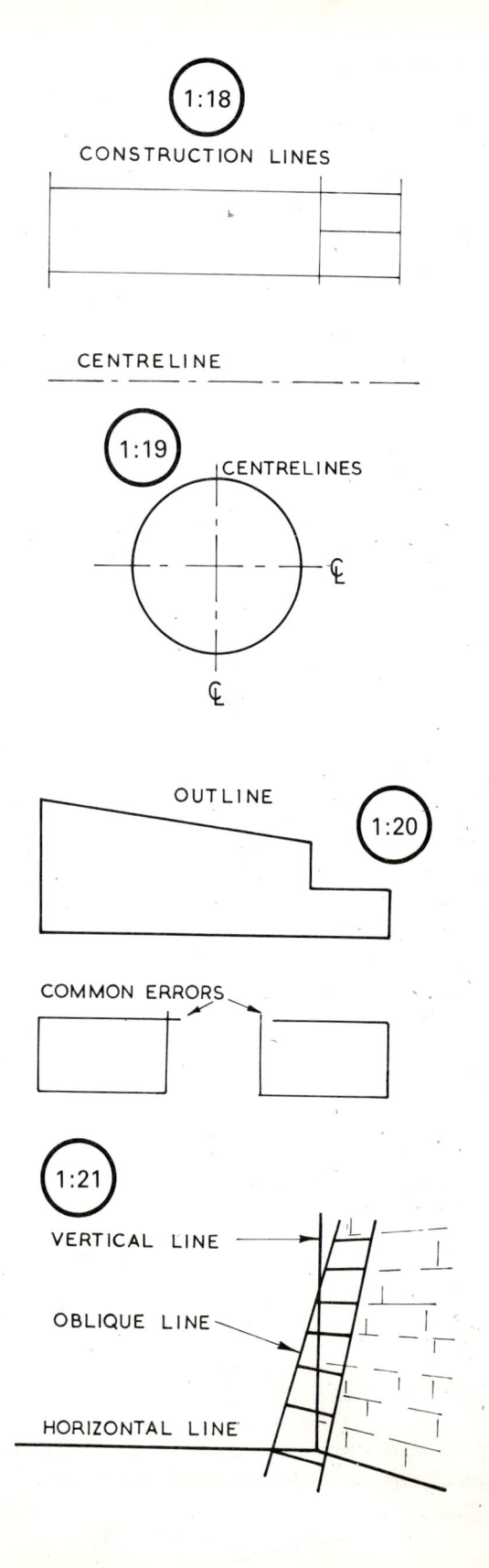

QUESTIONS

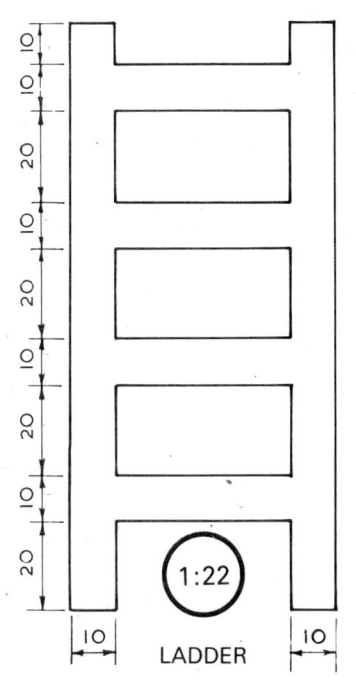

Q1 Copy the outline of a short ladder shown in Fig. 1:22.

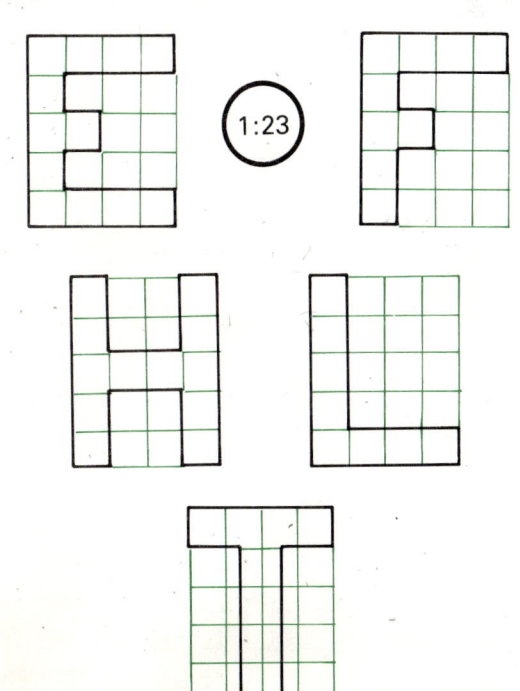

Q2 Copy the letters in Fig. 1:23, black lines only. The green guide lines represent 10 mm squares.

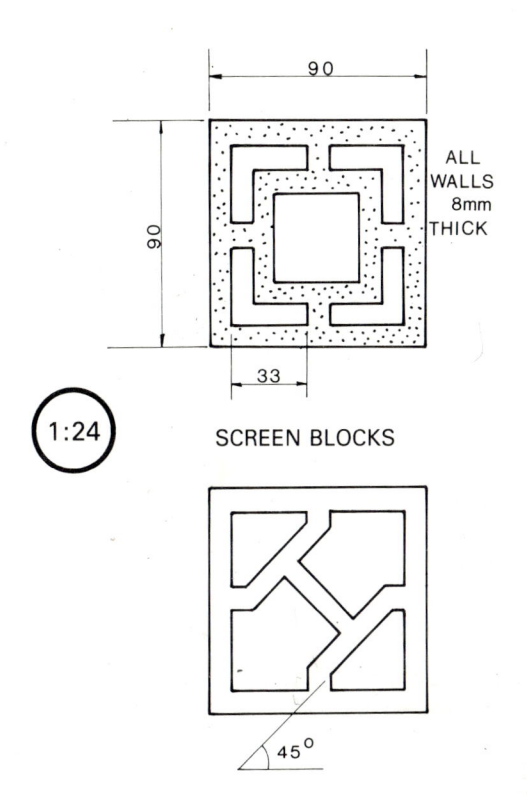

Q3 Copy the textured screen block from the dimensions given in Fig. 1:24, then design and colour another for a garden wall.

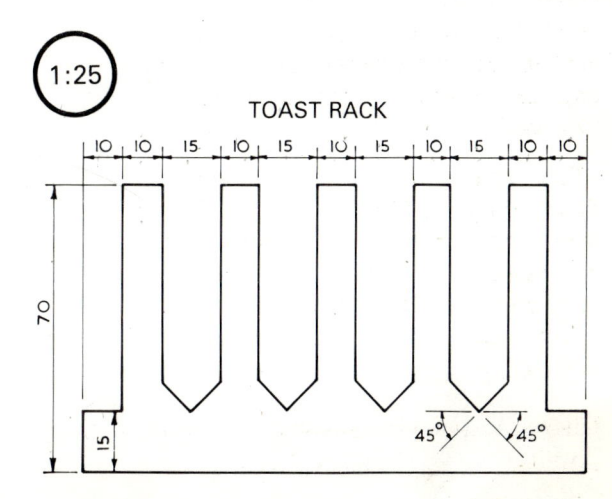

Q4 Make a full size drawing of the toast rack (Fig. 1:25).

TABLE LAMP

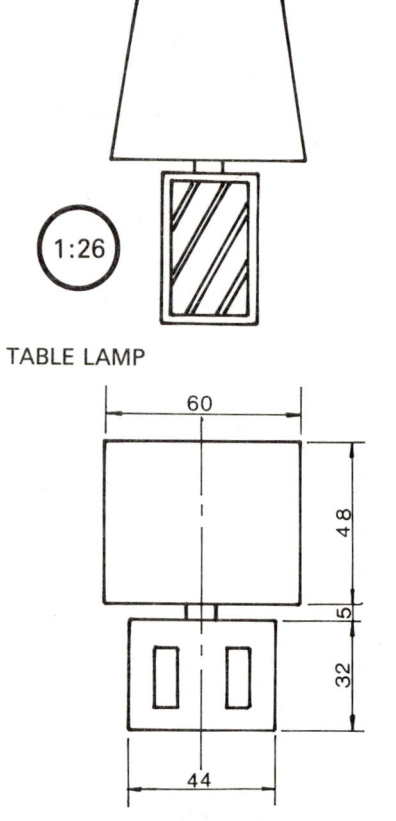

Q5 Draw a table lamp using the diagrams and dimensions in Fig. 1:26 as a guide. Place your own design on its base and use colour (sparingly) to highlight its shapes.

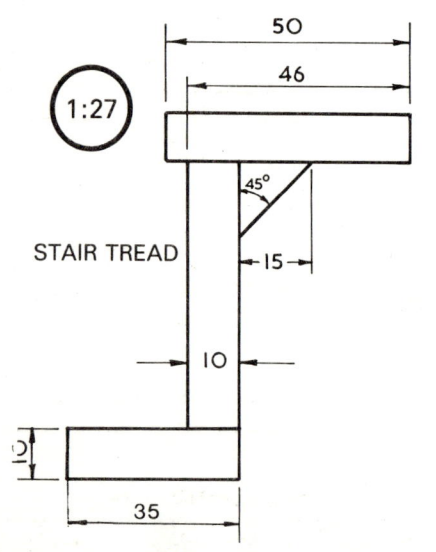

STAIR TREAD

Q6 Figure 1:27 shows a section through a stair tread. Copy the given view.

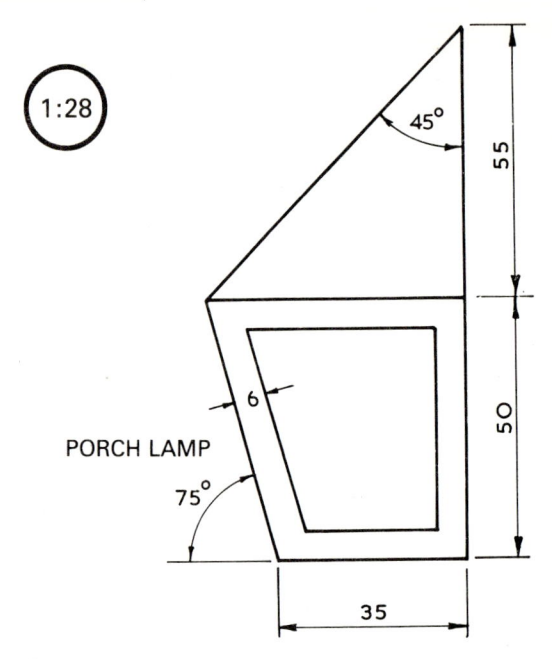

PORCH LAMP

Q7 Copy the end view of the porch lamp shown in Fig. 1:28,, obtaining the 75° angle as shown below.

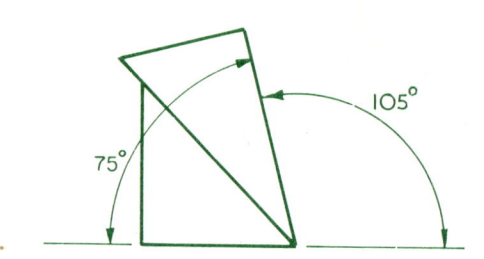

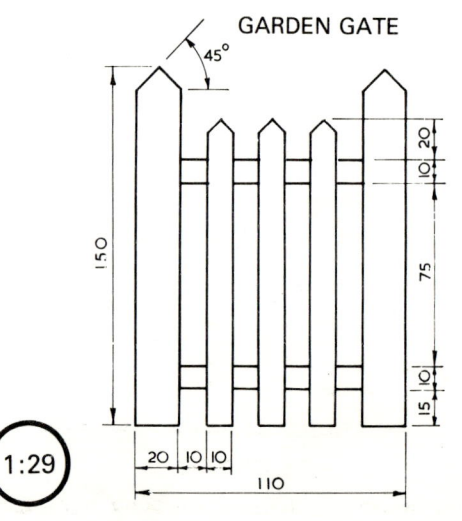

GARDEN GATE

Q8 Copy the elevation of a garden gate (Fig. 1:29).

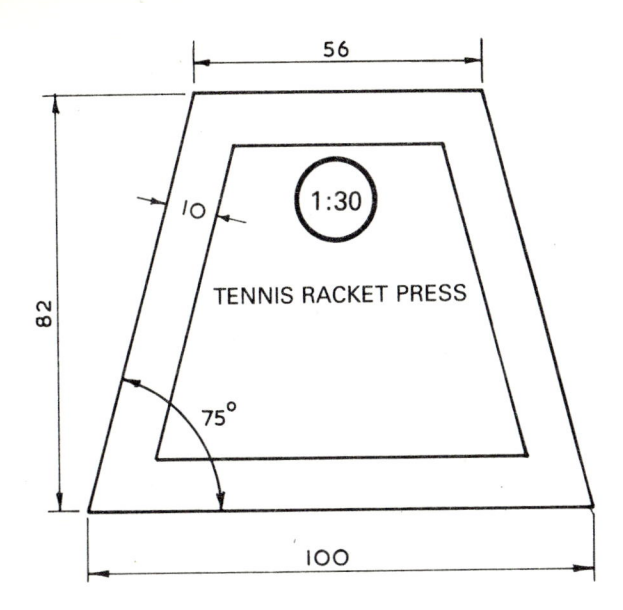

Q9 Draw the frame of the tennis racket press as shown in Fig. 1:30.

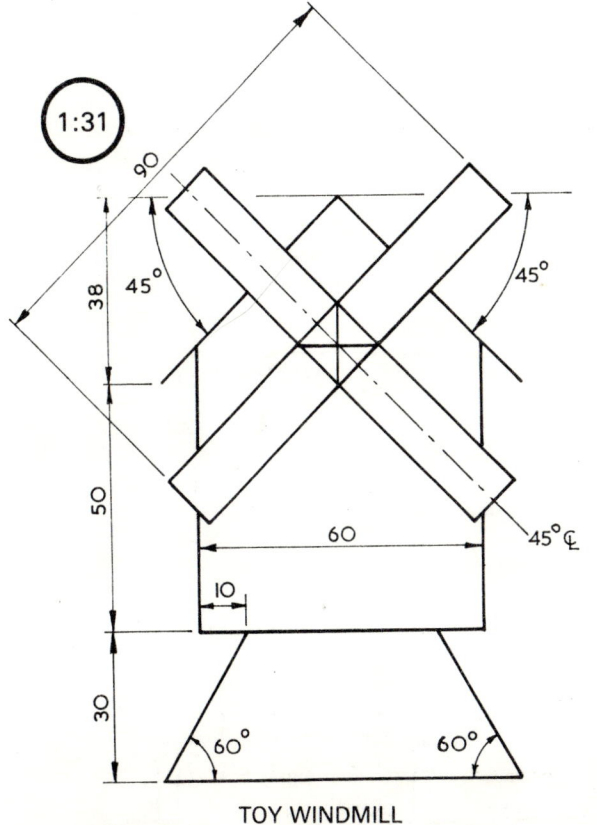

Q10 Copy the elevation of a toy windmill shown in Fig. 1:31.

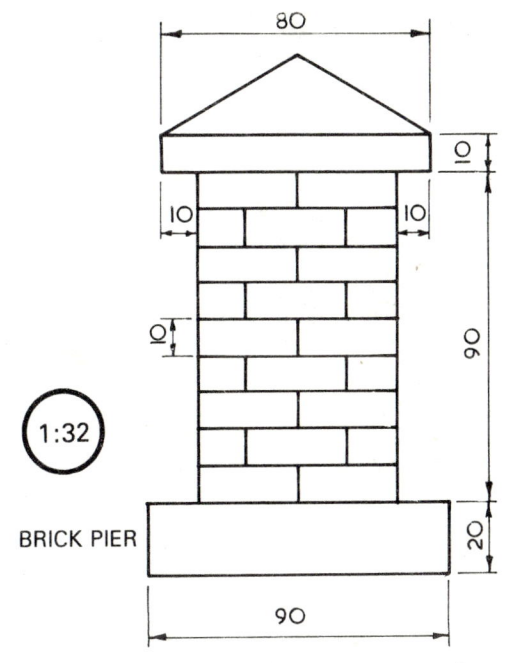

Q11 Make a drawing of the brick pier as shown in Fig. 1:32.

Q12 Copy the front view of a dormer window (Fig. 1:33). Take measurements directly from the drawing and make your drawing three times this size.

2 Introducing Graphics

Graphics is a method of transmitting information visually. Lines and curves, patterns and shapes can all be given a specific meaning which is understood by everyone who sees them.

Graphic communication has been used for thousands of years. Ancient civilisations such as the Egyptians used simple pictures to record and pass on important events and information. These pictures were painted on walls or carved in stone, wood or clay, each picture representing a different thing or idea.

For instance, ☼ could represent the **sun**. It looks quite like the sun, and doesn't look much like anything else. ⛵ could represent a **boat**, again because it looks like a boat.

However, more complicated ideas could also be transmitted in simple pictures. A boat with a billowing sail, for example, ⛵ could also represent the idea **the wind**. It would be very difficult to draw wind, but you can show some of its effects.

The Egyptians and others developed this method of communication so that each picture or shape represented a single **sound**; e.g. ∿ represented an 'n' sound, ◁ a 'q' sound, ⊬ an 's' sound, ᗉ a 't' sound. By combining shapes such as these, the sound of the **spoken** word could be represented in pictures, and a much larger number of ideas could be conveyed.

The printed words that you are now reading are simply a development of these early beginnings. Each word has a specific meaning. It can be **seen** in print or writing, or **heard** in speech. The letters which make up the printed word are just simple shapes which represent sounds in speech.

Graphics involves many other things apart from words, however. Engineering and architectural drawings, perspective and pictorial views, symbols, shapes for emphasis and flow diagrams all convey information that words alone cannot convey. The language of Graphics is therefore the drawn line, used as a totally separate form of communication.

2:1

Sketching

This was the very first method of graphic communication. Inside the caves of southern Europe, pre-historic men sketched pictures of their most important activities such as hunting animals for food. Figure 2:1 is an archaeologist's copy of a 20 000-year-old cave drawing which tells the story of just such a hunt in which the wounded bison turned on the hunter and killed him. Figure 2:2 shows a few of the graphic symbols that were widely used in Europe some 7000 years ago, before writing was invented.

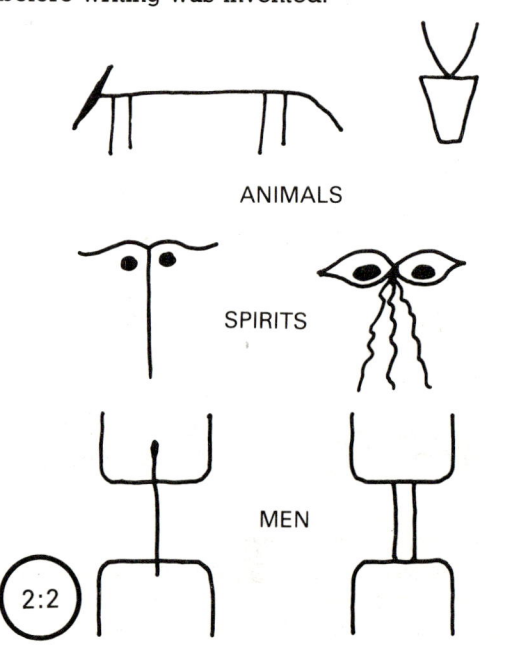

ANIMALS

SPIRITS

MEN

2:2

Graphics should be Clear and Simple

Just as written information can be made difficult to understand by the use of too many long and complicated words, so may graphic communication also be made difficult by cramming in too much information, thus producing complicated drawings. Graphical methods of communication should, by their very nature, be made as simple and as clear as possible and should always fit the following criteria:

1 The drawings and symbols should be clear and easy to read.
2 They should convey the information or idea simply.

Some colours or shapes can add emphasis to the presentation, but the misuse or overuse of colour can cause confusion.

Bad presentation of correct material can produce inaccurate information.

PICTOGRAMS

A pictogram is a picture or symbol which **suggests, warns, informs, directs,** without using words. These have proved to be of immense value to the public because, firstly, they enable people to absorb information quickly, and secondly, they cut out language difficulties for travellers in foreign countries.

There are many uses of pictograms including advertising, instructions, notices, warnings, identification and danger signs, all of which give the public, in one way or another, information that they may, or should, use. For instance, motorway travel is made easier by the service stations that provide various facilities. These are shown on a pictogram well beforehand, thus giving the driver time to decide if the area has the facilities he or she needs. These service area pictograms are in use all over Europe and much of America, as are the symbols illustrating the various services available at camp sites.

Use of Colour

Pictograms are often coloured and have the following uses:

1 Give information of a service available (blue/black/white).
2 Inform the public of safety regulations (blue/white).
3 Indicate industrial hazards and the need for caution (yellow/black).
4 Show where emergency services can be found (green/white).
5 Warn of danger as well as restrictions (red/black on white).

The signs and symbols may be contained in circles, triangles, squares and rectangles. You need to observe this when you draw your own graphics.

(i)   *(ii)*   *(iii)*   *(iv)*

Some examples of pictograms: *(i)* A North American graphic showing how to operate pedestrian crossing lights. *(ii)* A sign directing people to a camping and caravan site. *(iii)* A North American sign denoting a conservation area with forest and lakes. *(iv)* A North American sign instructing cyclists to turn *right,* even though it shows the cyclist going the other way! An example of misleading graphics.

Motion

Symbols and lines which are themselves stationary can be used to give an impression of movement. The well known British Rail symbol (Fig. 2:3) is a good example of this, where one simple clear sign gives the impression of fast, smooth transportation.

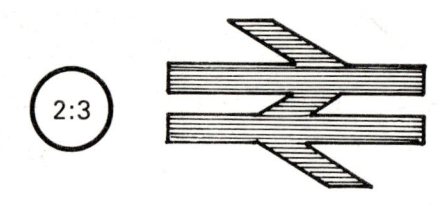

2:3

Figure 2:4 clearly shows the invisible field of forces about a bar magnet and the various directions in which they act.

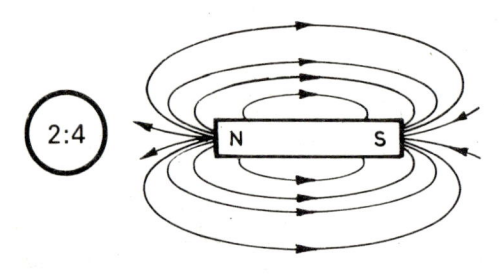

2:4

The arrow in Fig. 2:5 also clearly indicates the direction of rotation in the cylinder.

2:5

Q1 Design and draw symbols that indicate the following: (i) a lighthouse; (ii) a speedboat lake; (iii) a radio beam; (iv) a spin drier; (v) a rocket launch pad.

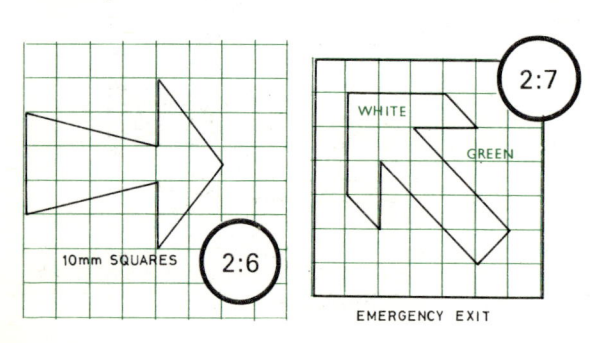

Arrows

One of the most common features of pictograms is the arrow, suggesting a direction of travel. It is also often accompanied by additional information to indicate what may be found there.

Arrows in pictograms take a wide variety of shapes and sizes; below are a few that may be found.

The dimension arrow is, however, the most frequently used and is shown first to indicate how an arrow should be drawn to give a size or measurement.

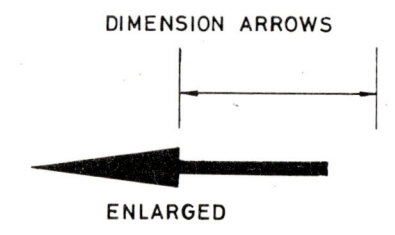

DIMENSION ARROWS

ENLARGED

Q2 Using a grid (10 mm squares) or plain paper, design and draw a pictogram (as Fig. 2:6) indicating direction flow for a particular purpose in a school. State the purpose of your pictogram. Colour should be used *only* where necessary.

Q3 Design and draw an arrow suitable for a road sign that indicates an acute bend in the road.

Q4 Draw Fig. 2:7 on 10 mm squares and colour in the areas as shown.

Q5 (i) Using Fig. 2:8 draw the pictogram for 'Way Out'. (ii) Design a different pictogram for 'Way Out' using Fig. 2:9 as the basis of the drawing. Include dimensions and dimension arrows as previously shown.

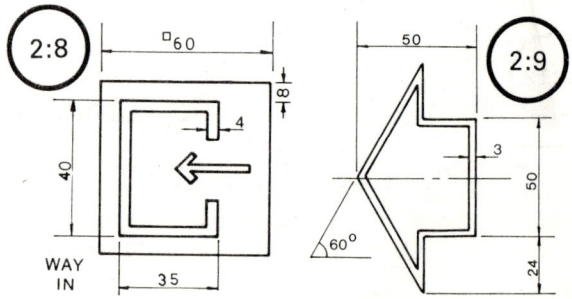

10mm SQUARES   2:6

2:7 WHITE GREEN
EMERGENCY EXIT

2:8 WAY IN

2:9

DRAWING BY THE GRID METHOD

Figure 2:10 shows the symbol of a well known petroleum company with 10 mm spaced lines drawn onto its surface in order for it to be drawn the **same size** onto drawing paper.

The lines on your drawing paper **must** be drawn very lightly so that your final drawing stands out clearly. This method can be used to draw a vast selection of objects so long as each square in turn has been located and the information found there copied into the square on your paper.

Q6 Use this method to copy Fig. 2:10 or a picture of your own choice.

Grid Enlargement

Original drawings may be enlarged or reduced by using the grid method. Examples may be readily seen in kits for model cars, space toys and aircraft. In all cases a grid is drawn on the original drawing as in Fig. 2:11 where a 10 mm grid is used. Drawing A is a traced original and drawing B is the result of using 20 mm squares to draw the same object.

2:10   10 mm squares

2:11

Figure 2:12 applies these techniques to a more complex drawing and clearly shows how the information from the 10 mm grid is transferred to each square in the 20 mm grid.

Q7 Using the example shown (Fig. 2:12), increase the whole front of the car, including the wheel, in 20 mm squares.

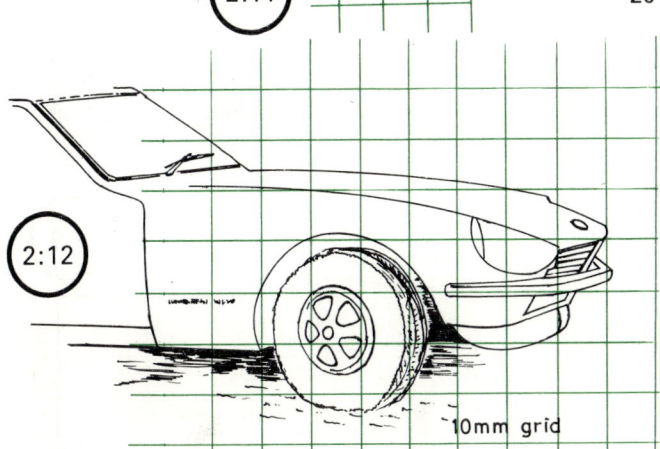

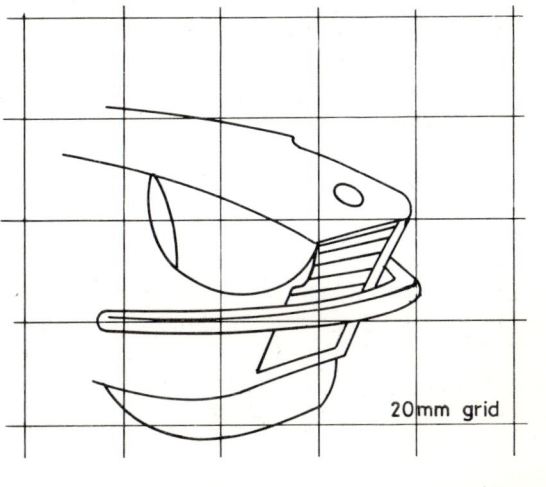

2:12   10 mm grid   20 mm grid

15

FURTHER QUESTIONS

Q8 Use the 'Escalator Service' pictogram in Fig. 2:13 as the basis for your own pictogram showing stairs to be used in the 'up' direction only.

Q9 Draw the 'Danger' sign (Fig. 2:14) and the 'Hazard' sign (Fig. 2:15). Refer to page 13 for the appropriate colour codes and colour your pictograms. The surrounds for these signs should not be less than 100 mm square. Choose the other dimensions yourself.

Q10 A large sports complex has facilities for almost every athletic sport. Figure 2:16 shows the sign for the weight-lifting area. Design a symbol for a sport of your own choice that clearly shows what the sport is. Keep the outline clear and simple. Avoid unnecessary detail. Grid paper may be used with 10 mm squares, and your drawing must have a minimum size of 90 × 50 mm.

Q11 Copy the international pictogram for 'Baggage Claim', using freehand curves where they are shown in the drawing (Fig. 2:17). A grid of 10 mm squares should be used as a guide to proportions. Colour your drawing with pencil, colour wash or felt pen.

Q12 Draw the 'First Aid' sign (Fig. 2:18) and enlarge it if you wish. Colour in the areas as indicated.

Q13 You are camping abroad and are looking for the following facilities: telephone, food, boating, petrol, a hospital. Draw the graphic signs you might expect to see.

Q14 Draw the signs you would display to show the following: danger, speed boats, fast water currents, downward-moving stairs, golf-club swing, rotating wheel, direction of cassette playback.

Q15 Draw signs within a rectangle, a circle or a triangle to illustrate within your school the following: Headmaster's office; workshops; science rooms; P.E. block; art rooms; secretary's office; playground.

Q16 Design a sign for a shop selling one of the following: model kits; boys' clothes; baby goods; sports equipment.

Q17 Reproduce the symbol used for one of the television channels.

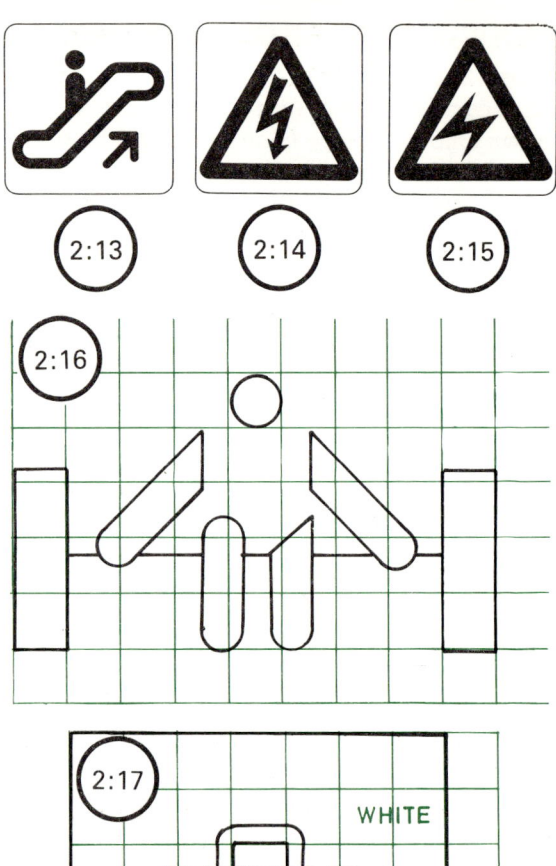

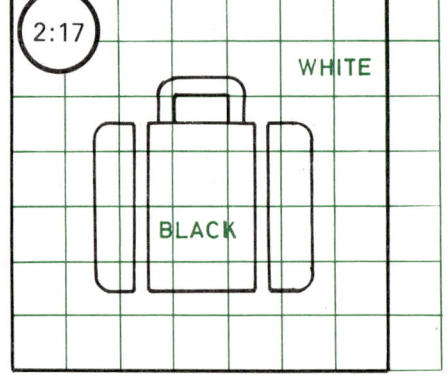

EGGS → CATERPILLAR

BUTTERFLY

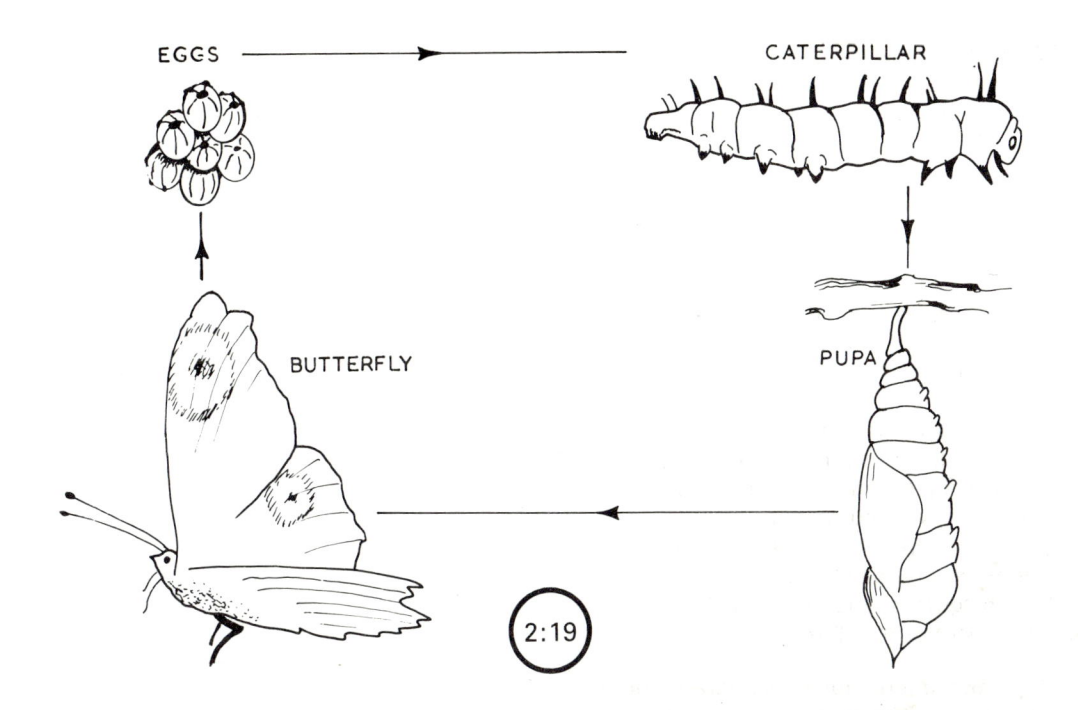

PUPA

2:19

Q18 Design symbols for the following items: fan; heater; spotlight; horn; 'turn clockwise'; 'push'.

Q19 A hood over a cooker is used to take away the heat rising from the cooker and cool it through a fan operating within the cooker hood itself. The cooker hood is also equipped with inset lights to shine down onto the cooking surface. Design symbols to be placed over the four switches that operate the following functions: light only; slow fan; fast fan; light + fast fan.

Q20 Figure 2:19 shows the life-cycle of a common butterfly in pictorial form. This pictorial method is very time-consuming as well as being difficult to produce. Redraw the sequence using a much simplified method. Set squares should be used.

Q21 Figure 2:20 is a flow diagram that shows, in simple stages, the growth of a tree and how it is converted into usable timber for the customer to adapt to his own use. Copy the diagram as shown, adding a few of the various uses to which the wood might be put.

Q22 Design and draw pictograms to indicate each stage shown in Fig. 2:20.

Q23 Show graphically (as in Fig. 2:20) the main stages of your life so far and the training you expect to need for a trade or profession of your choice. (Example—not to be used—Dentist: infant; primary; secondary; entry exams; college; assistant; exams for full qualification; dental practice.)

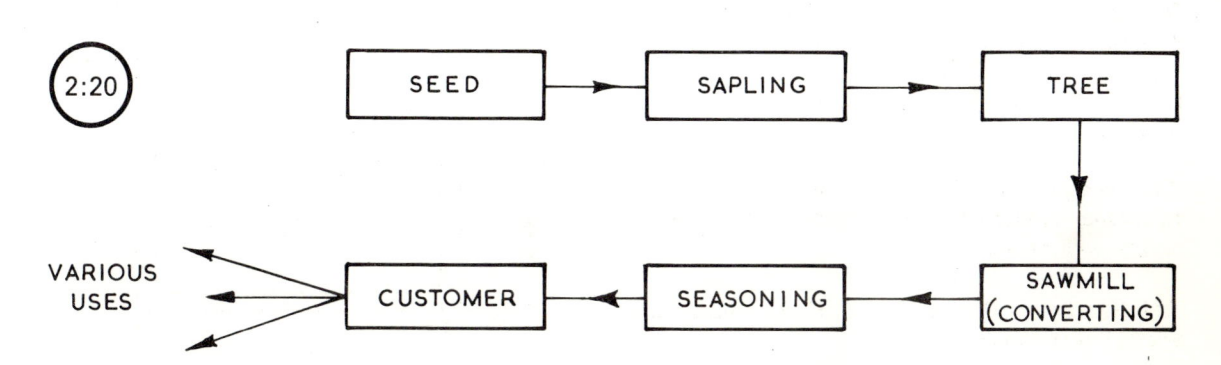

2:20 SEED → SAPLING → TREE → SAWMILL (CONVERTING) → SEASONING → CUSTOMER → VARIOUS USES

3 Lines, Arcs and Angles

The construction and division of both lines and angles form the very foundations of Technical Graphics for all trades and their allied professions.

Perpendicular means 'at right angles' to a given line or surface. For instance, when two lines form a right angle (Fig. 3:1) they are said to be 'perpendicular to each other'. Good examples of this can be seen in the floor and wall joint lines in blocks of flats and office blocks. 'Perpendicular' does not necessarily mean 'straight up'. Our telephone poles are both straight up and perpendicular to our view, but to the Australians on the other side of the world, our telephone poles are merely perpendicular, and to our view, theirs are both perpendicular and straight down!

Parallel lines are those which throughout their length are always the same distance apart. These need not be straight lines; for example, the circles of latitude on the globe form parallel lines.

An **angle** can be regarded as a corner, or as the space between two straight lines which meet at a point. The point is called the **vertex** and the space between the lines is stated in **degrees**. Degrees have nothing to do with length but are a measurement of turning movement between the two lines. For example, on board a ship, the navigating officer measures all turning movements by degrees of angles reading clockwise from the North.

BISECTING A LINE

1 Draw a line AB of any convenient length (Fig. 3:1).
2 Set the compass point in A and open it to a distance greater than half the length of the line; draw an arc.
3 Turn the compass round, placing the point in B; using the same radius, draw a second arc cutting the first at C and D (Fig. 3:2).
4 Join C and D. The line CD is the perpendicular bisector of AB and is always at right angles to the given line.

A bisector always cuts and passes through the given line. Note that regular curved lines may be similarly bisected.

ERECTING PERPENDICULARS

(a) From a point O within the given line AB (Fig. 3:3):
1 With O as centre and any radius, draw the semicircle marking equal distances OC and OD.
2 Set the compass in D and with any radius greater than DO, draw an arc at E.
3 Using C as centre and with the same radius, draw a second arc cutting the first at E.
4 Draw line EO—the required perpendicular.

(b) From a point O at or near the end of the line (Fig. 3:4):
1 With O as centre and any radius, draw the arc CDE.
2 With E as centre and using the same radius, cut this arc at D.
3 With D as centre and using the same radius, cut the arc again at C.
4 Still using the same radius and C and D as centres, draw the two arcs at F.
5 Draw line OF—the required perpendicular.

(c) From a point O outside the line (Fig. 3:5):
1 With O as centre and any radius, draw the arc cutting the line at C and D.
2 Using C and D as centres and any radius, draw arcs on the opposite side of the line at E.
3 Draw line EO—the required perpendicular.

(d) From a point O over the end of the line (Fig. 3:6):
1 Join O to any point C near to the end B.
2 Bisect OC to obtain point D.
3 Using D as centre and DO as radius, draw a semicircle OC cutting AB at E.
4 Join E to O to obtain the required perpendicular.

A perpendicular always meets the given line at 90°.

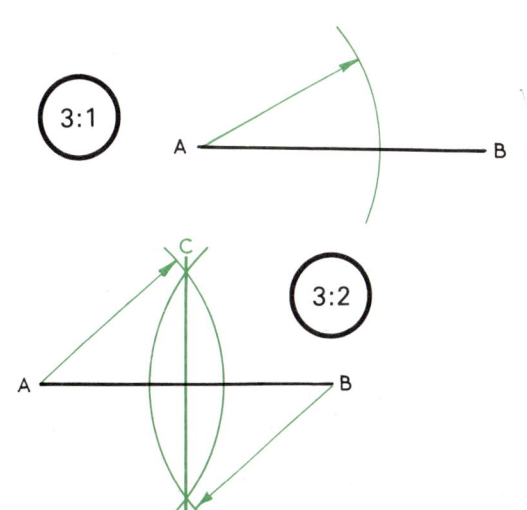

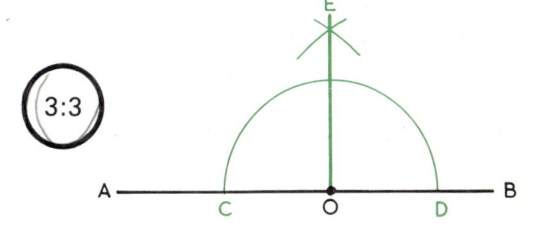

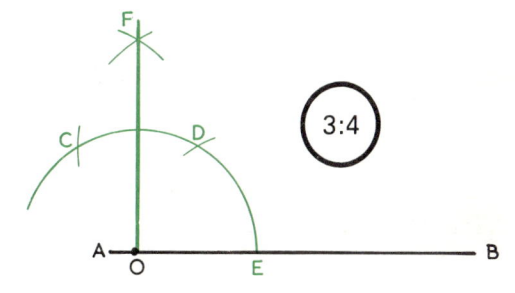

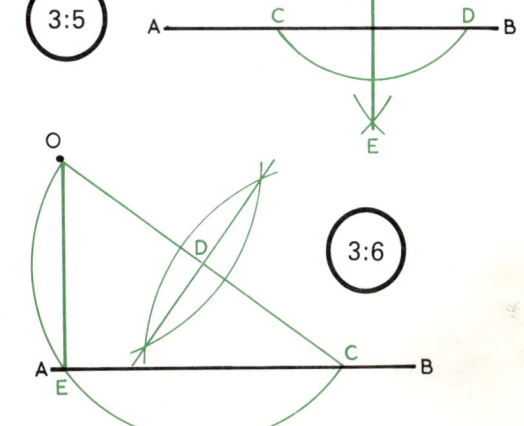

PARALLEL LINES

Parallel lines are the same distance apart throughout the whole of their lengths.

Parallel lines may be horizontal, vertical, oblique, or curved, as shown in Fig. 3:7.

(a) Drawing a line parallel to a given line and at a given distance from it (Fig. 3:8):

AB is the given line and CD the given distance.
1 Using any points E and F near the ends of the line as centres and a radius equal to CD, draw the two arcs GH.
2 Draw a line touching both arcs (a tangent). This is the required parallel.

A more accurate method is to erect perpendiculars from E and F. The line XY should then be drawn through the intersections of the arcs and perpendiculars.

(b) Drawing a line through a given point O and parallel with a given line AB (Fig. 3:9):

1 Using any suitable point C for centre and CO as radius, draw an arc from O cutting AB at D.
2 Using the same radius and D as centre, draw an arc CE.
3 Using OD as radius and C as centre, cut this arc at F.
4 The line FO is the required parallel.

(c) A quick and easy way to draw parallel lines (Fig. 3:10):

1 Place your set square exactly on the given line and hold it firmly on the paper.
2 Bring your ruler up to the set square to form a right angle with the given line.
3 Hold the ruler firm and stationary and slide the set square down the ruler for the distance required. Draw the line.

(d) Using parallel lines to divide a line into a number of equal parts:

For example, divide the line AB, 100 mm long, into 7 equal parts (Fig. 3:11).
1 Draw the line AC at an acute angle to AB and of a length that is exactly divisible by 7 (say 84 mm).
2 Mark off AC into 7 equal parts (84 ÷ 7 = 12 mm).
3 Join C to B.
4 Draw lines parallel to CB through points 6, 5, 4, 3, 2 and 1, cutting AB into 7 equal divisions.

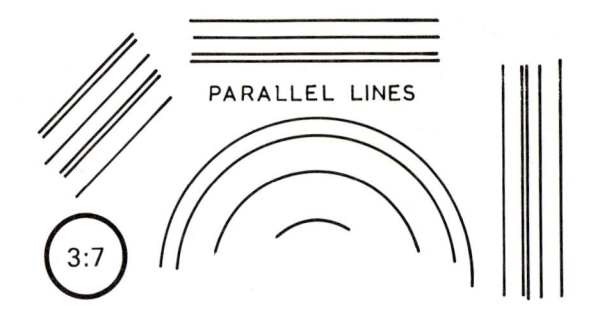

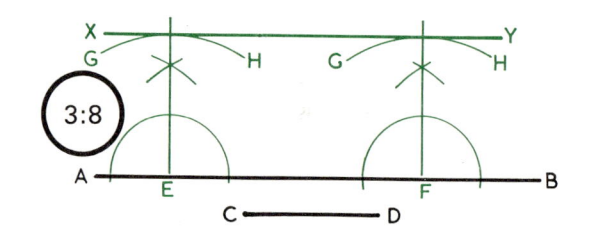

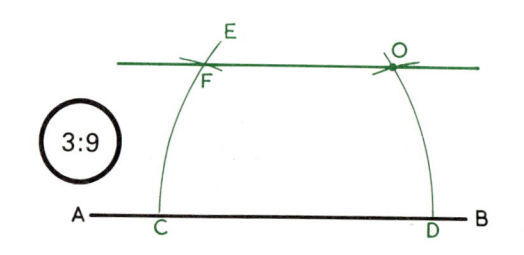

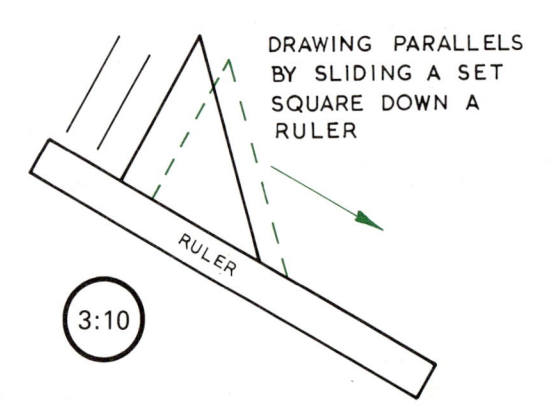

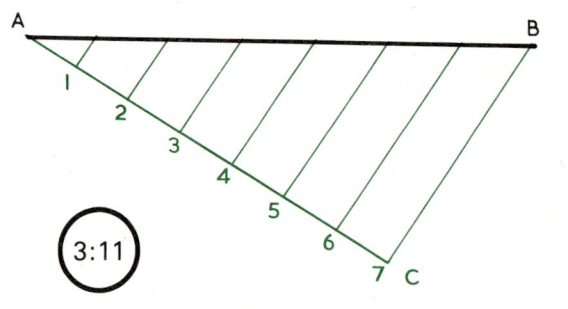

ANGLES

An angle is the inclination to each other of two straight lines meeting at a point (or, the amount of turn between them).

If a line turns through a complete circle (like the hands of a clock) it is said to have passed through 360 degrees (Fig. 3:12). Similarly, if the line passes through a quarter of the circle it will have passed through 90 degrees (or 90°). Thus the magnitude, or size, of an angle is measured in degrees.

From Fig. 3:13, we can see that the two angles formed on each side of the perpendicular CD are 90° angles. A right angle contains 90°, therefore four right angles equal 360° (4 × 90°) and these equal one complete revolution.

Degrees are a measurement of turning movement and not of linear distance.

SPECIAL ANGLES

Six types of angles are given special names to describe their shapes. These are shown in Fig. 3:14.

Right angles contain 90°.
Acute angles contain less than 90°.
Obtuse angles contain more than 90° and less than 180°.
Reflex angles contain more than 180°.
Supplementary angles are two adjacent angles which together total 180°.
Complementary angles are two adjacent angles that together total 90°.

An angle of 180° forms a straight line.

To save time in writing and drawing, the sign ∠ can be used in place of the word 'angle', and the sign ∠s in place of 'angles'. Angles can also be described by using three letters only, as shown in Fig. 3:15 and 3:16. The point of the angle is called the vertex. The letter placed at this point is always quoted as the middle one of the three.

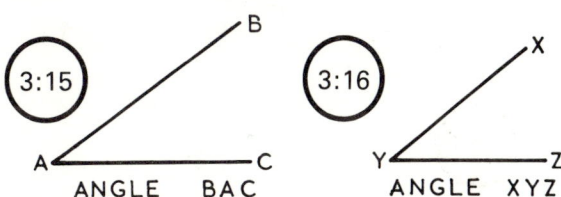

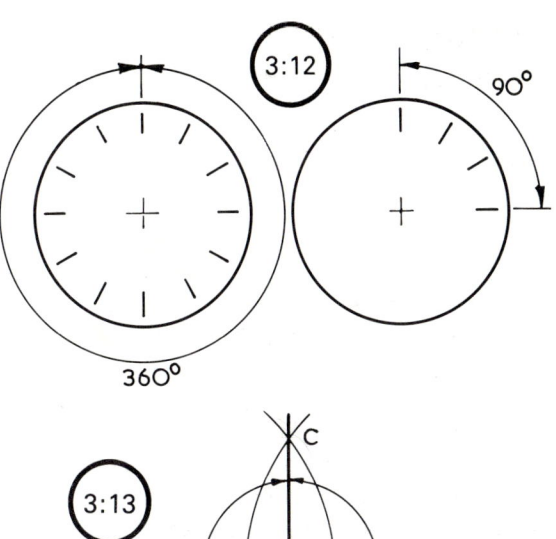

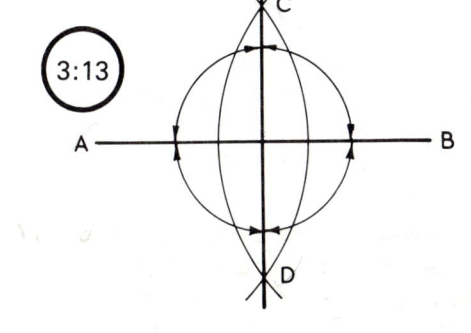

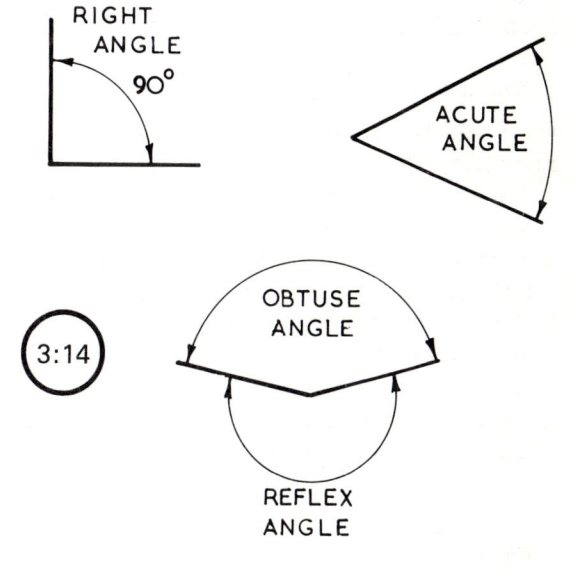

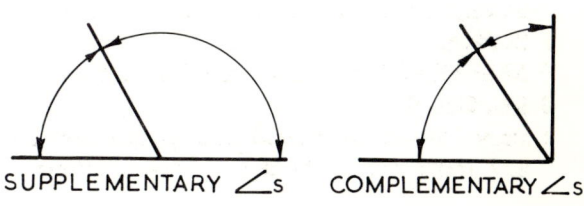

BISECTING AN ANGLE

For any type of angle BAC (Fig. 3:17):
1. Using A as centre and any convenient radius, draw an arc cutting the two arms of the angle at B and C.
2. Using B and C as centres and a convenient radius, draw the two intersecting arcs at D.
3. Join AD. This line bisects the angle.

The bisector of any acute or obtuse angle also bisects its reflex angle.

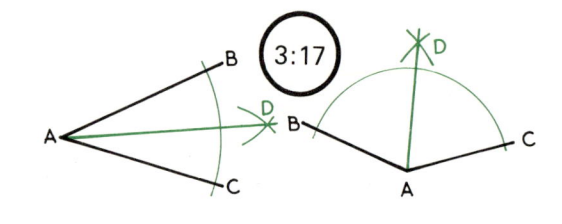

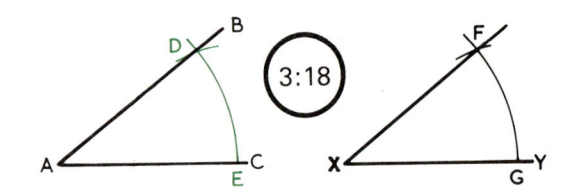

CONSTRUCTING ANGLES

(a) Drawing an angle equal to a given angle BAC (Fig. 3:18):
1. Using A as centre, draw arc DE.
2. Draw line XY to any convenient length.
3. Using radius AD and X as centre, draw arc GF.
4. Mark off an arc at GF of equal radius to ED.
5. Draw a line from X through the intersecting arcs at F to complete the angle.

Q1 A speedometer dial is shown (Fig. 3:19) with facilities to cover speeds from 0–160 km/h. The positions for 0, 80 and 160 have been found. Draw the given view (radius 45 mm) and include the points for speeds, 20, 40, 60, 100, 120 and 140 km/h.

(b) Constructing an angle of 60° (Fig. 3:20):
1. Draw line AB.
2. Using A as centre and any radius, draw arc CD.
3. With D as centre and using the same radius, draw a second arc cutting the first at C.
4. Join A to C to complete the 60° angle.
5. Bisecting the 60° angle will produce two 30° angles and bisecting one of these will produce two 15° angles, and so on.

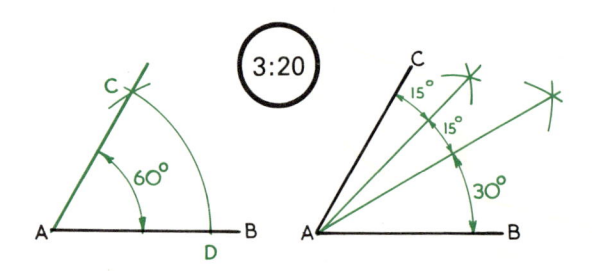

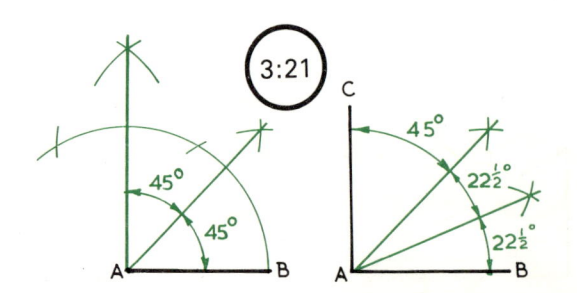

(c) Constructing an angle of 45° (Fig. 3:21):
1. Draw line AB and erect a perpendicular (see page 19), thus constructing a right angle (90°).
2. Bisecting this right angle will produce two 45° angles. Bisecting one of these will produce two $22\frac{1}{2}°$ angles.

You can divide a semicircle into three equal angles by stepping off the radius AB around the curve as in Fig. 3:22.

Note also that each angle has a magnitude of 60°. Since $3 \times 60° = 180°$, a semicircle contains 180°. Because a semicircle contains 180° its base-line must also indicate an angle of 180°. This can be proved by drawing any triangle, as in Fig. 3:23, cutting off the corners, A, B and C, and then fitting them together in the order shown in Fig. 3:24, when they will always produce a straight base-line.

A straight line indicates an angle of 180°.

Drawing Angles with Set Squares

While it is essential to know how to draw angles by using geometric constructions, the production of a working drawing can be speeded up considerably by using set squares to obtain certain specified angles and oblique lines. Figures 3:25 and 3:26 show the shapes of the standard 60/30° and 45° set squares. Figures 3:27 to 3:32 show how these can be used to obtain a number of other angles.

Points to Remember

1. The utmost accuracy is essential in all geometric drawings. To obtain this, divider points, compass points and pencil points must all be needle sharp at all times.
2. Never rub out construction lines on geometric drawings. These form an integral part of the drawings and always carry high marks in examinations.

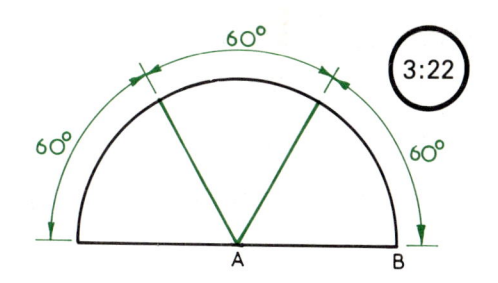

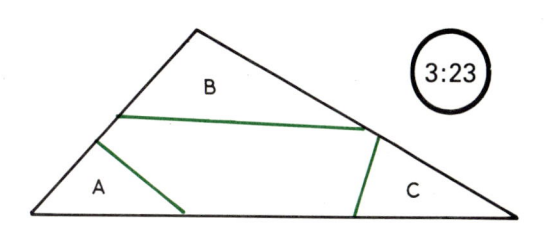

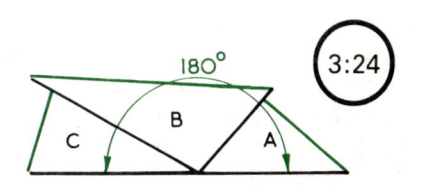

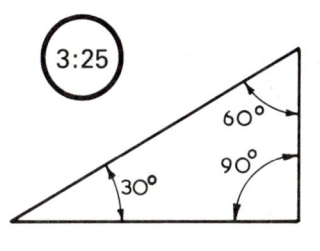

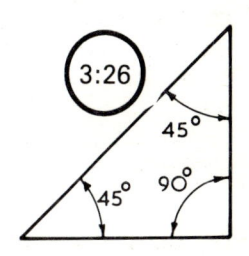

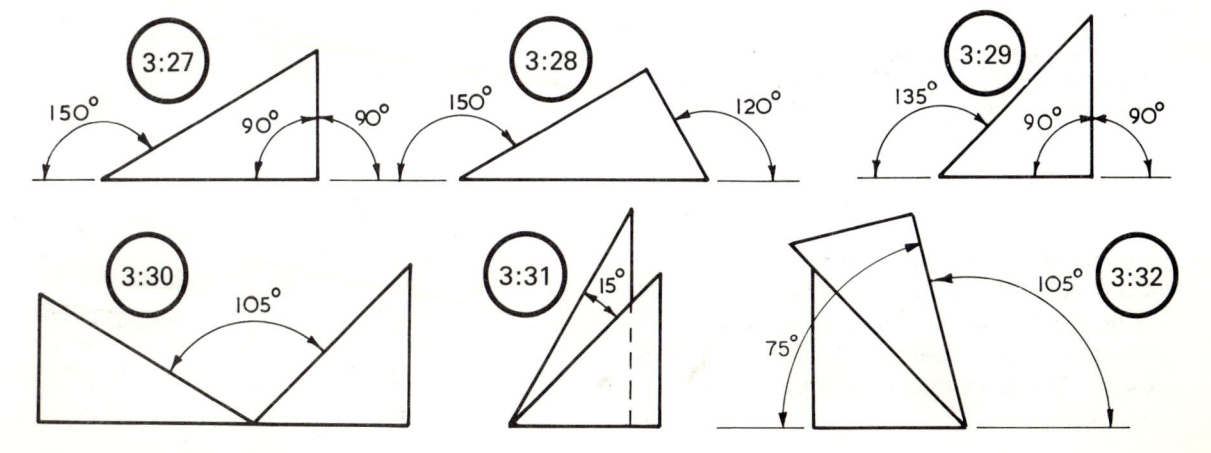

FURTHER QUESTIONS

Q2 A metal plate for hanging utensils is screwed to the wall through holes A and B (Fig. 3:33). The three hooks are equally spaced over the length of the plate. Locate their centres by construction as shown. Use your own judgement for holes A and B.

Q3 The coin slots in a pay-phone are shown with the centre-lines for locating the slots (Fig. 3:34). Draw the plate full size with slots 5 mm wide.

Q4 The top of a fence post has an angled support for the wire to pass through (Fig. 3:35). Draw the post and support, and locate by construction the centre position for the wire to pass through. Draw to a scale of 2:1.

Q5 The top view of a TV aerial is shown (Fig. 3:36) with five bars. If the bars are 1 mm thick and equally spaced, draw the given view of the aerial **twice** full size.

Q6 The fine tuning adjustment dial on a radio is shown surrounded by its 'window' (Fig. 3:37). Draw the complete unit and by construction find the **equal** positions from the centre to each end of the arc. Measurements not given are left to your discretion.

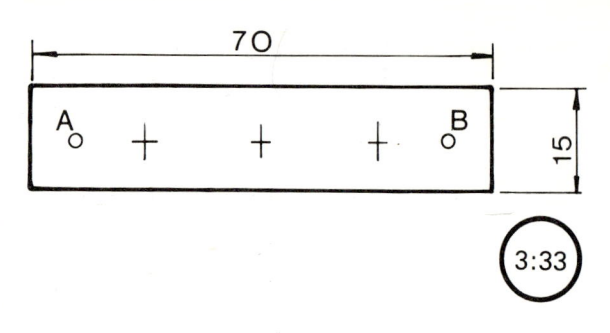

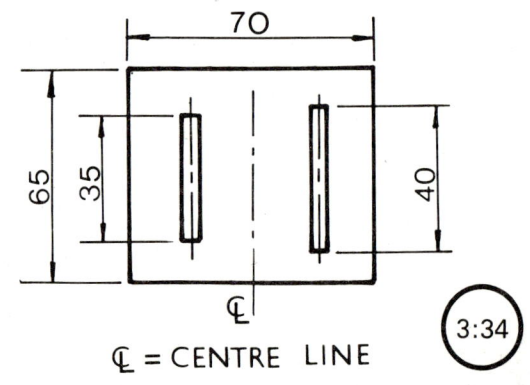

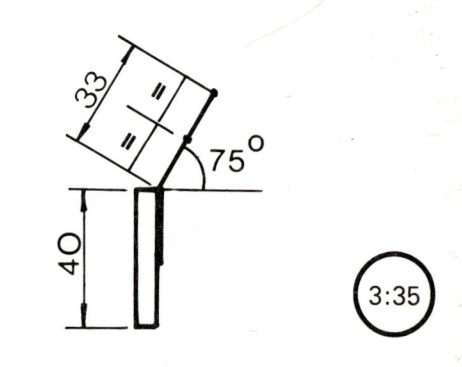

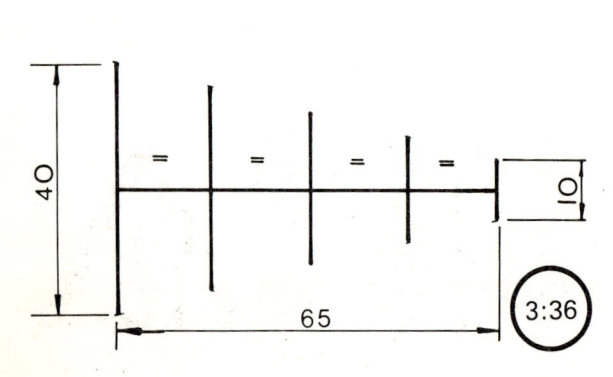

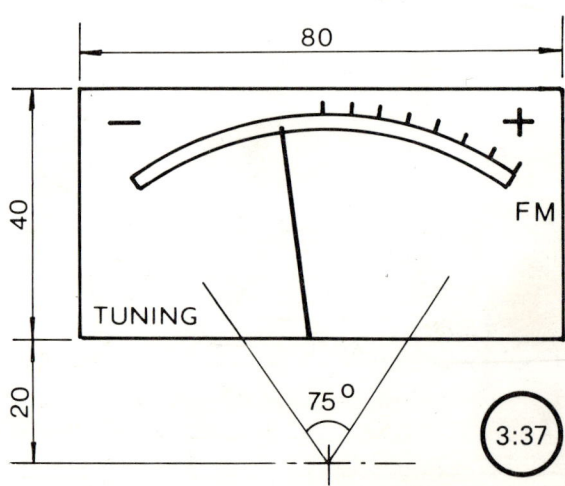

3:33

3:34

₵ = CENTRE LINE

3:35

3:36

3:37

24

Q7 Figure 3:38 shows alternative constructions for the 'Mail' pictogram (colour coding black on white). Draw both and for each design add a suitable backplate.

Q8 (i) Copy Fig. 3:39 and the table, inserting the names of the angles shown. (ii) Using your set squares *only*, draw angles of 75°, 105°, 120°, 150°, 165° and 180°. Check with a protractor and state any errors. Neat printing is required.

Q9 Transfer the two angles A and B (approximate will do) to your paper (Fig. 3:40). Draw a third angle C equal to their sum, and a fourth angle D equal to their difference (A + B = C; B − A = D).

Q10 A pictogram has been drawn within a triangle where all angles are 60° (Fig. 3:41). Using the measurements given and your 60° set square for sloping lines, draw the pictogram.

Q11 Draw the pictogram showing 'Caution, Laserbeam' (Fig. 3:42). Locate the centre of the triangle by bisecting two angles, then construct the radiating lines as shown. Use colour to indicate a warning sign.

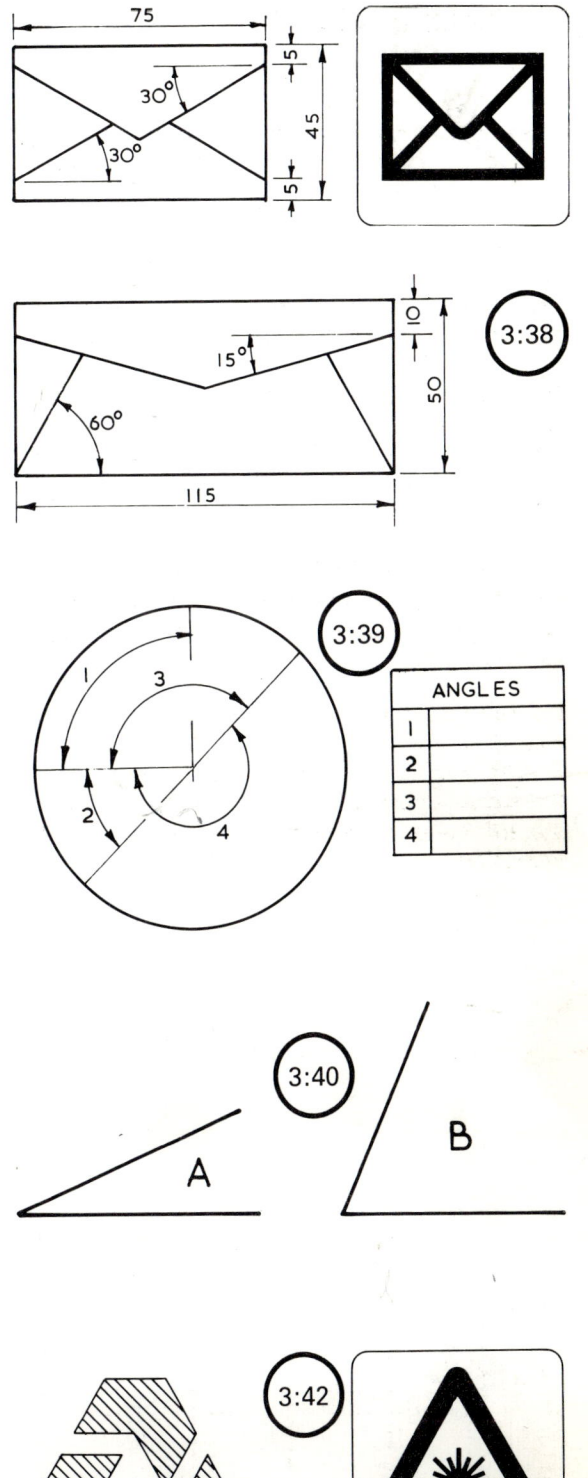

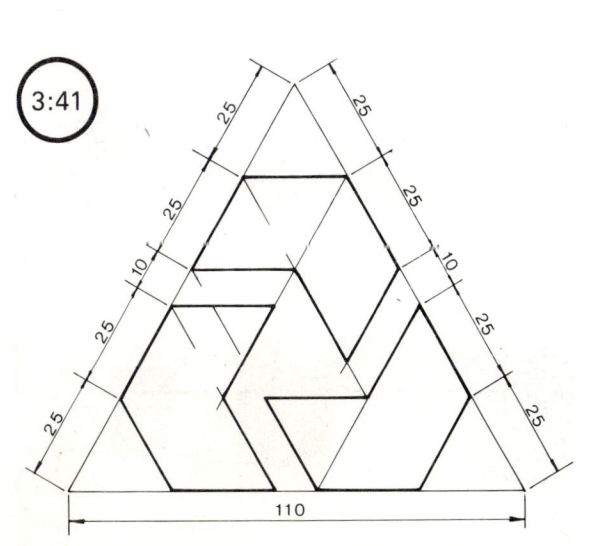

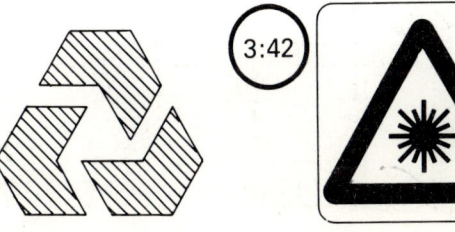

3:38

3:39

ANGLES	
1	
2	
3	
4	

3:40

3:41

3:42

4 Triangular Structures

A triangle is a plane figure having three sides and three angles. The sum of the angles in any triangle is always 180°.

The triangle is a simple shape but when it is made from steel girders it is strong and rigid. This is why so many roof trusses, bridges and cranes are built up from a series of steel triangles. It is one of the most important and useful shapes used in building constructions.

The illustration below shows a well designed spectator stand for a modern sports arena. The triangular structure ensures adequate strength and it is pleasing to the eye.

A parkland shelter for children

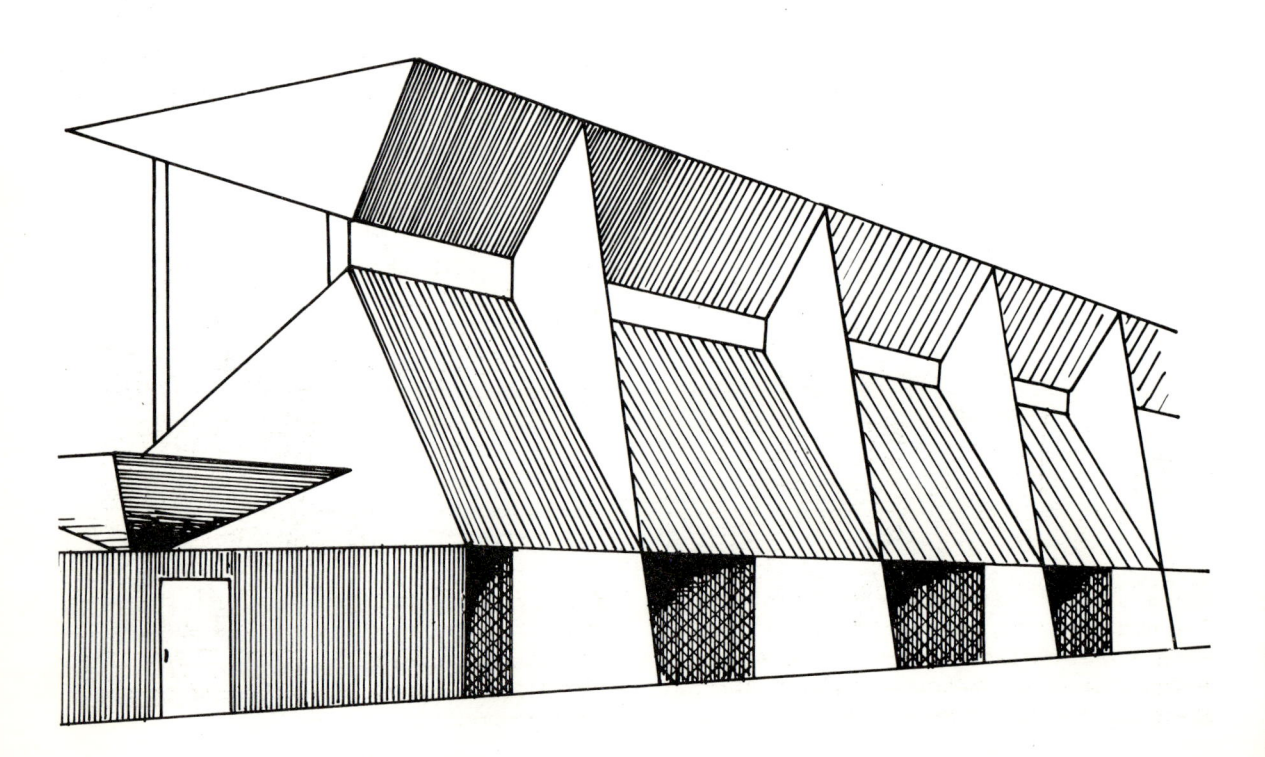

TYPES OF TRIANGLES

There are six different shapes of triangles. Three of these are named by the length of their sides and three by the magnitude of their angles:

(a) **Equilateral** triangles have three equal sides and three equal angles (Fig. 4:1).
(b) **Isosceles** triangles have two equal sides and two equal angles (Fig. 4:2).
(c) **Scalene** triangles have three unequal sides and three unequal angles (Fig. 4:3).
(d) **Acute-angled** triangles have three acute angles (Fig. 4:4).
(e) **Right-angled** triangles have one right angle and two acute angles (Fig. 4:5).
(f) **Obtuse-angled** triangles have one obtuse angle and two acute angles (Fig. 4:6).

Above is shown a part of a playing field fence. Note how the posts are strengthened by the inclined supports (forming triangles) just where the fence changes direction to form a corner.

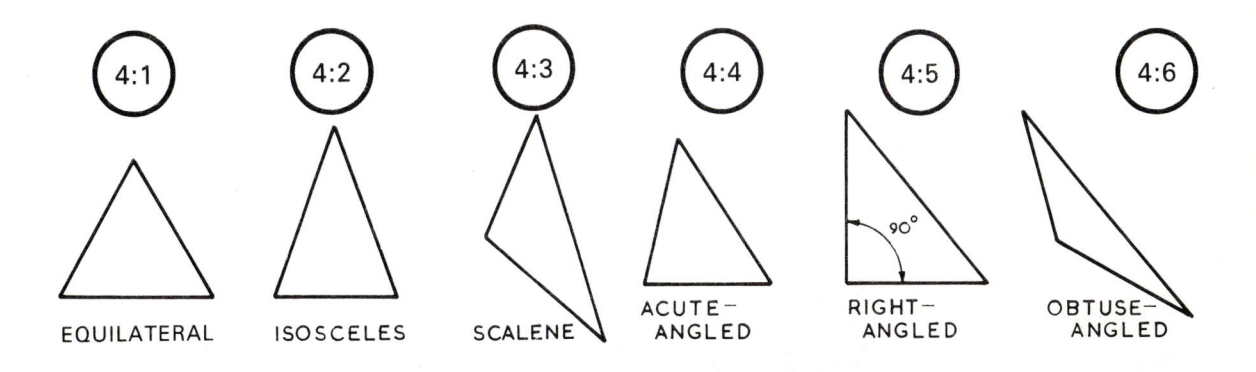

4:1 EQUILATERAL
4:2 ISOSCELES
4:3 SCALENE
4:4 ACUTE-ANGLED
4:5 RIGHT-ANGLED (90°)
4:6 OBTUSE-ANGLED

The photograph above shows the end of the horizontal jib of a tower crane such as the ones used on building sites. The triangular frame is specially designed for lightness and strength.

Here is a view of the main structure of the crane, which shows the control cabin for the operator, the trolley and crane hook, the slewing ring and the straining cables; note the large number of triangles in the structure.

PROPERTIES OF TRIANGLES

Triangles have separate names for their parts as shown in Fig. 4:7.

The **vertex** or **apex**, is the point of the angle opposite to the base.

The **altitude** is the perpendicular height from the base to the vertex.

The **hypotenuse** is the longest side in a right-angled triangle and is always opposite to the right angle.

A **median** is a line drawn from any angle to the centre of the opposite side (Fig. 4:8).

The **perimeter** is the sum of the lengths of the three sides.

Similar triangles (Fig. 4:9) have corresponding angles of equal magnitude, even though the lengths of the corresponding sides are different.

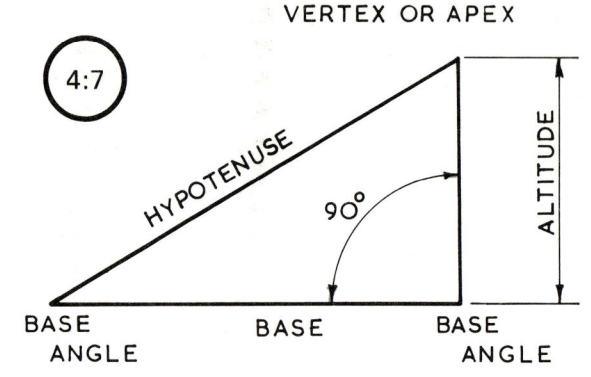

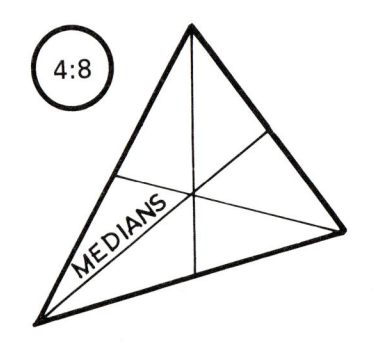

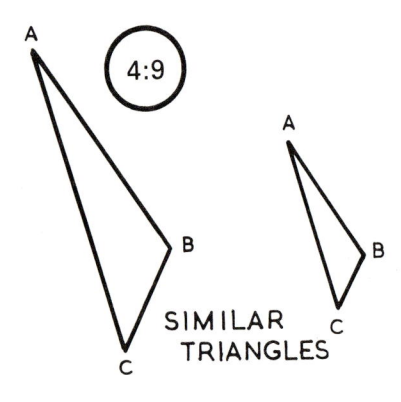

CONSTRUCTING TRIANGLES

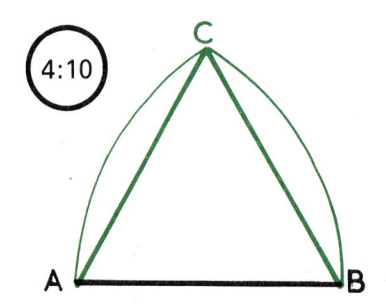

Equilateral Triangles

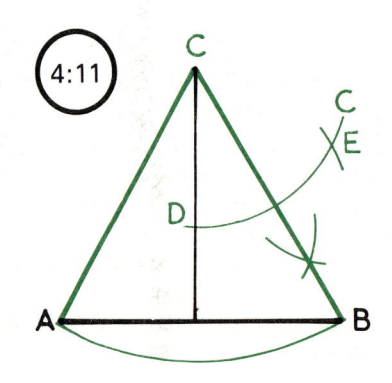

(a) Given the length of side (Fig. 4:10):

1 Draw a line AB, 60 mm in length.
2 Using A and B as centres, and AB as radius, draw two arcs intersecting at C. Join AC and BC.

(b) Given the length of the altitude (Fig. 4:11):

1 Draw the base AB, any length. Construct the perpendicular bisector.
2 Mark off point C 60 mm above the base-line.
3 Construct a 30° angle at DCB (see Fig. 3:20). Repeat the construction at DCA.

Isosceles Triangles

Given the base and the vertex angle (Fig. 4:12):
1. Draw the base AB, 40 mm long, and its perpendicular bisector.
2. Draw a semicircle CD, with A as centre and half the base as radius.
3. Draw the line AE, forming a 40° angle with the line CA.
4. Bisect the angle EAD to cut the perpendicular at F.
5. Join B to F to complete the triangle.

The two equal angles in an isosceles triangle need not be the two base angles (see Fig. 4:13).

4:12 ISOSCELES TRIANGLE

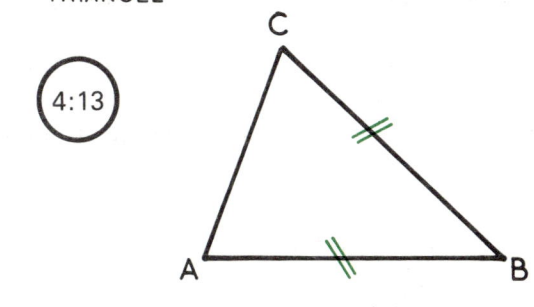

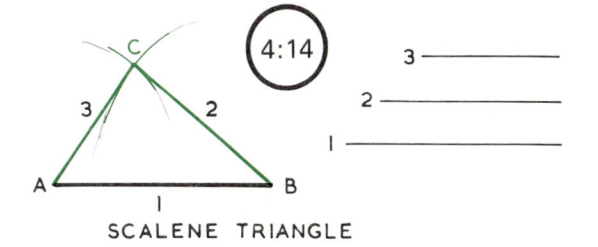

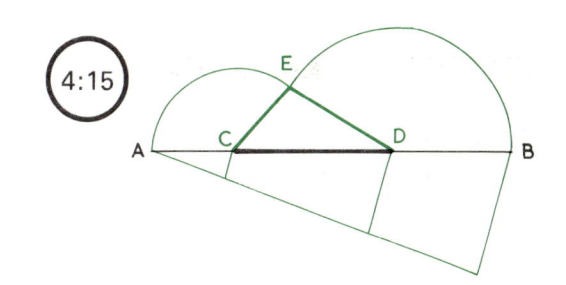

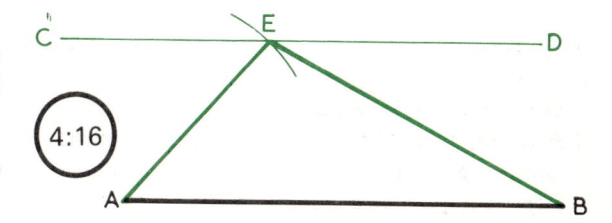

4:13

Scalene (and Acute-angled) Triangles

(a) Given the lengths of the three sides (Fig. 4:14):
1. Draw AB, equal in length to line 1.
2. Using A as centre and a radius equal to the length of line 3, draw an arc at C.
3. Using B as centre and line 2 as radius, draw a second arc cutting the first at C. Join A and B to C.

(b) Given the perimeter and the proportionate lengths of the sides (Fig. 4:15):
1. Draw the line AB, 100 mm in length, and divide it into three parts in the proportion of 2:3:4 (see Fig. 3:11).
2. Using C and D as centres and CA and DB as radii respectively, draw the two arcs intersecting at E. Join EC and ED.

4:14 SCALENE TRIANGLE

4:15

(c) Given two sides and the altitude (Fig. 4:16):
1. Draw AB, 75 mm in length (side 1).
2. Draw CD parallel to AB and 35 mm distant (see Fig. 3:8). This is the altitude.
3. Using A as centre and a radius of 50 mm (side 2), draw the arc cutting CD at E. Join E to B and A.

Always use this parallel line method when the altitude is given.

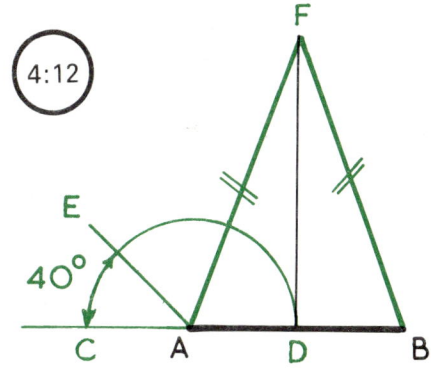

4:16

29

RIGHT-ANGLED TRIANGLES

The right-angled triangle is especially useful in surveying and in the building industry. For well over a thousand years this has been the basis on which the foundations of rectangular buildings have been laid. A simple practical method of setting out a right-angled triangle that has come down to us from ancient times is the use of the 3, 4, 5 rule.

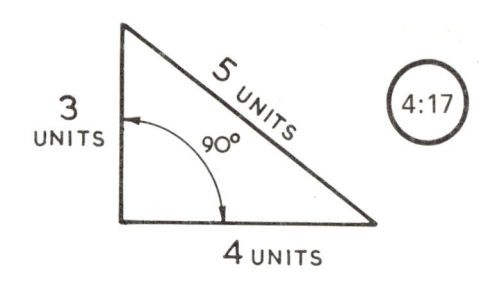

A triangle whose sides are in the proportion of 3, 4, 5, is a right-angled triangle (Fig. 4:17).

Constructing Right-angled Triangles

(a) Given the length of the hypotenuse and the length of one side (Fig. 4:18):
1 Draw the hypotenuse AB, 75 mm long. Bisect it and draw the semicircle, using C as centre and AC as radius.
2 Using B as centre and a radius of 35 mm, draw an arc cutting the semicircle at D. Join D to A and B.

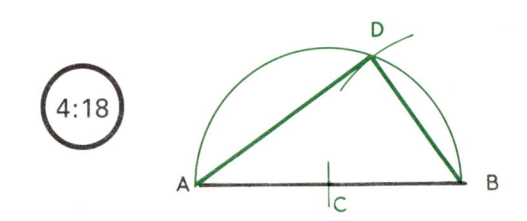

This solution (Fig. 4:18) depends on an important property of the semicircle—that the angle contained in a semicircle is always a right angle.

(b) Given the hypotenuse and an acute base angle (Fig. 4:19):
1 Draw the hypotenuse AB, 70 mm long. Bisect it and draw the semicircle.
2 Draw AC, making an angle of 30° with AB and cutting the semicircle at C. Join BC.

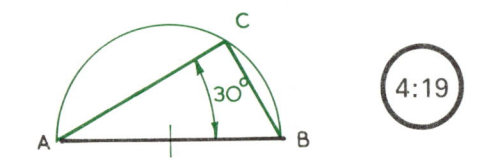

(c) Given the hypotenuse and the altitude to vertex, which is a right angle (Fig. 4:20):
1 Draw the hypotenuse AB, 80 mm long. Bisect this and draw the semicircle.
2 Draw a line parallel to the hypotenuse and 35 mm distant (the altitude) cutting the semicircle at C and D.
3 Joining either of these points to A and B will produce the required triangle.

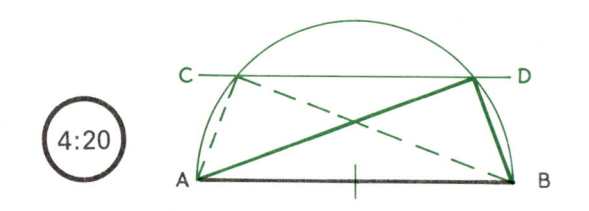

Constructing a Similar Triangle

Given the original triangle (ABC) and a new base-line (Fig. 4:21):
1 Draw the new base-line, 50 mm long.
2 Transfer angle CAB (see Fig. 3:18).
3 Repeat with angle CBA, intersecting at D to complete the triangle.

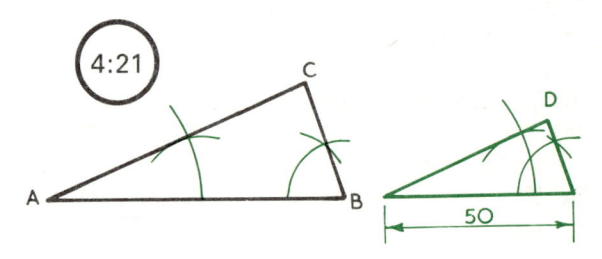

General Methods of Construction for all Triangles

(a) Given the altitude and the two sides (Fig. 4:22):
1 Draw a base-line AB and erect a perpendicular CD to equal the altitude (50 mm).
2 Using D as centre and a radius of 80 mm (side 1), cut the base at A.
3 Using D as centre and a 60 mm radius (side 2), cut the base at B.
4 Join AD and BD. Then ADB is the required triangle. ADE is a second triangle that satisfies the same requirements.

(b) Given the base and the base angles (Fig. 4:23):
1 Draw the base AB, 60 mm in length.
2 Transfer the base angles C and D using the method detailed in Fig. 3:18.

(c) Given the two base angles, and the altitude (Fig. 4:24):
1 Draw the altitude AB, 35 mm. Draw a base-line CD perpendicular to AB and passing through A.
2 Draw EF parallel to CD and passing through B.
3 Construct the two angles (45° and 30°) from EF about BA. The angles produced will cut the base at C and D to give the required triangle. (Angle EBC = angle BCA, and angle FBD = angle BDA.)

(d) Given the altitude, one base angle and the vertex angle (Fig. 4:25):
1 Draw a base-line AB of any convenient length.
2 Draw a parallel line 50 mm distant from this, to mark the altitude.
3 Construct a 60° angle (base angle) at A, cutting the altitude line at C.
4 Construct a 75° angle (the vertex angle) about AC to cut the base-line at B.

Points to Remember
Any triangle can be constructed providing three properties are known. These may be any of the following:
  (i) The lengths of the three sides.
  (ii) The lengths of two sides and the size of their included angle.
  (iii) The length of one side and the size of two angles.

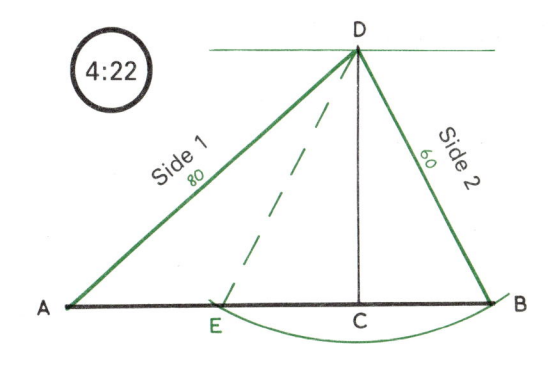

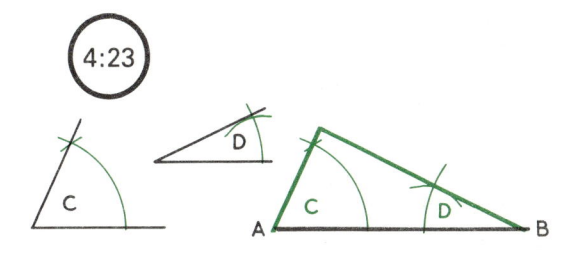

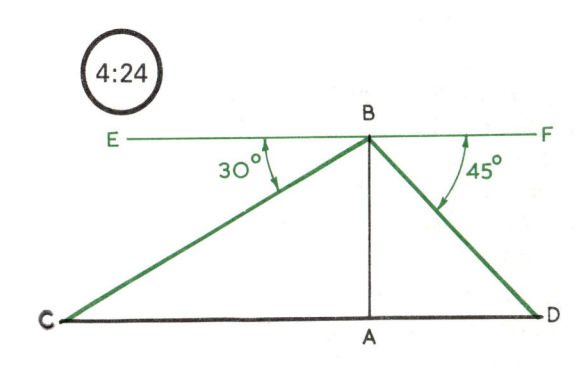

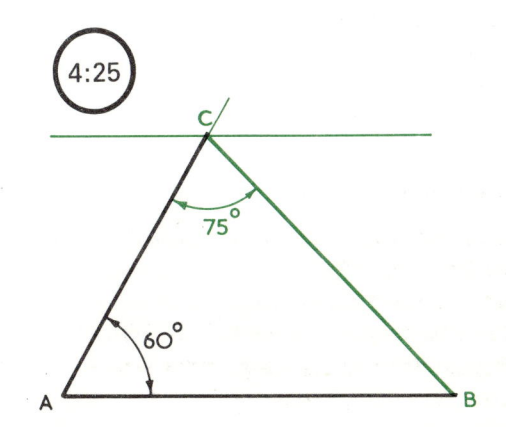

QUESTIONS

Q1 The children's playground shelter is drawn (Fig. 4:26) giving roof dimensions only. Draw the roof from the sizes given and then design or copy the base, working from the centre of the roof. In all cases, constructions should be shown. A protractor should not be used.

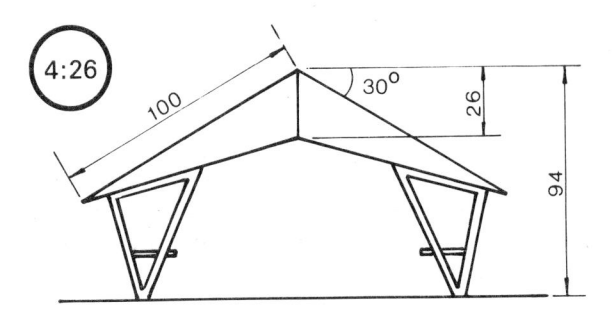

Q2 The symbol for 'British Aerospace' is shown in a simplified form (Fig. 4:27). The basic shape is an equilateral triangle of side 50 mm, i.e. the *inner* triangle, with a tapered tail added to indicate an arrow. Observe carefully that the dimensions lead to the inner triangle surrounded by the 2 mm edging. The largest area is coloured *red*, the four smaller areas *blue* and the narrow strips are *white*. Draw the symbol and colour it.

Q3 A tent is shown with a flysheet covering that is pegged to the ground (Fig. 4:28). Copy the drawing, given that the shape of both inner and outer tents is isosceles.

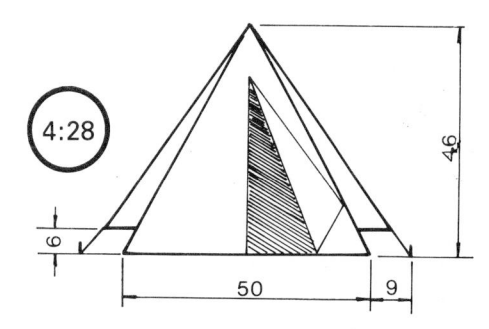

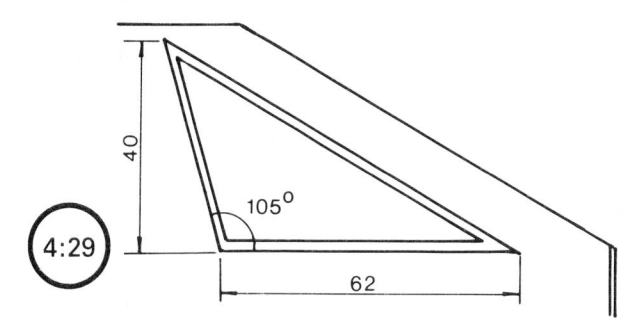

Q4 The rear quarter-light window of a hatchback car is shown in Fig. 4:29; only the window is dimensioned. Copy the drawing and, from the proportions given, complete the side view of the car using your own dimensions.

Q5 The enlarged drawing (Fig. 4:30) of a typical 'hazard lights' switch on a car console is given with the symbol in the form of two equilateral triangles with a thickness of 2 mm. (i) From the measurements shown, draw and colour the given view. (ii) Provide an alternative design that should be suitably dimensioned.

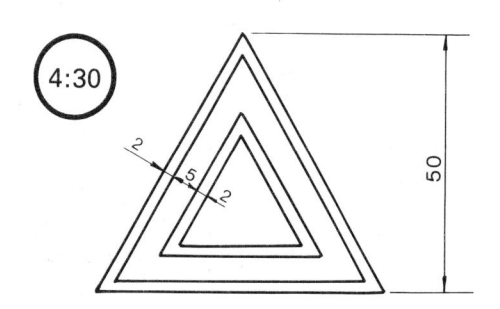

Q6 A foot bracket commonly found on telegraph poles is shown in Fig. 4:31, with the hypotenuse dimension given. Copy the drawing and leave all construction lines on your drawing. Note the points to which the dimension lines lead.

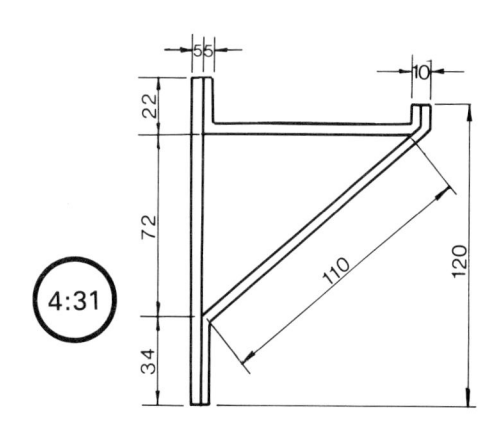

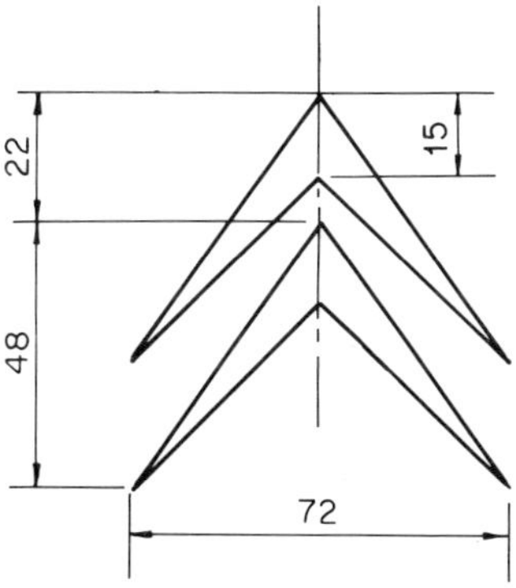

Q7 The emblem of the Citroën car is shown (Fig. 4:32). From the information given, copy the drawing, showing all construction lines. You will notice that the emblem is *symmetrical* (the same shape on either side of the centre-line), and by careful observation two interlocking isosceles triangles may be seen.

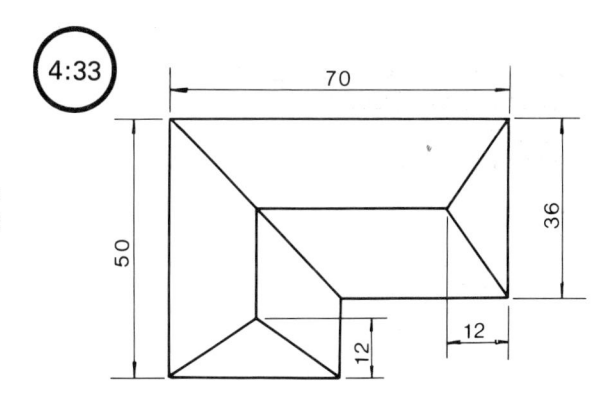

Q8 Figure 4:33 is a scaled drawing of the roof of a house seen from above. Copy the view but draw it **twice** the given size.

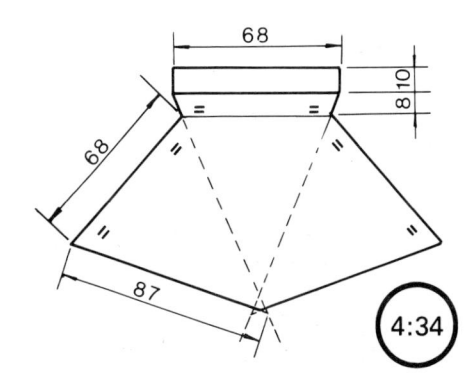

Q9 Figure 4:34 shows the outline of a ceiling lampshade made up of three isosceles triangles. Copy the drawing but do *not* add any dimensions. You should start with the central triangle and by using the construction for copying angles, construct the others.

33

Q10 The outline of a plastic shuttlecock is given in Fig. 4:35, with a suggested arrangement of the flight 'feathers' added on one half only. Draw the shuttlecock from the information given, showing *all* flight feathers. Dimensions not given are left to your discretion. Note that the angles of the feathers originate from the centre-line.

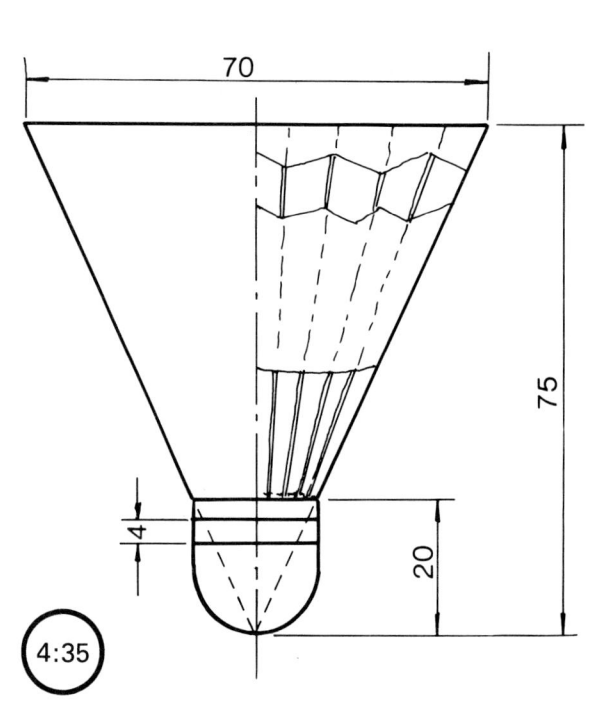

Q11 Figure 4:36 shows the flights of a dart when seen at right angles. If the shaft is 4 mm diameter, draw the flights and shaft with the given dimensions and add a suitable pattern or design to the two visible flights. Colour should be added with felt pen or crayon.

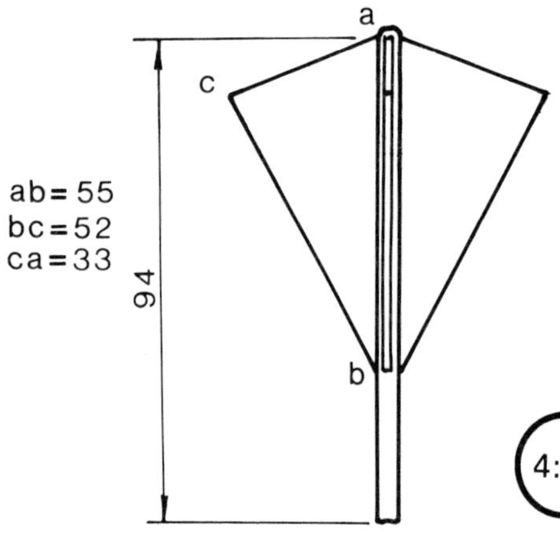

ab = 55
bc = 52
ca = 33

Q12 The dial of a fuel gauge is shown in Fig. 4:37, with the indicator at present off the scale. Draw the dial and on it place the quarter, half and three-quarters full positions. The indicator should be placed in the three-quarters position. A suitably designed surrounding enclosure should be added.

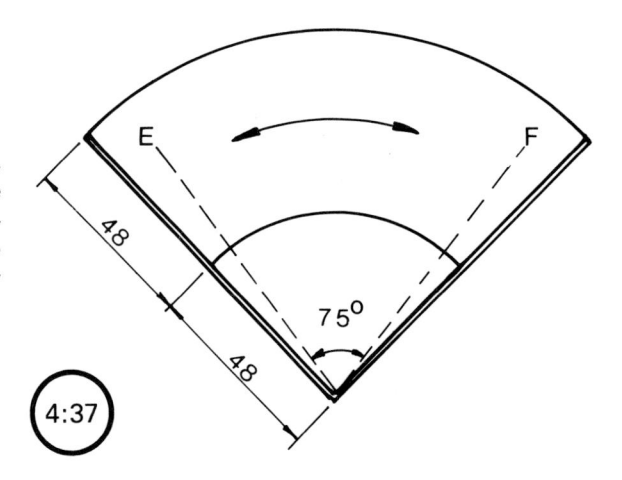

5 Quadrilaterals and Polygons

A **quadrilateral** is a plane figure bounded by **four** straight lines. A **polygon** is a plane figure bounded by **more than four** straight lines.

The illustration below shows a simplified plan of part of a modern school, designed from a variety of quadrilaterals and polygons. Combining the various shapes in this way is a very economical use of space.

Quadrilaterals are the commonest shapes we see about us in our daily lives. We are surrounded by hundreds of examples: door frames, windows, books, newspapers, football pitches, tennis courts, packing cartons for shoes, matches, cornflakes and so on. Their number and variety are endless.

There are seven different shapes of quadrilateral, each with a special name: (i) parallelogram; (ii) rhombus; (iii) rectangle; (iv) square; (v) trapezium; (vi) trapezoid; (vii) deltoid.

Shapes (ii)–(iv) are, in fact, special types of shape (i), the 'parallelogram'. A **parallelogram** is a quadrilateral whose opposite sides are parallel.

Squares and rectangles are the most widely used shapes. They are essential to all kinds of building and construction work.

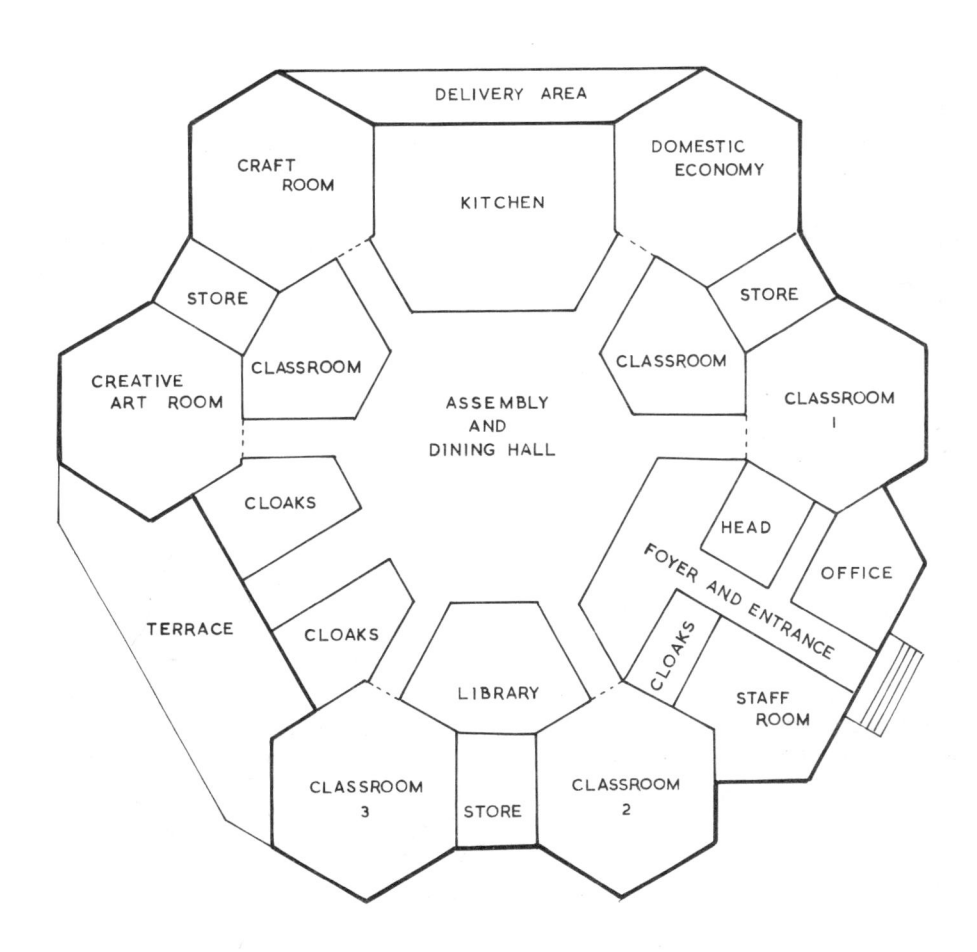

PARALLELOGRAMS

Constructing a Square

A square is a parallelogram with four equal sides (equilateral) and four right angles.

(a) Given the length of one side (Fig. 5:1):
1. Draw the base AB (70 mm) and erect the perpendiculars from A and B.
2. Using AB as radius and each point in turn as centre, cut off the perpendiculars at C and D. Join C and D.

(b) Given the base and using the tee square and 45° set square (Fig. 5:2):
1. Draw the base AB (60 mm).
2. Draw a 45° diagonal from A and a perpendicular from B.
3. From the intersection of these two, draw a line parallel to the base.
4. Complete the square with a perpendicular from A.

(c) Given the diagonal (Fig. 5:3): The straight line joining two opposite angles of a square is called the **diagonal**. The diagonals always bisect each other at right angles.
1. Draw the diagonal AB (70 mm).
2. Using the 45° set square, draw in the four sides as shown; or
3. Bisect the diagonal and draw the circumscribing circle, cutting the vertical centre-line at C and D.

(d) Given (i) the inscribed circle or (ii) the circumscribing circle (Fig. 5:4): An **inscribed** circle is inside a square and touching each side; a **circumscribing** circle is outside the square and touching each corner.

The circles are drawn first, then the centre-lines; the square is completed by using the 45° set square.

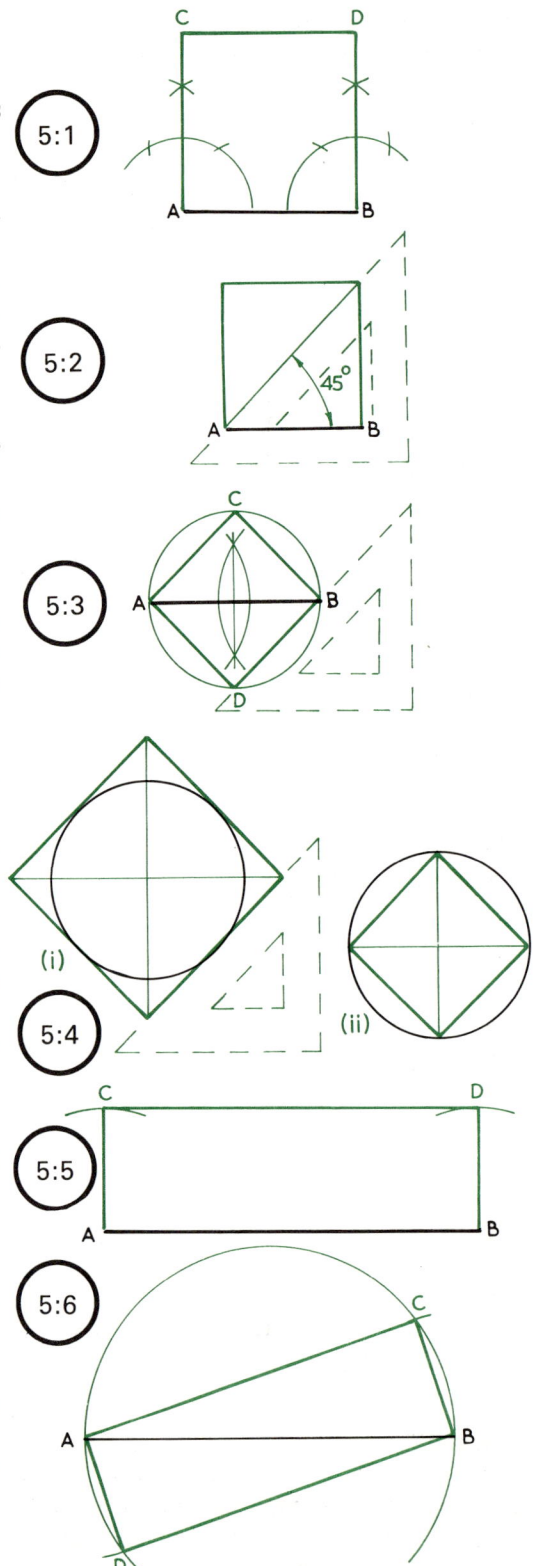

Constructing a Rectangle

A rectangle is a parallelogram with two pairs of equal sides and four right angles.

(a) Given two adjacent sides (Fig. 5:5):
1. Draw the base AB (75 mm).
2. Erect perpendiculars from both A and B, cutting them at 25 mm at C and D. Join C and D.

(b) Given the diagonal and one side (Fig. 5:6):
1. Draw the diagonal AB (75 mm). Bisect this and draw the circle.
2. Using A as centre and a radius of 25 mm, draw an arc cutting the circle at D.
3. Repeat this from B, cutting the circle at C.
4. Draw the lines AC, AD, BC and BD.

Constructing a Rhombus

A rhombus is an equilateral parallelogram (four equal sides) with no right angles.

(a) Given the diagonal and a side (Fig. 5:7):
1 Draw the diagonal AB (75 mm).
2 Using A and B as centres and a radius of 60 mm, draw arcs on both sides of the diagonal AB intersecting at C and D.
3 Join C and D to both A and B to obtain the required rhombus.

(b) Given one side and one angle (Fig. 5:8):
1 Draw the side AB (50 mm). Draw AC making an angle of 60° with AB.
2 Using A as centre and AB as radius, cut off AC equal to AB.
3 Retaining the same radius and using both B and C as centres, draw intersecting arcs at D. Join D to B and C.

OTHER QUADRILATERALS

Constructing a Trapezium

A trapezium is a quadrilateral having two of its sides parallel (Fig. 5:9). If the other two sides are of equal length as in Fig. 5:10, then it is called an **isosceles trapezium**.

Given three sides and one included angle
(Fig. 5:9):
1 Draw AB to a length of 60 mm.
2 Construct an angle of 135° at B (the included angle). The external angle between BD and AB produced is 45°.
3 Cut off BD at 40 mm.
4 Draw DC parallel to AB and 90 mm in length.
5 Join A to C, thus completing the figure.

The Trapezoid

The trapezoid (Fig. 5:11) is a quadrilateral where no sides are equal or parallel.

The Deltoid

The deltoid (Fig. 5:12) is a quadrilateral having two pairs of adjacent sides equal. Although the pairs are of different lengths, the diagonals still intersect at right angles as in the rhombus.

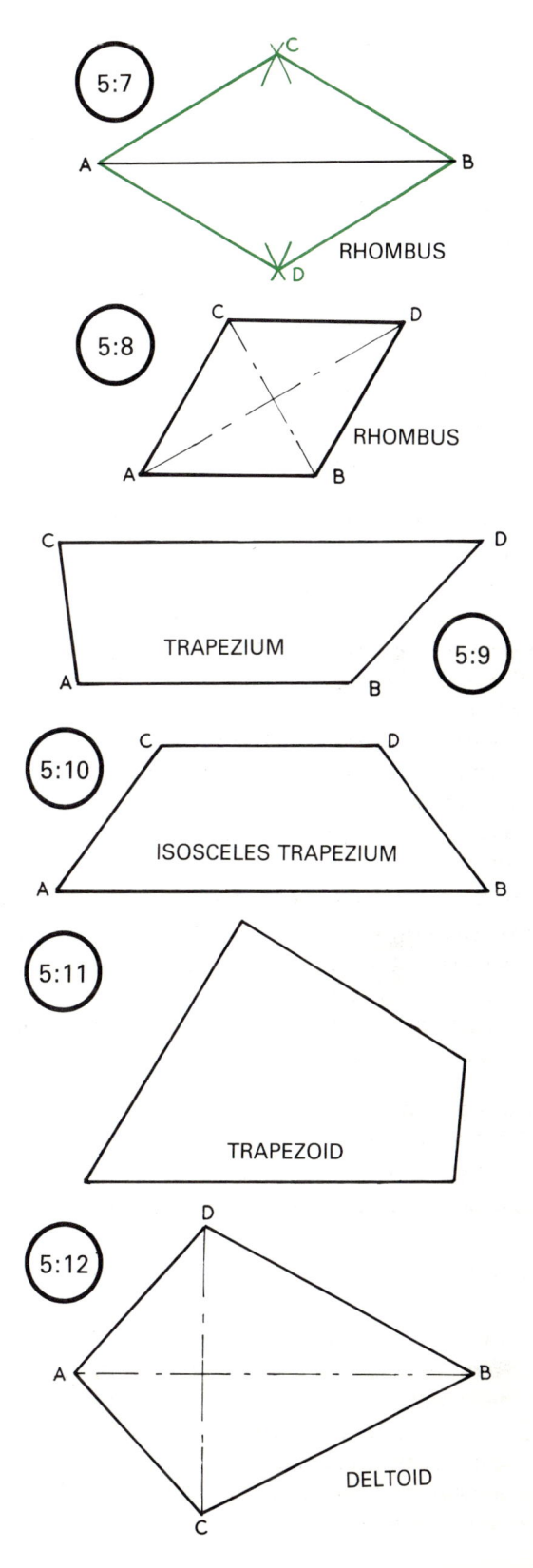

POLYGONS

A polygon is a plane figure bounded by more than four sides. When the sides and the angles are **equal**, it is a **regular polygon**; when they are **unequal** it is **irregular**.

The photographs show children's playground structures which have regular polygon shapes. This is a practical use of polygon design. Note the strength of these structures.

Polygons are known by the number of their sides (and angles):

Pentagons have **five** sides and **five** angles.
Hexagons have **six**
Heptagons have **seven**
Octagons have **eight**
Nonagons have **nine**
Decagons have **ten**
Undecagons have **eleven**
Dodecagons have **twelve** sides and **twelve** angles.

Figure 5:13 shows four of the regular polygon shapes that are in widespread daily use in structure and packaging designs.

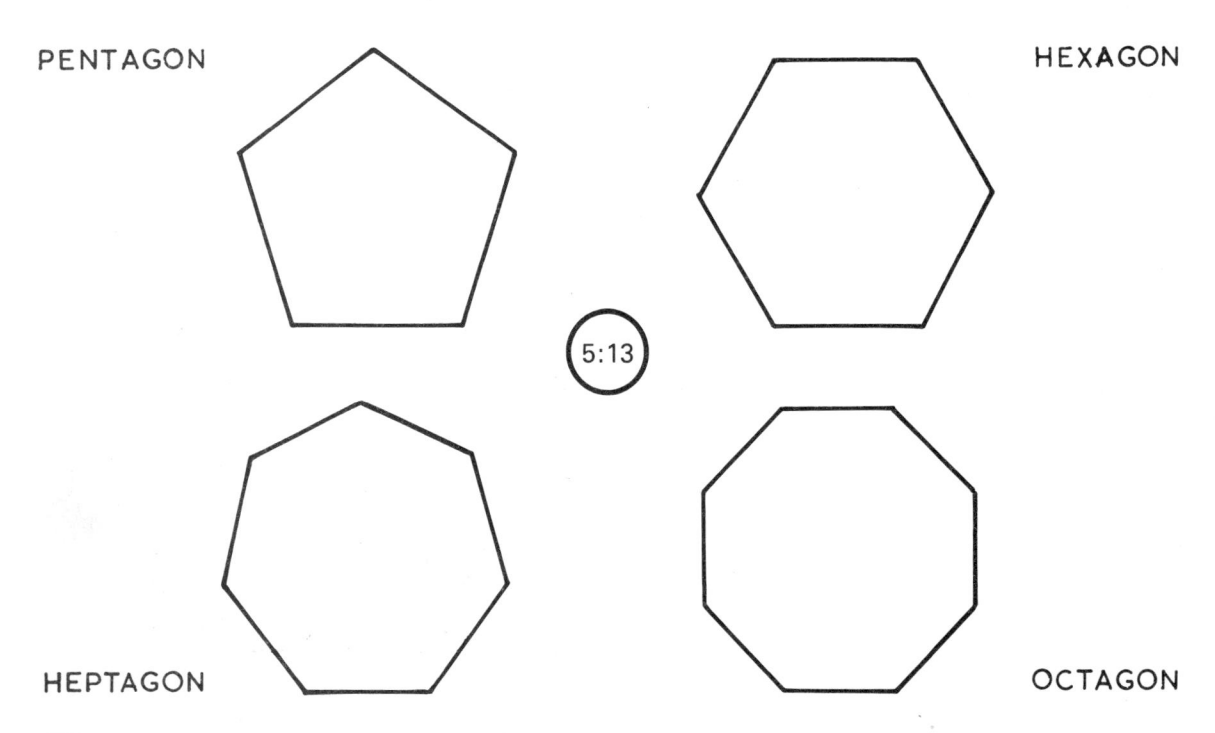

PENTAGON   HEXAGON

5:13

HEPTAGON   OCTAGON

General Methods of Construction for all Regular Polygons

Given the length of one side (Figs 5:14 and 5:15):
1 Draw side AB (50 mm).
2 Bisect this and erect the perpendicular bisector which forms a centre-line.
3 Draw a 45° line from A. This forms the diagonal of the square on AB and cuts the perpendicular at 4, which is the centre of the square.
4 Draw a 60° line from A. This forms the diagonal of the hexagon and cuts the centre-line at 6, which is the centre of the hexagon.
5 Bisect the distance between 4 and 6 to obtain point 5, which is the centre of the pentagon.
6 Step off up the centre-line from point 6 distances equal to the distance 4 to 5. Number these as shown. These are the centres of the remaining polygons named above which have lengths of sides equal to AB.
7 In each case the polygon is drawn by stepping off the distance AB round the circumscribing circle.

An alternative start to the construction is to draw an arc using B as centre and AB as radius. This will cut the centre-line at 6, the centre of the hexagon. It will also cut a perpendicular from B at C, meeting the 45° line from A, making a second side to the square.

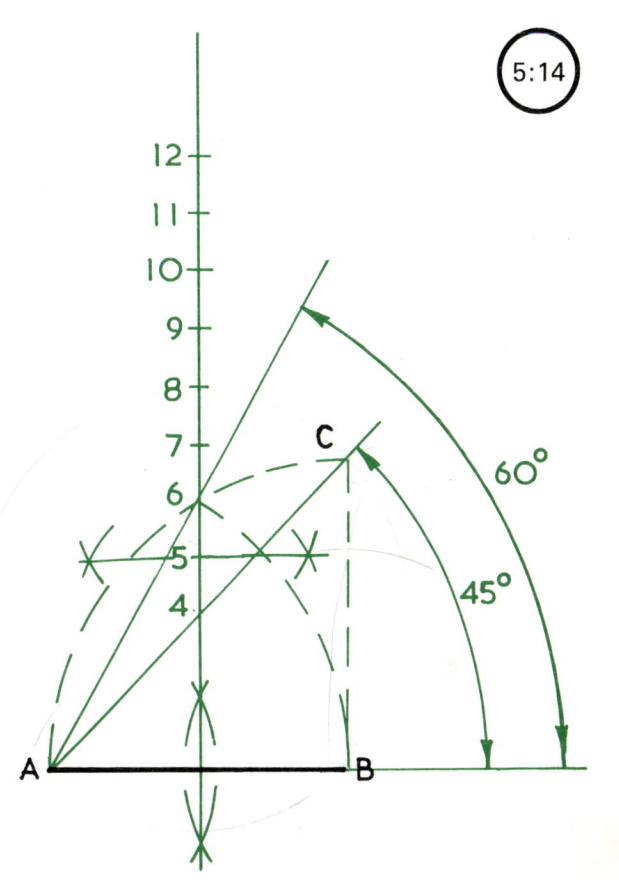

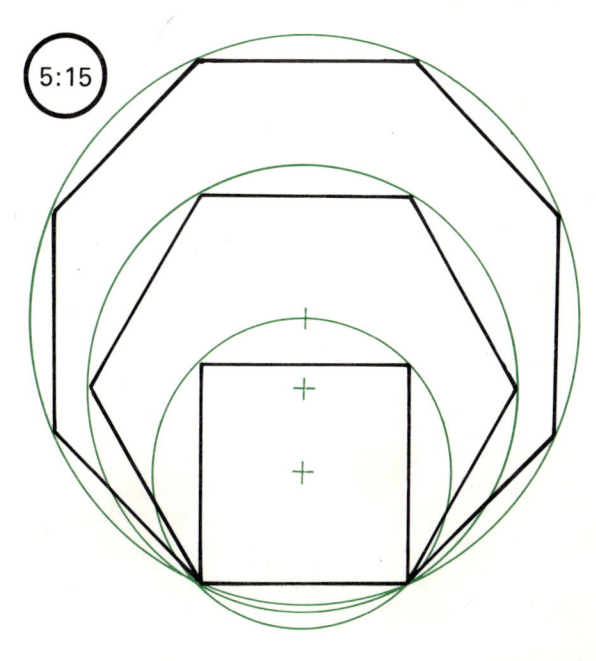

5:14

5:15

39

Constructing a Regular Hexagon

The regular hexagon is probably the most frequently used of all the polygons, appearing as the standard hexagon nut on most engineering drawings.

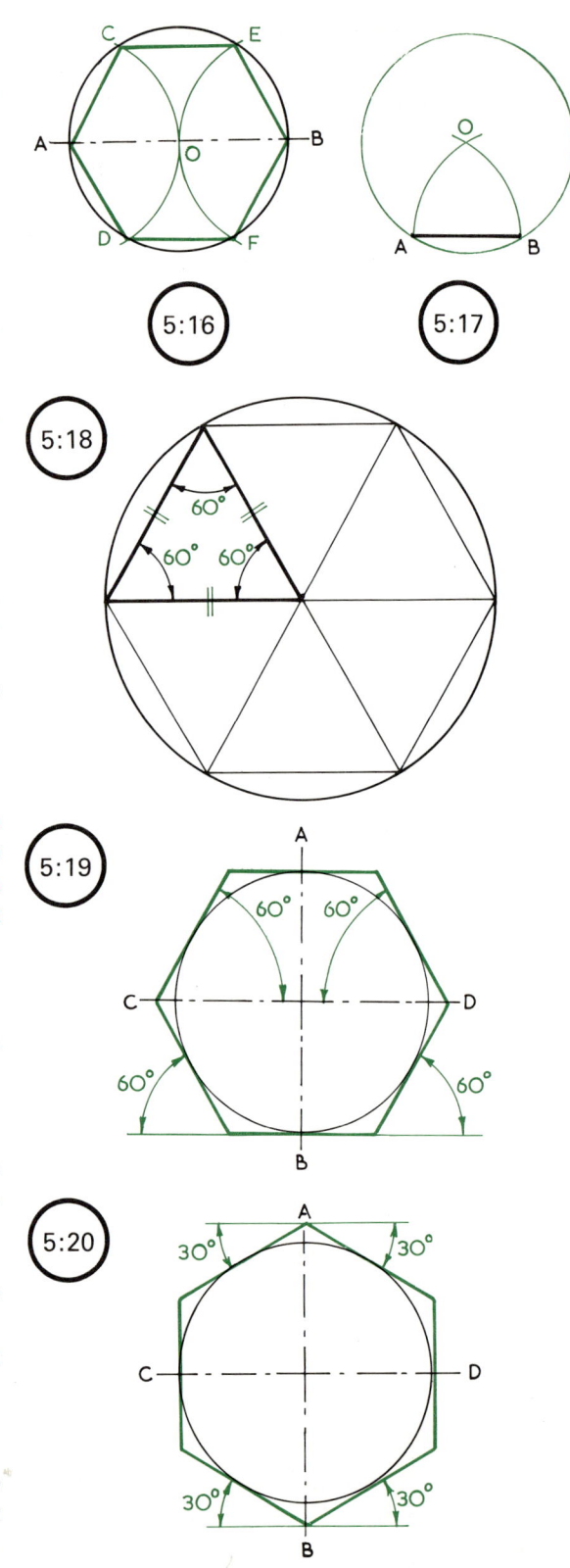

(a) Given the circumscribing circle (Fig. 5:16):
1. Draw the circle (60 mm diameter) and a centre-line AB.
2. Using A as centre and AO as radius, draw the arcs C and D.
3. Repeat this from B to obtain points E and F.
4. Join the six points so obtained to complete the hexagon.

(b) Given the length of one side (Fig. 5:17):
1. Draw the side AB (30 mm).
2. Using A and B as centres and AB as radius, draw the two arcs. These intersect at O, the centre of the circumscribing circle.
3. Draw the circle and step off the remaining five sides (chords) similar to AB.

Drawing the two exercises above and inspection of Fig. 5:18 demonstrates that the radius of the circumscribing circle equals the lengths of each of the sides of the hexagon and of the six equilateral triangles formed by its diagonals.

(c) Two quick methods for drawing hexagons (Figs 5:19 and 5:20):
In both cases:
1. Draw the centre-lines AB and CD.
2. About their intersection draw a circle with its diameter equal to the given distance across the flats of the hexagon (50 mm).

Then either (Fig. 5:19):
3. Using the tee square, draw horizontal lines touching the circle at the top and bottom.
4. Draw the four remaining sides with the 60° set square.

Or (Fig. 5:20):
3. Draw the four 30° sides with the set square.
4. Turn the set square round and add the two vertical sides. Make sure that all six sides just touch the circle and do not miss it or cut into it.

Constructing a Regular Octagon

(a) Given the circumscribing circle (Fig. 5:21):
1. Draw a circle (80 mm diameter) and its two centre-lines AB and CD intersecting at O.
2. Bisect the angles AOC and COB and produce the bisectors fully across the circle.
3. Join the points where the centre-lines and bisectors cut the circumference.

(b) Given the length of one side (Fig. 5:22):
1. Draw side AB (40 mm) and from B draw a line using the 45° set square.
2. Using B as centre and AB as radius, cut this line to length by the arc AC.
3. Then AB and BC form the first two sides of the octagon.
4. Bisect these to obtain the centre of the circumscribing circle.
5. Step the distance AB round the circle and join the points so obtained.

(c) Within a given square (Fig. 5:23):
1. Draw the square (80 mm side) and insert its diagonals.
2. Using each corner of the square in turn as centres and half the diagonal as radius, draw in the four arcs.
3. Join up the points where the arcs cut the sides of the square to obtain the required octagon.

This is a most useful practical method of setting out octagonal shapes in woodworking and constructional work.

Constructing a Regular Dodecagon

Given the circumscribing circle (Fig. 5:24):
1. Draw the circle (80 mm diameter), and its two right-angled centre-lines AB and CD.
2. Using A as centre and AO as radius, draw the arc EF.
3. Repeat this from points B, C and D, thus obtaining the twelve equal divisions of the circle.
4. Join all these twelve points to produce the required figure.

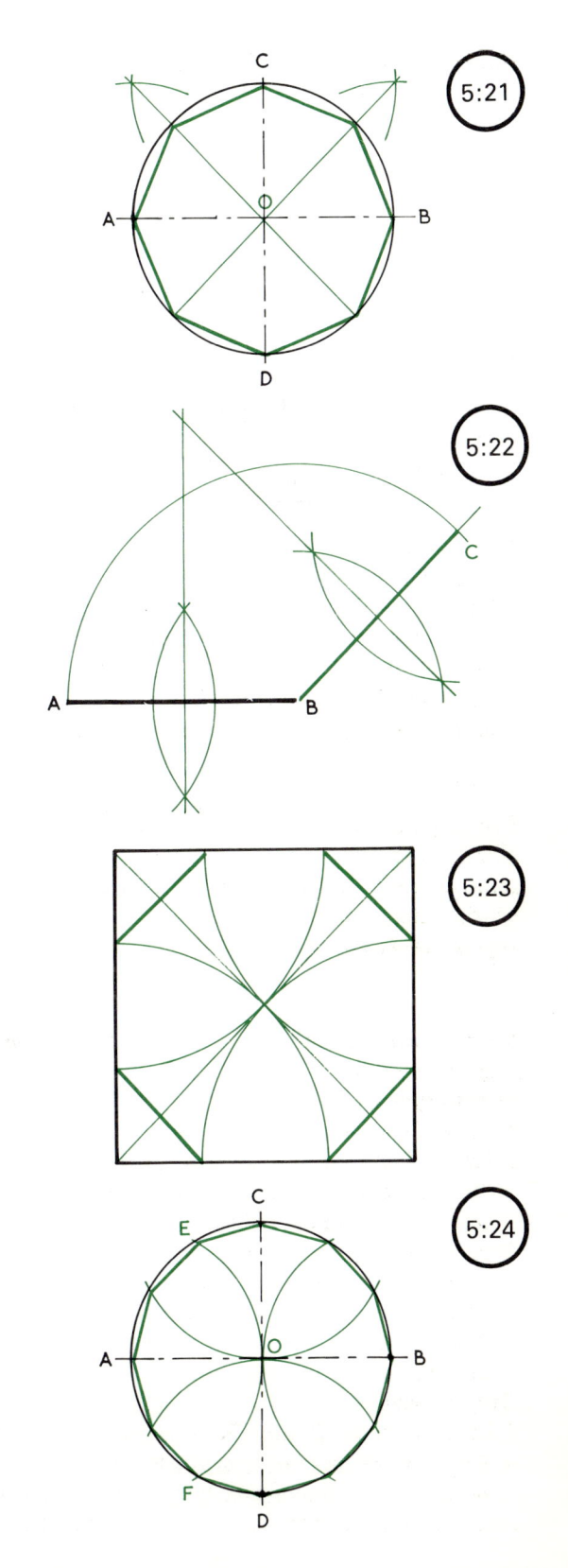

Constructing a Regular Pentagon

(a) Given the length of one side (Fig. 5:25):
1. Draw side AB (50 mm) and produce it to O.
2. Using B as centre, draw a semicircle of any suitable radius.
3. Divide this into as many equal parts as there are sides in the polygon. (This may be done by trial and error with dividers or by measuring with a protractor.)
4. Draw BC through division 2 on the semicircle and equal in length to AB. Division 2 is used because the external angle of any polygon is

$$\frac{360°}{\text{No. of sides}} \text{ or } \frac{180°}{\text{No. of sides}} \times 2.$$

5. Bisect AB and BC to obtain D, the centre of the circumscribing circle.
6. Using D as centre and DA as radius, draw the circle. Step off the remaining three sides from A and C.

(b) Within a given circle (Fig. 5:26):
1. Draw the circle and its diameter AB (80 mm).
2. Divide the diameter into as many equal parts as there are sides in the polygon, in this case five. Look at Fig. 3:11 to remind you how to do this.
3. Using A and B as centres and AB as radius, draw two arcs intersecting at C.
4. Draw a line from C through division 2 to cut the circle at D. the line joining A and D is the first side of the polygon. Step off this distance AD round the circle to obtain the remaining sides.

This method can be applied to all regular polygons.

(c) Given the length of one side (Fig. 5:27):
1. Draw the side AB (30 mm).
2. Using A as centre and AB as radius, draw circle X.
3. Repeat with B as centre to draw circle Y, cutting the first circle at C and D.
4. Using C as centre and AB as radius, draw the bottom circle cutting the first two at E and F.
5. Join C to D, thus obtaining G.
6. Draw lines from E and F through G to cut the upper curves of circles X and Y at H and K.
7. Using H and K as centres and AB as radius, mark in the two intersecting arcs at L. Join up LK, LH, HA and KB.

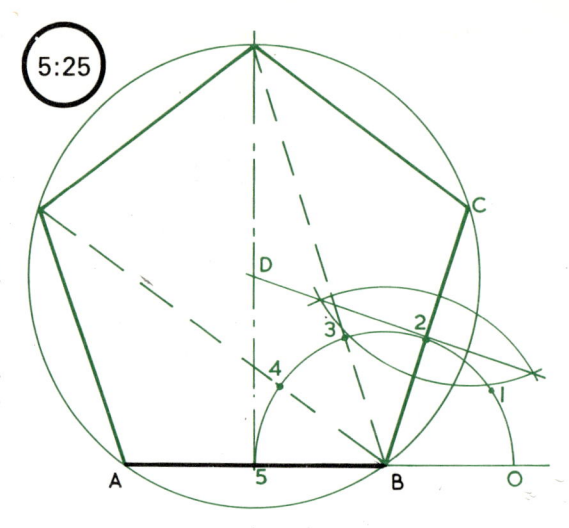

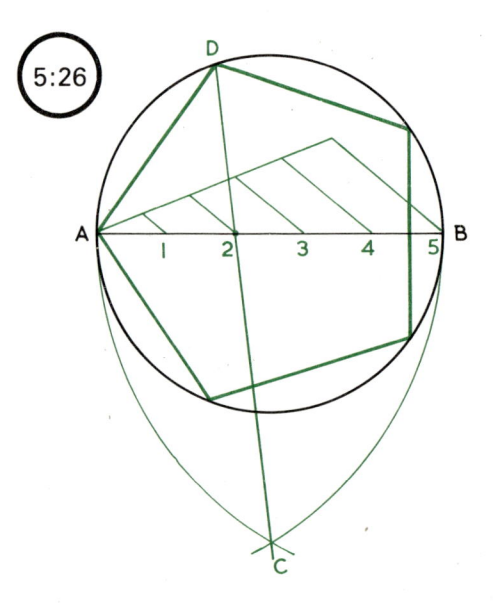

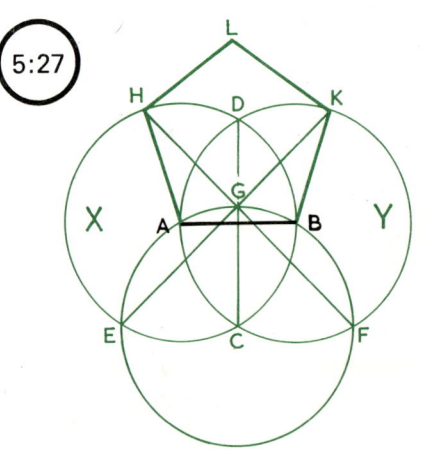

QUESTIONS

Q1 The diagonal of a square is 60 mm. Draw the square.

Q2 Construct a rectangle having a diagonal of 70 mm and a side of 30 mm.

Q3 The diagonal of a rectangle is 75 mm and it forms an angle of 35° with one side. Draw the rectangle.

Q4 Draw a parallelogram having sides of 50 mm and 75 mm and diagonals that intersect at 35°.

Q5 Draw a rhombus of 50 mm side and 75 mm diagonal.

Q6 Draw a rhombus with sides 40 mm long and the acute angles 50°.

Q7 Construct a hexagon with all its corners touching the inside of a 50 mm diameter circle. Draw a second hexagon with all its sides touching the outside of a 70 mm circle.

Q8 Construct a regular hexagon on a 70 mm diagonal.

Q9 Draw a hexagon of 30 mm sides standing on one of its corners.

Q10 Construct a hexagon 45 mm across the flats (between the parallel sides).

Q11 Draw a hexagon 50 mm across the corners.

Q12 Construct a regular octagon inside a square having 70 mm diagonals.

Q13 The perimeter of an octagon is 200 mm. Draw the figure.

Q14 Construct a regular octagon 60 mm across the flats.

Q15 Draw two lines 30 mm long to form an angle of 135°. Add six other lines of similar length to complete a regular octagon.

Q16 Construct a regular pentagon on a diameter of 70 mm.

Q17 The two interlacing triangles in Fig. 5:28 form the ideogram (advertising sign) for an independent airline. Draw this within a 120 mm diameter circle. Figure 5:29 gives details of the construction. The centre circle is 20 mm diameter.

Q18 Construct the five pointed gear wheel centre shown in Fig. 5:30, within a 100 mm diameter circle. The centre circle is 8 mm radius.

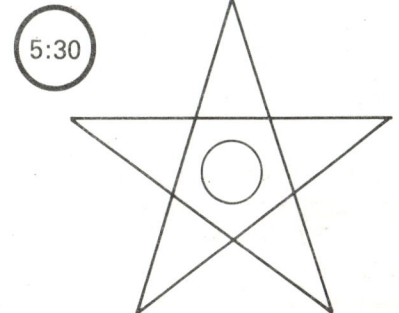

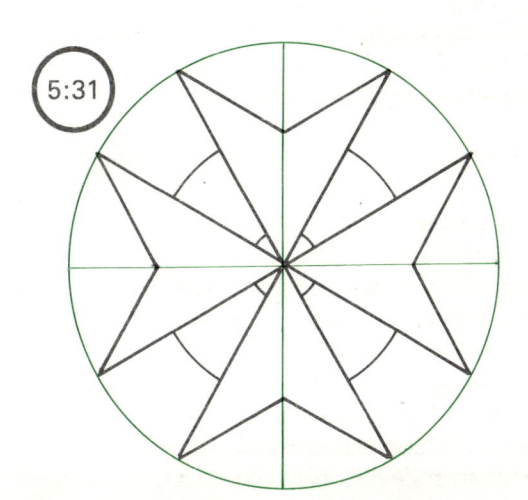

Q19 Copy the St John's cross shown in Fig. 5:31. Start with a 90 mm diameter circle and then use the 30/60° set square. The internal support circles are 50 mm and 16 mm diameter respectively.

43

Q20 Figure 5:32 shows a precious gem stone seen from underneath. The flat faces that reflect the light are called facets and are all contained within an octagon which fits into a circumscribing circle. The octagon is divided into two squares and these are cut into triangles meeting in the centre of the figure. Copy the given view within a 120 mm circle.

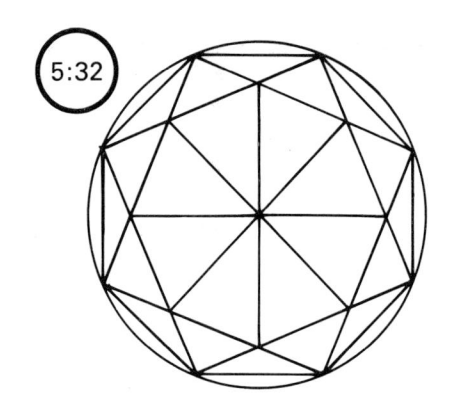

Q21 Figure 5:33 is a front view of a moon buggy which could be adapted for travelling in desert conditions. The main cabin is hexagonal and the top half of the rear storage space is a dodecahedron. All the chassis measurements are given. Copy the view making the diameter 110 mm.

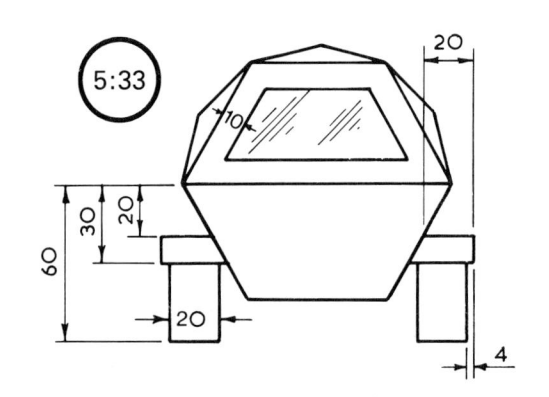

Q22 Figure 5:34 shows a double-ended box spanner standing on its larger end. The view on the right is looking down from above the spanner. Copy this view making the larger hexagon 116 mm across its diameter, the top end 90 mm diameter with a wall thickness of 6 mm.

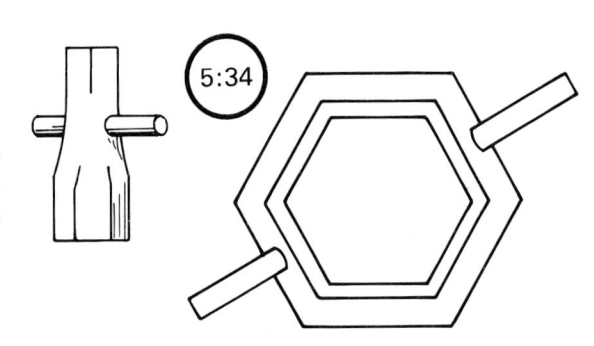

Q23 Figure 5:35 shows a wristwatch face within a hexagonal case. Draw this case inscribed in a 90 mm diameter circle. Include the hands and the twelve hour figures as shown.

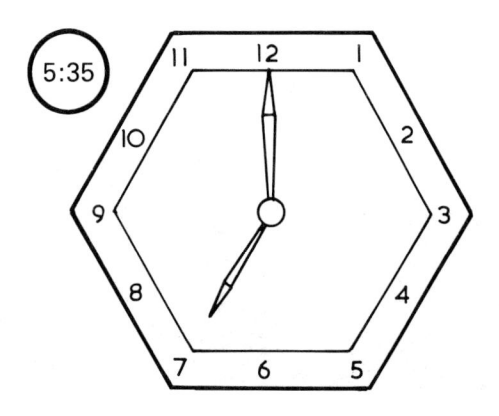

6 Circles in Design

The circle is a plane figure bounded by a curved line, all points on which are equidistant from its centre.

Just as the square is essential to all building work so the circle is equally essential to all engineering work. Most land transport rolls on wheels. Helping the smooth flow of this transport are the many roundabouts (circles again!) as shown by the photograph below which indicates a road taking off at a right angle (normal) and another one tangentially.

The bicycle contains many circles in the form of wheels, bearings, hubs, crank wheels, the pump and even washers and valves, probably running into hundreds of circular components if we really looked.

It can truly be said that our present way of life is built upon the square and the circle.

PARTS OF A CIRCLE

Arc
Any portion of the circumference.

Chord
A straight line, shorter than the diameter, joining two points on the circumference.

Circumference
The outline of the circle.

Diameter
A straight line across the centre of the circle ending at the circumference.

Normal
A straight line drawn outside the circle but radiating from its centre. (The continuation of the radius.)

Quadrant
The part enclosed by two radii at right angles and an arc. A quarter of the circle.

Radius
A straight line from the centre to the circumference. (Plural = **radii**; abbreviation *R* or *r*.)

Sector
The part enclosed by two radii and an arc, and covering less than 180°.

Segment
The part of a circle enclosed by a chord and its arc.

Semicircle
One of the halves into which a diameter divides a circle.

Tangent
A straight line touching the circumference but not entering the circle. (Always perpendicular to the normal.) See page 49.

The circle contains a total of 360° at its centre; therefore a quadrant (quarter-circle) contains 360 ÷ 4 = 90°.

46

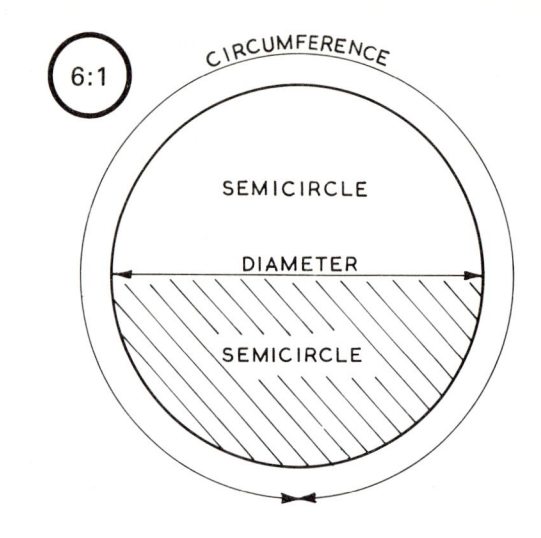

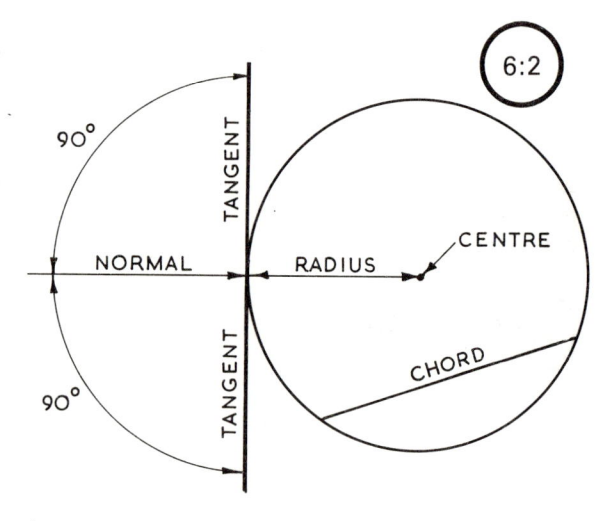

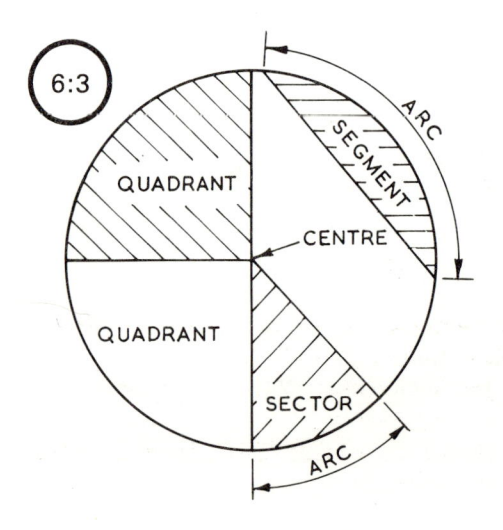

Circles drawn from the same centre are known as **concentric**; those from different centres, **eccentric**.

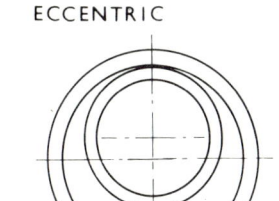

CONCENTRIC   ECCENTRIC

Q1 Draw the Mercedes car emblem shown in Fig. 6:4, with circle diameters of 90 mm and 100 mm and where each division is equal. The distance either side of the centre-line for each spoke is 3 mm at centre.

Q2 Draw the symbol for the radio beacon shown in Fig. 6:5, with concentric arcs 8 mm apart.

Q3 Draw the Audi car emblem shown in Fig. 6:6, making the outer circles 40 mm diameter, and where all circles are drawn from the one common horizontal centre-line. Choose the remaining dimensions yourself.

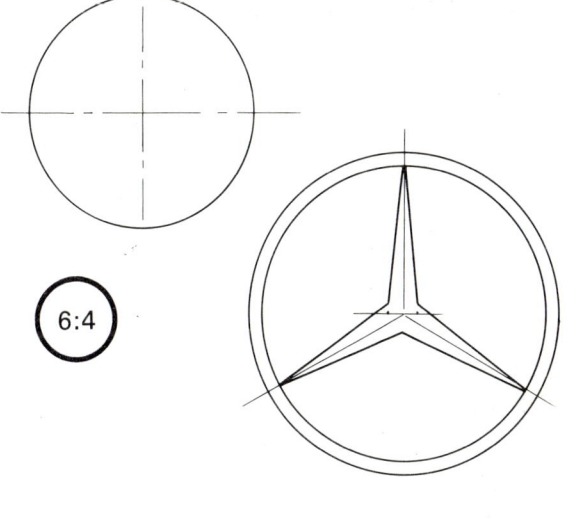

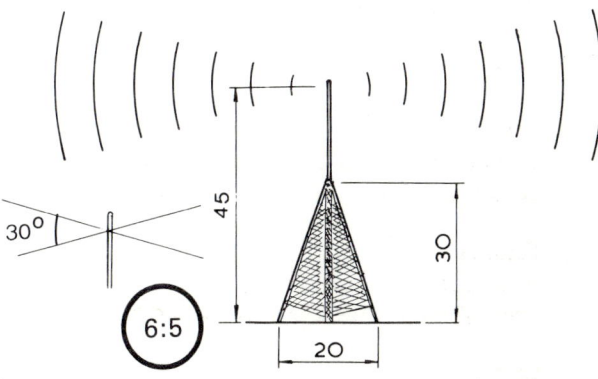

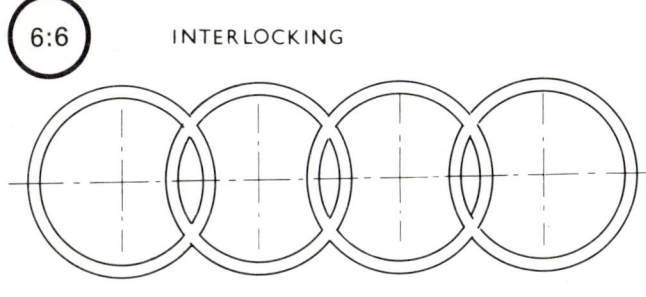

INTERLOCKING

Finding the centre of any circle (Fig. 6:7):
1 Draw any two chords as AB and CD. It helps accuracy if the chords are approximately at right angles to each other.
2 Bisect the chords.

The perpendicular bisector of a chord passes through the centre of the circle.

Drawing a circle (or an arc) to pass through three points (A, B, C) (Fig. 6:8):
1 Join AB and BC. These lines form chords of the required circle.
2 Bisect the chords. The bisectors cross at the circle centre.

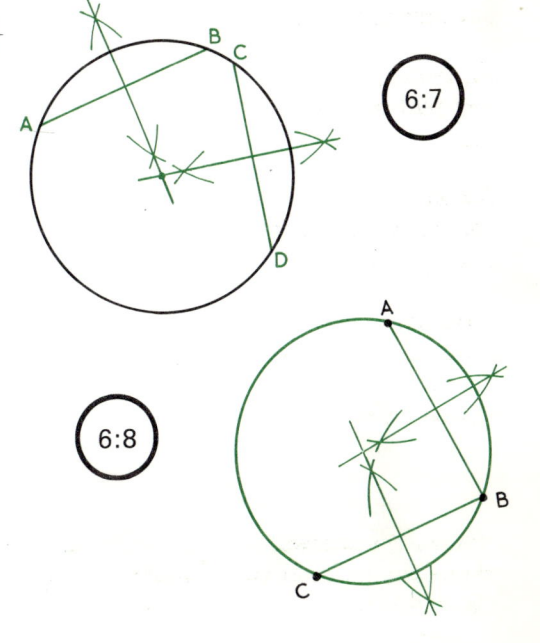

47

TANGENTS

A tangent is a line that touches the circumference of a circle without entering it.

Tangency has many important functions in engineering design; for example, bicycle spokes are tangential to the hub: this gives added strength, particularly when braking.

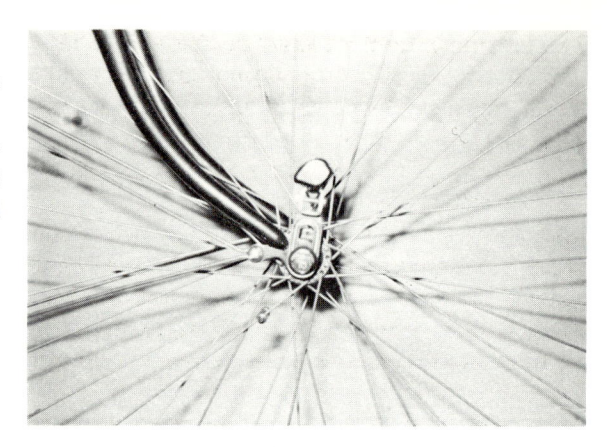

Drawing Tangents

(a) From a point P on the circumference (not given the circle centre) (Fig. 6:9):
1. Draw a circle 50 mm in diameter.
2. Using P as centre and any convenient radius, step off equal distances either side at A and B. P may be any point on the circumference.
3. Join A and B to form a chord. Bisect the chord.
4. Produce the bisector to give the normal.
5. Erect a perpendicular to the normal from point P.

(b) From a point P outside the circle (Fig. 6:10):
1. Draw a circle 60 mm in diameter.
2. Join P to the centre of the circle. P may be any point outside the circle.
3. Bisect this line and draw the semicircle cutting the circumference at A. This is the point of tangency.
4. Draw a line from P through A. This is a tangent from P. A second one can be drawn through the opposite curve as shown in dotted line.

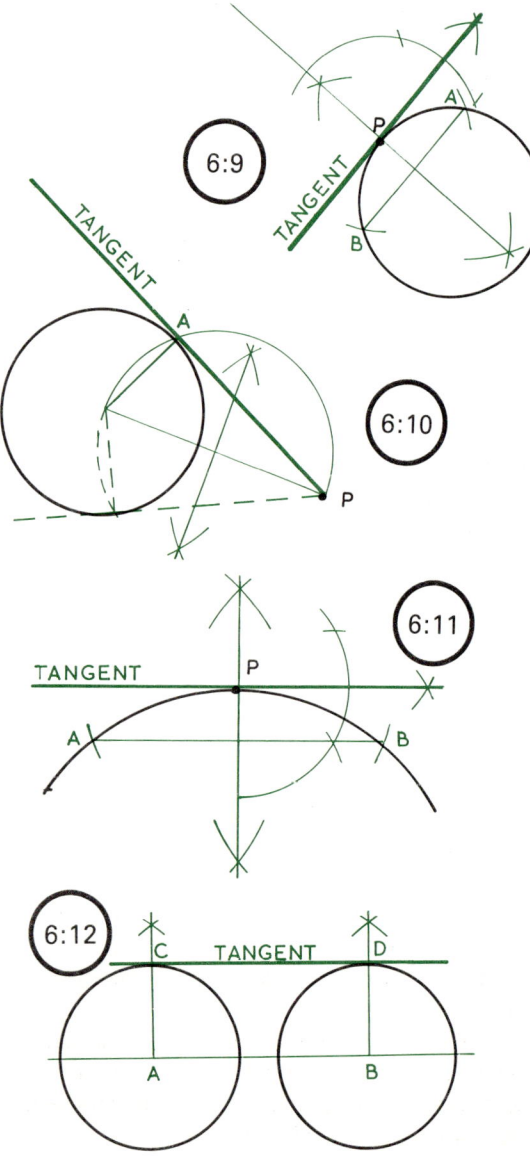

This solution depends on the right angle in a semicircle (see Fig. 4:18). Note also that the tangent forms a right angle with the radius from A to the centre.

(c) To an arc having an inaccessible centre (Fig. 6:11):

The solution to this problem is similar to that shown in Fig. 6:9.

COMMON TANGENTS

Drawing an External Tangent

(a) Common to two equal circles (Fig. 6:12):
1. Draw two circles, each 40 mm diameter.
2. Joint the centres A and B. Erect perpendiculars from both these points to C and D.
3. Draw a line through C and D. This is the required tangent and C and D are points of tangency.

(b) Common to two unequal circles (Fig. 6:13):
1. Draw two circles, one 40 mm diameter, the other 60 mm diameter, with centres 80 mm apart.
2. Join the centres A and B, bisect AB and draw the semicircle.
3. About the centre A draw a circle of radius equal to the difference between the radii of the given circles. This will cut the semicircle at C.
4. Draw a line from A through C cutting the circumference of the larger circle at D, the point of tangency.
5. Draw BE parallel with AD to obtain the point of tangency at E. The line ED is the required tangent.

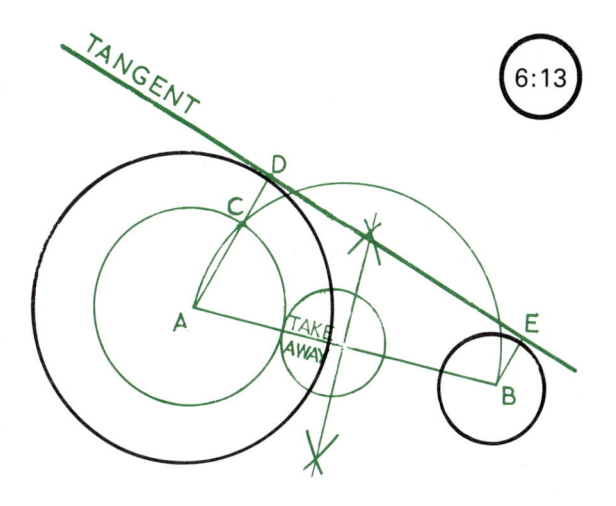

Drawing an Internal Tangent

(a) Common to two equal circles (Fig. 6:14):
1. Draw two circles, each 60 mm diameter, with centres 90 mm apart.
2. Join the centres A and B. Bisect AB and bisect each half to obtain points C and D.
3. With each in turn as centre and AC as radius, draw the two small circles cutting the large circles at E and F. These are the points of tangency on the internal tangent. A second internal tangent is shown in dotted line.

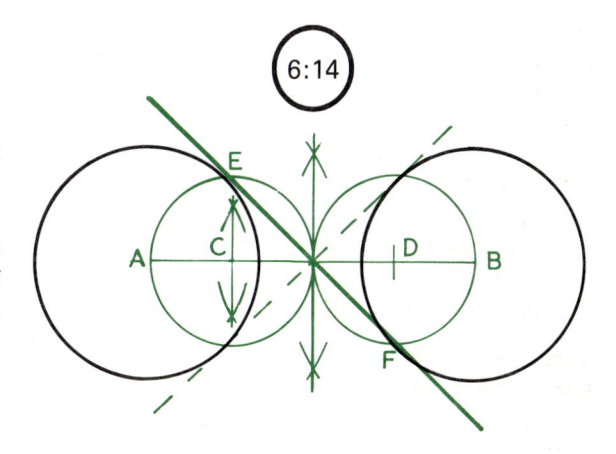

(b) Common to two unequal circles (Fig. 6:15):
1. Draw two circles, one 40 mm diameter, the other 70 mm diameter, with centres 95 mm apart.
2. Join the centres A and B. Bisect AB and draw the semicircle.
3. With B as centre and a radius equal to the sum of the two radii, draw the large circle cutting the semicircle at C.
4. Join B to C, cutting the circumference of the given circle in D.
5. Draw a line parallel to this from A, cutting the small circle in E. D and E are points of tangency and the line DE is a common interior tangent. A second tangent is shown in dotted line.

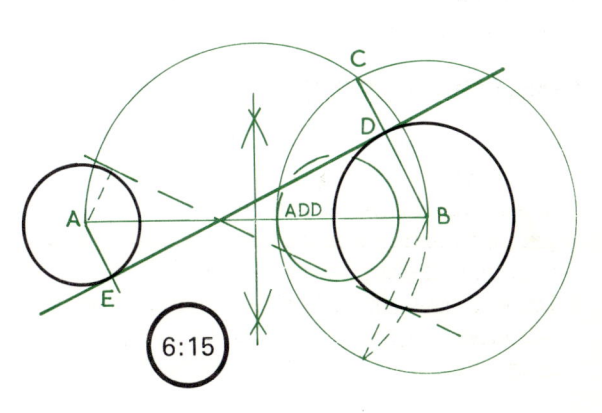

TANGENTIAL CIRCLES AND ARCS

When circles touch without penetrating they are called **tangential circles**, and the exact point at which they make maximum contact is called the **point of tangency**. This can be determined by drawing a line through the centres of both circles, when it will cut their circumferences at the common point of tangency (Fig. 6:16). Tangential circles form the basis for geometrical tracery and the profiles of mouldings, as well as the outlines of machinery guards.

(a) Drawing a reversed curve from two equal radii (Fig. 6:17):
1 Draw the centre-line and on it mark off a distance AB equal to the sum of the two equal radii. (Use radii of 20 mm each, so AB = 40 mm.)
2 Draw the semicircles.

(b) Drawing a reversed curve from two dissimilar radii (Fig. 6:18):
Follow the same procedure as detailed above in Fig. 6:17, but use radii of 45 mm and 15 mm.

(c) Blending two arcs of equal radius ($R = 35$ mm) to two parallel lines where $2R$ is greater than the distance between the lines (Fig. 6:19):
1 Draw the parallel lines AB and CD, 50 mm apart, and a centre-line EF.
2 Erect a perpendicular from any point G.
3 Using G as centre and $R = 35$ mm, mark point H.
4 Using point H as centre and $R = 35$ mm, draw the first arc cutting the centre-line at J.
5 Draw a line from G through J to cut line AB at K. Erect a perpendicular from K.
6 Using K as centre and $R = 35$ mm, mark point L.
7 Draw the second curve using L as centre.

(d) Blending two arcs of unequal radii in a given ratio to points A and B on two parallel lines (Fig. 6:20).
1 Draw the lines, mark off two points A and B, and join A to B.
2 Divide the line AB to the ratio 1:2 at point X.
3 Bisect AC and BX to cut perpendiculars drawn from A and B at O_1 and O_2.
4 Using O_1 as centre and O_1A as radius draw the first arc.
5 Repeat for the second arc using O_2B.

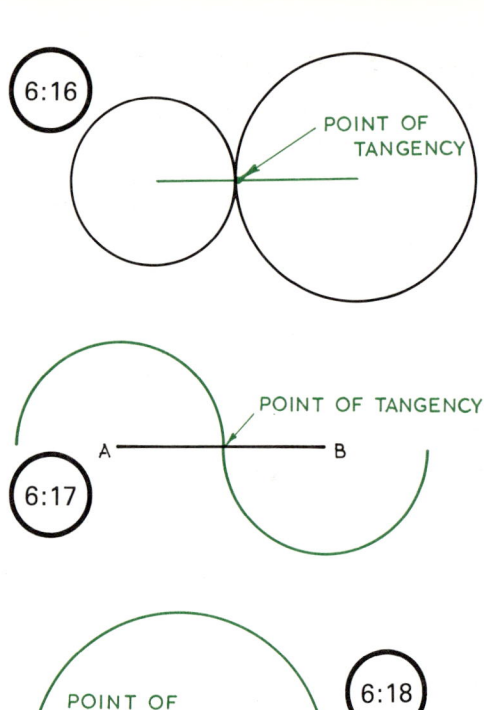

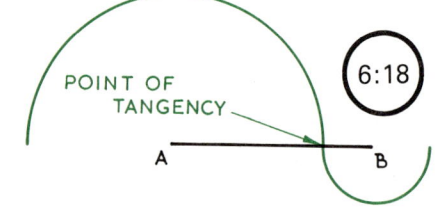

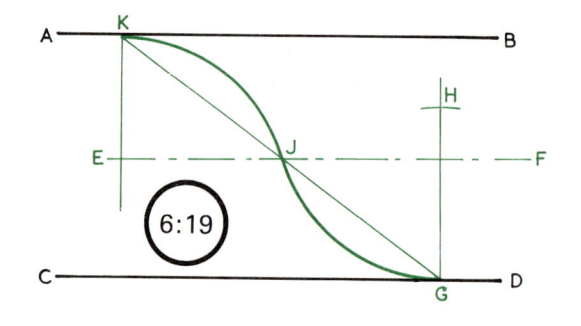

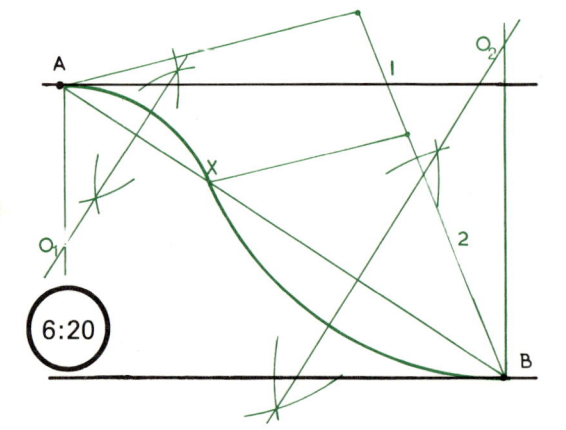

BLENDING ARCS TO CIRCLES

(a) Drawing an arc ($R = 35$ mm) **which blends internally with two circles** (Fig. 6:21):
1 Draw a circle with centre A, radius $r_1 = 15$ mm.
2 Draw a second circle, with centre B 60 mm from A, radius $r_2 = 25$ mm.
3 Using A as centre and $R + r_1$ as radius ($35 + 15 = 50$), draw an arc at C.
4 Using B as centre and $R + r_2$ as radius ($35 + 25 = 60$), draw a second arc cutting the first at C. An arc of $R = 35$ mm drawn from this will blend into the two given circles.

(b) Drawing two arcs of equal radius to join and blend with any two given circles (Fig. 6:22): Draw two circles with centres A ($r_1 = 12$ mm) and B ($r_2 = 20$ mm) where AB = 50 mm. Proceed as in Fig. 6:21, drawing arcs of $R = 20$ mm on both sides of the centre-line.

(c) Drawing an arc ($R = 65$ mm) **which blends externally with two given circles** (Fig. 6:23):
1 Draw two circles with centres A ($r_1 = 15$ mm) and B ($r_2 = 25$ mm), where AB = 60 mm.
2 Using A as centre and $R - r_1$ as radius ($65 - 15 = 50$), draw an arc at C.
3 Using B as centre and $R - r_2$ as radius ($65 - 25 = 40$), draw a second arc cutting the first at C. An arc of 65 mm radius drawn from this will blend into the two given circles.

(d) Drawing two arcs of equal radius enclosing two given circles (Fig. 6:24): Using circles with radii of 15 mm and 50 mm, centres 60 mm apart, proceed as in Fig. 6:23, drawing arcs of $R = 60$ mm on both sides of the centre-line.

Q4 The photograph shows a park bench, the end frames of which consist of series of curves blending together. Using your own dimensions, design one end frame for a bench similar to the one shown. Leave in your construction lines.

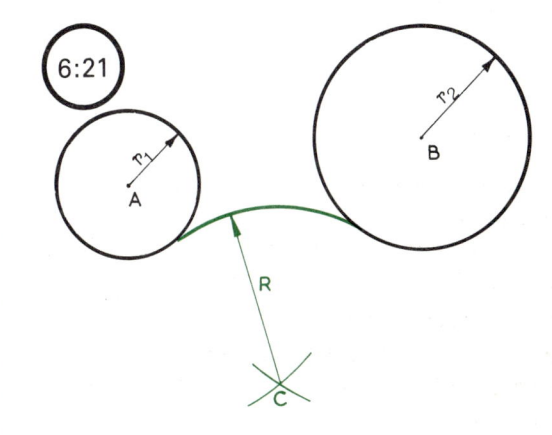

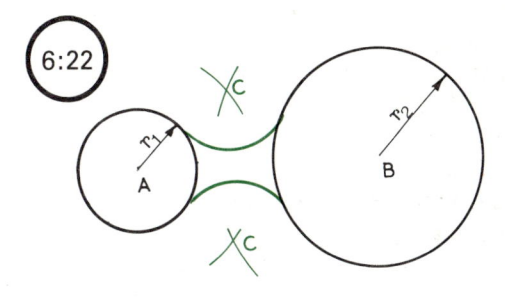

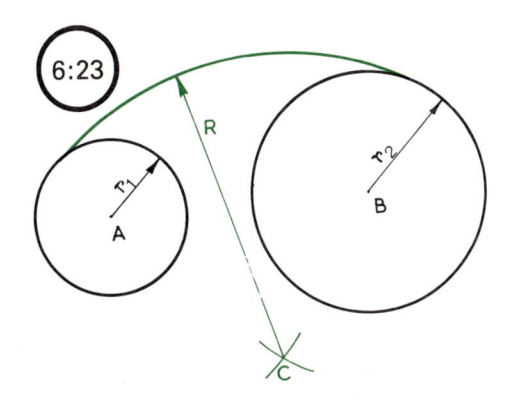

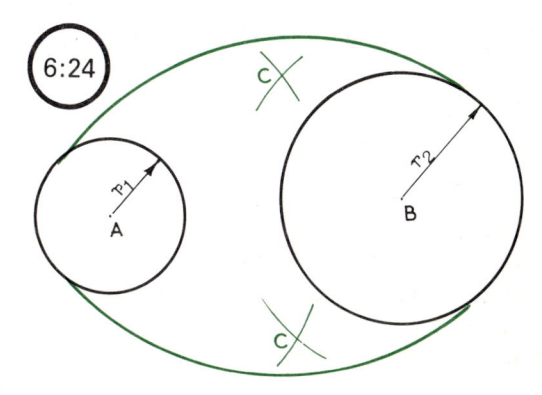

51

TANGENTIAL CIRCLES

(a) Drawing a circle of given radius ($R = 50$ mm) to enclose two other given circles (Fig. 6:25):
1. Draw two circles with centres 45 mm apart, $r_1 = 20$ mm, $r_2 = 10$ mm.
2. Using A as centre and $R - r_1$ as radius, draw an arc at C.
3. Using B as centre and $R - r_2$ as radius, draw a second arc cutting the first at C. This is the centre of the circumscribing circle.

(b) Drawing a circle of given radius ($R = 15$ mm) internally tangential to two other given circles (Fig. 6:26):
1. Draw two circles with centres 60 mm apart, $r_1 = 25$ mm, $r_2 = 15$ mm.
2. Using A as centre and $R + r_1$ as radius, draw an arc at C.
3. Using B as centre and $R + r_2$ as radius, draw a second arc cutting the first at C. This is the centre of the tangential circle.

(c) Drawing a circle of given radius ($R = 20$ mm) tangential to a second circle and a straight line (Fig. 6:27):
1. Draw circle C, radius $r = 15$ mm.
2. Draw line AB, 30 mm below the centre of circle C.
3. Draw line DE parallel to AB and 20 mm above it.
4. Using C as centre and a radius equal to the sum of the radii of the two circles ($r + R = 15$ mm + 20 mm), cut DE at F. This is the centre of the required circle.

(d) Drawing three tangential circles of given radius (Fig. 6:28):
($R_A = 35$ mm, $R_B = 25$ mm, $R_C = 15$ mm)
1. Draw circle A ($R_A = 35$ mm) and from its centre draw line ab equal in length to the sum of radii R_A and R_B (35 mm + 25 mm).
2. Using b as centre and the sum of radii R_B and R_C as radius (25 mm + 15 mm) draw an arc at C.
3. Using a as centre and the sum of radii R_A and R_C as radius (35 mm + 15 mm), draw a second arc cutting the first at C.
4. Draw the third circle about c.

The three lines joining the centres of the circles cross the three points of common tangency marked T.

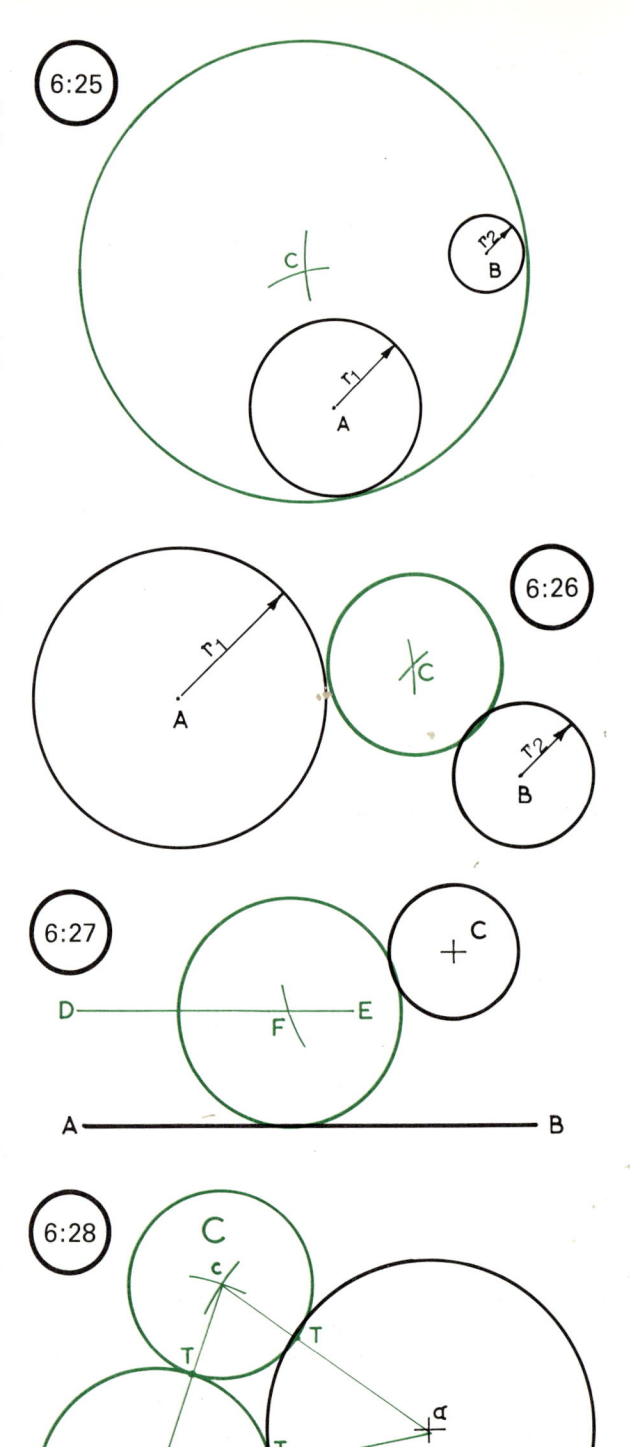

FURTHER QUESTIONS

Q5 Draw a circle of 25 mm radius. Construct the tangent and normal from a point P set anywhere in the circumference.

Q6 Draw a circle of 30 mm radius. Mark a point 60 mm from its centre. From this point construct two tangents to the circle. Measure and state the magnitude of the angle between them.

Q7 Draw two circles with 30 mm and 60 mm diameters respectively and with their centres 75 mm apart. Construct a common *external* tangent to both.

Q8 Draw the two circles as detailed in Q7 and then construct one of their common *internal* tangents.

Q9 Draw two lines meeting at an angle of 30°, AB 60 mm in length and AC 50 mm in length. Construct a circle to pass through points A, B and C.

Q10 Draw a circle of 30 mm diameter touching internally a second circle of 50 mm radius. Draw a third circle of 25 mm radius, inside the larger circle and outside the smaller circle, yet touching them both.

Q11 Draw a circle of 30 mm diameter tangential to the two circles given in Fig. 6:29.

Q12 Copy the design (Fig. 6:30) for the facets of a gem stone (80 mm diameter).

Q13 Copy the compass card shown in Fig. 6:31 (70 mm diameter).

Q14 Copy the view of a car brake drum shown in Fig. 6:32. Do not draw the small circles but indicate their positions by short centre-lines.

Q15 Copy the views of Cyma Reversa mouldings shown in Figs 6:33 and 6:34.

Q16 Copy the view of a car seat adjuster plate shown in Fig. 6:35, using set squares to draw the 15° tangential lines.

Q17 Design a pie chart (100 mm diameter) showing how you use the 24 hours of a normal weekday, e.g. sleeping, eating, travel, schoolwork, other activities.

Q18 Design a pie diagram (100 mm diameter) to show the year divided proportionally between work and leisure using the following figures:
    Saturdays and Sundays   104 days
    Bank Holidays   8 days
    Working days   193 days
    Other school holidays   60 days

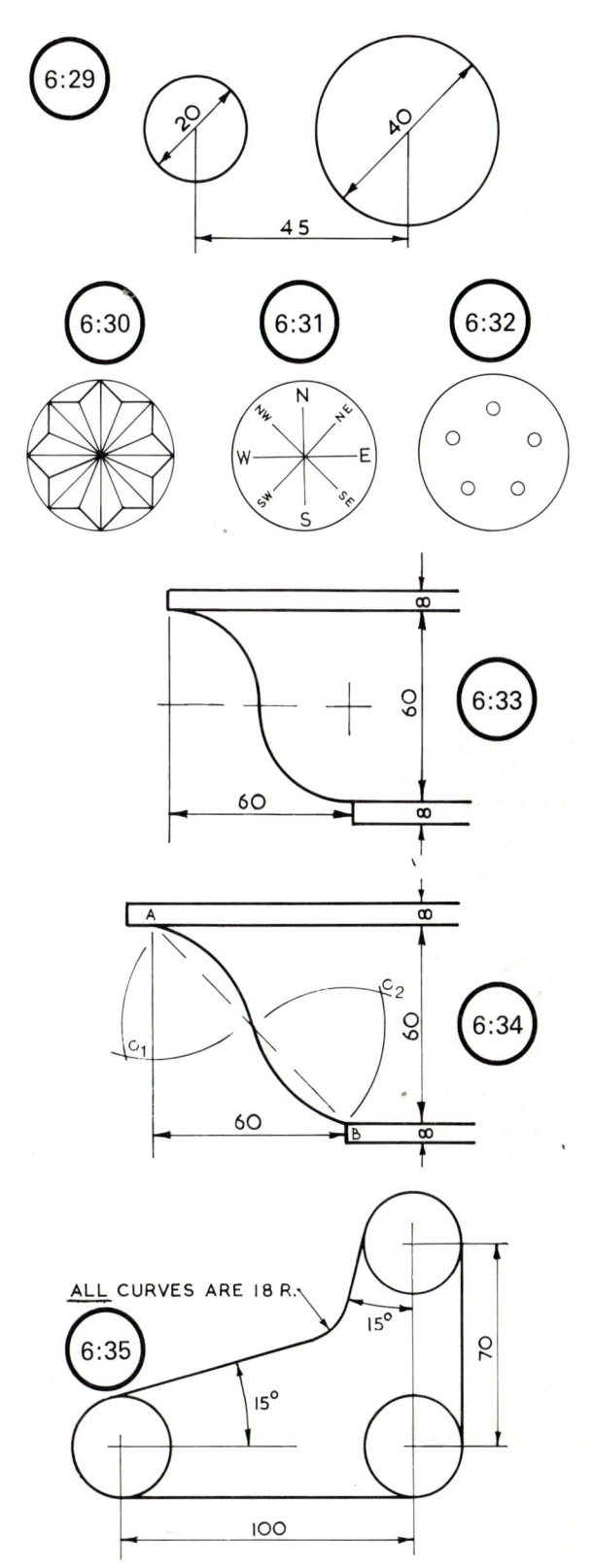

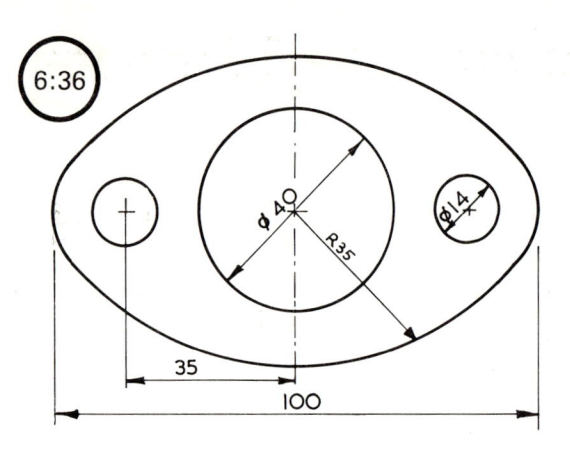

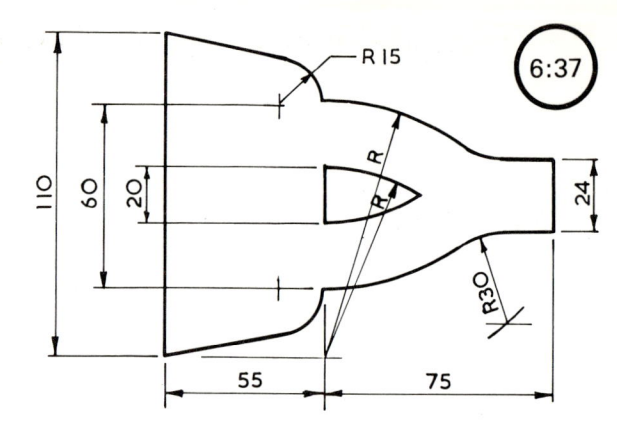

Q19 Copy the motor cycle carburettor flange (Fig. 6:36). Start from a centre line.

Q20 Copy full size the view of the Dutch hoe (Fig. 6:37).

Q21 Make a full size drawing of the machine link (Fig. 6:38).

Q22 Copy the drawing of a gear lever trigger (Fig. 6:39).

Q23 Copy the given view of a lathe slide handle (Fig. 6:40).

Q24 Copy the outline of the hexagon spanner (Fig. 6:41). The radii, R, can be found from the sides of the hexagon as shown.

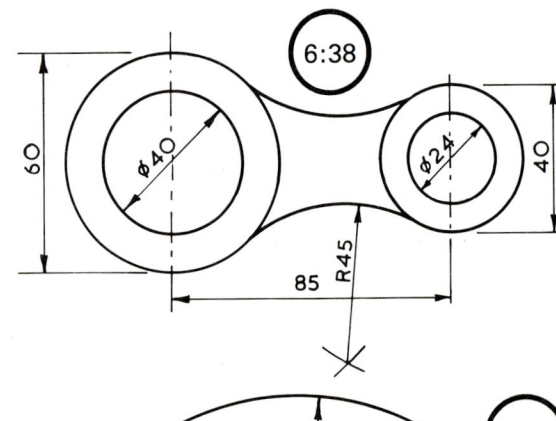

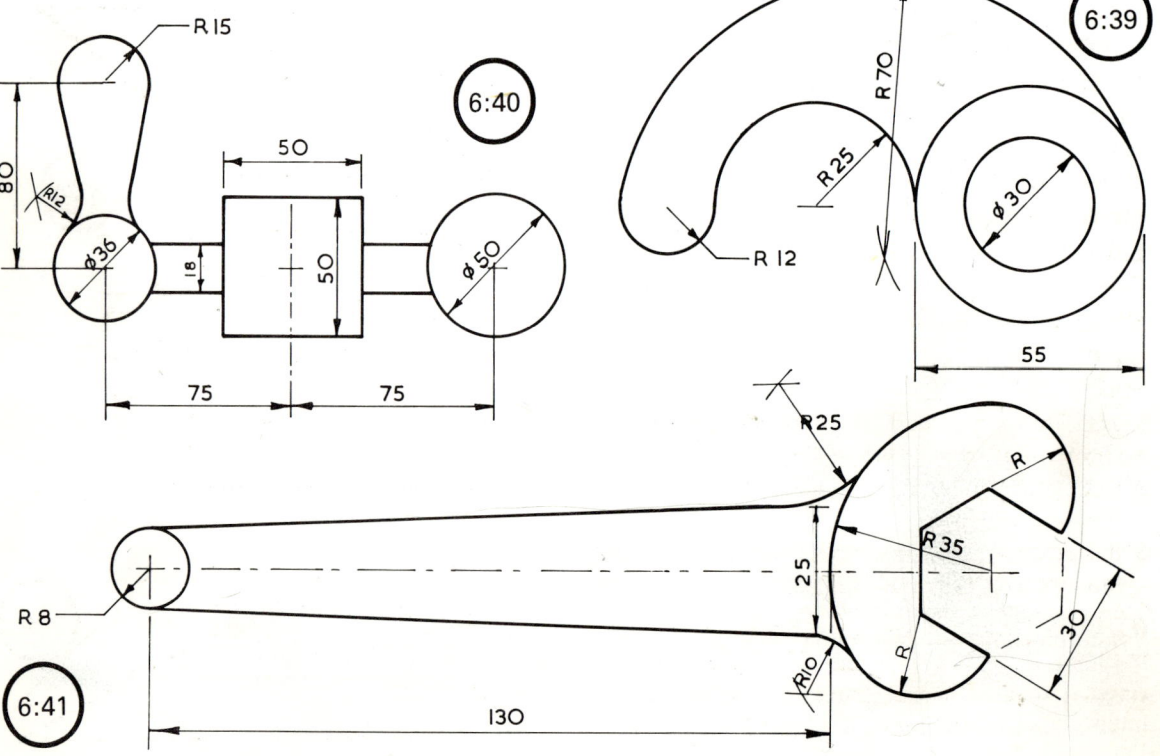

7 Inscribed and Circumscribed Figures

INSCRIBED FIGURES

An inscribed figure is the largest figure of the required shape that will fit into a given outline.

Inscribed figures form an important part in the design and ornamentation of many everyday articles.

Inscribing Circles

(a) In a given square (Fig. 7:1) Draw a square with sides of 50 mm. The diagonals of the square bisect the angles; the intersection of the diagonals is therefore at the centre of the inscribed circle.

(b) Four equal circles in a given square (Fig. 7:2):
1 Draw a square with sides of 80 mm.
2 Bisect the sides, thus producing four smaller squares.
3 Draw the diagonals across each square. The centres of these diagonals mark the centres of the inscribed circles.

(c) In an equilateral triangle (Fig. 7:3) Draw an equilateral triangle with 60 mm sides. The bisectors of any two angles intersect at the centre of the inscribed circle.

(d) In a given rhombus (Fig. 7:4) Draw a rhombus with sides of 60 mm. The intersection of the diagonals marks the centre of the inscribed circle, as indeed it does with all regular polygons.

(e) Four equal circles, each touching two others and one side only of a given square (Fig. 7:5):
1 Draw a square with 80 mm sides.
2 Draw the diagonals, thus dividing the square into four triangles.
3 Inscribe a circle in each of these triangles using the method shown in Fig. 7:3.

(f) In a scalene triangle (Fig. 7:6) Draw a triangle with sides of 60 mm, 90 mm and 120 mm. As in Fig. 7:3, the bisectors of any two angles intersect at the centre of the inscribed circle.

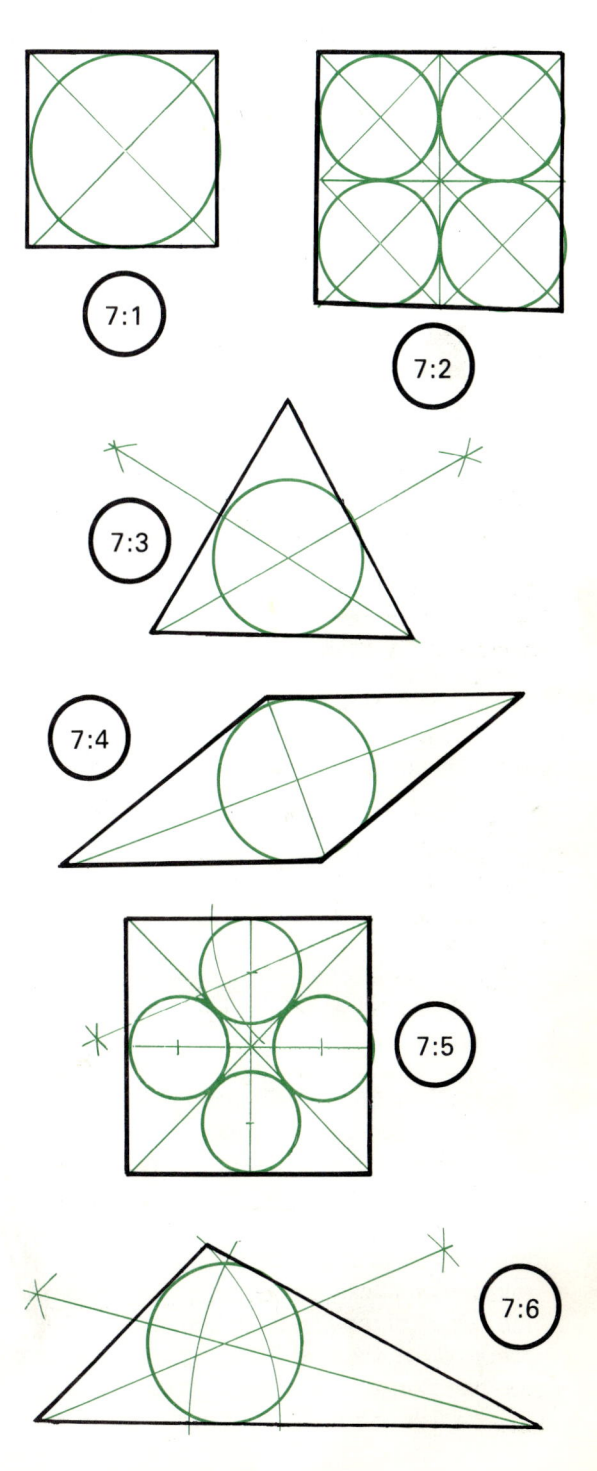

55

The basic construction shown on page 55 can be expanded into more elaborate geometric patterns that have provided the foundation for much decorative work on the pottery, woodwork and architecture of many countries throughout the ages.

(g) Inscribing three equal circles in an equilateral triangle (Figs 7:7 and 7:8):
1 Draw a triangle with 100 mm sides and bisect all three angles (Fig. 7:7).
2 Bisect the angles ABC and BCA as shown in Fig. 7:8. These bisectors cross at D, the centre of the first inscribed circle.
3 Mark off the distance CD along the bisector AB from point A as in Fig. 7:8. This gives the centre of the second inscribed circle.
4 Mark the distance CD along the bisector from the apex E. This establishes the centre of the third inscribed circle.

(h) Inscribing six equal circles in an equilateral triangle (Fig. 7:9):
1 Draw a triangle with 120 mm sides and bisect all three angles.
2 Bisect angle BAC to obtain D, the centre of the first circle.
3 Draw EF through D and parallel to BC to obtain the centres of the other two base circles at E and F.
4 Draw EG and FG parallel to the other two sides of the triangle to obtain the three remaining centres.

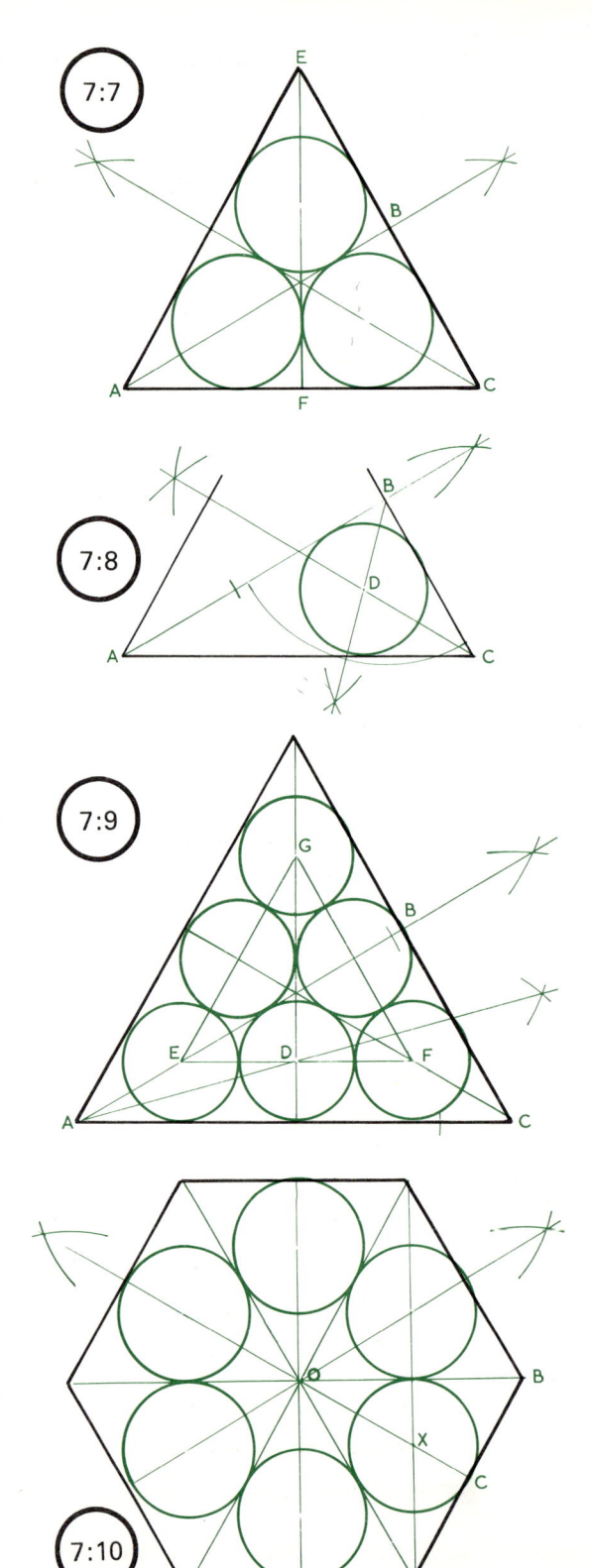

(i) Inscribing six equal circles in a given regular hexagon (Fig. 7:10):
1 Draw a regular hexagon (60 mm sides) and bisect all the angles, thus dividing the hexagon into six equilateral triangles.
2 Bisect each side of the hexagon, thus bisecting the vertex angles of each of the six triangles.
3 Bisect a base angle of one of the equilateral triangles as at angle OAB. The intersection of this bisector with the bisector OC establishes the centre of the first inscribed circle.
4 Mark off the distance OX along each appropriate bisector to obtain the centres of the other five circles.

(j) Inscribing three equal circles in a given circle (Figs 7:11 and 7:12):
1 Draw a circle 70 mm in diameter.
2 With CO extended as the vertical centre-line, divide the circle into six equal parts (60°/30° set square).
3 Produce the two division lines OA and OB (Fig. 7:12).
4 Join A to B by a horizontal line touching the circle at C, making this line tangential to the circle.
5 Bisect the angle OBC cutting OC at E, the centre of the first inscribed circle.
6 Transfer the distance OE to the radius lines 2 and 3, to obtain the centres of the other two circles.

CIRCUMSCRIBING FIGURES

A circumscribing figure is the outline that touches and envelopes the given figure.

Circumscribed Triangles
Bisect any two of the sides, then the bisectors cross at the centre of the circumscribing circle. (See Figs 7:13 and 7:14.)

When the triangle is obtuse-angled, the centre of the circle lies outside the triangle, opposite to the obtuse angle.

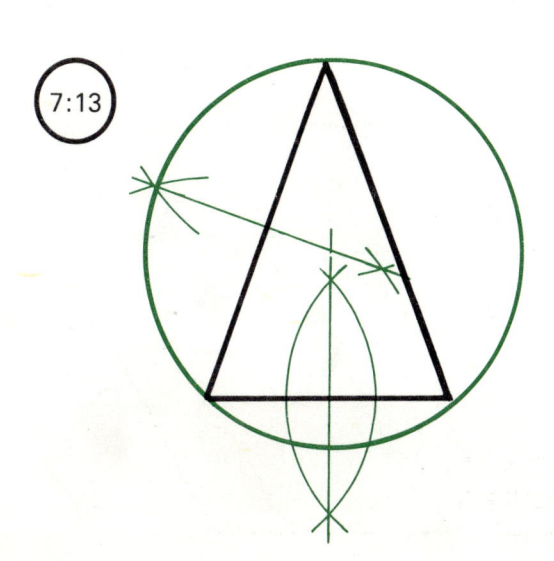

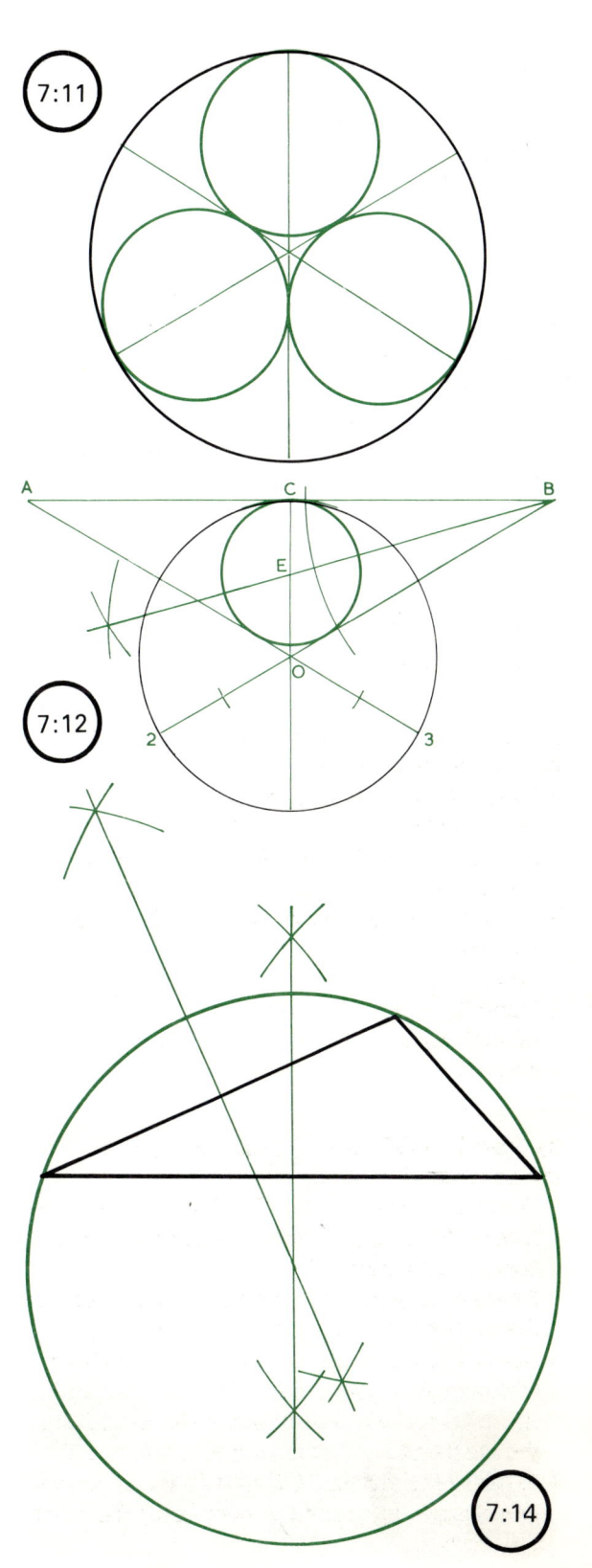

57

QUESTIONS

Q1 The plastic cutlery holder shown in the photograph on the right has four circular compartments. Copy the top view (Fig. 7:15). Show all construction lines. The outer radii, including the blending arcs, are all 25 mm.

Q2 The retaining plate shown in Fig. 7:16 is in the form of an equilateral triangle. The three fixing holes are equally spaced on a 60 mm diameter circle. Copy the given view using your own dimensions for the radius corners.

Q3 A ceramic tile is shown below. This carries a pattern of two rhomboids. (i) Copy the tile 90 mm × 90 mm and insert the pattern given. Colour may be used to highlight the pattern. (ii) Design a second tile to the same size but using an alternative repeating pattern.

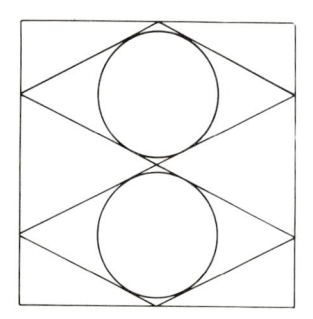

Q4 The two photographs show a camera tripod head. Draw the outline of the white central cross within a 90 mm square. Use your own dimensions.

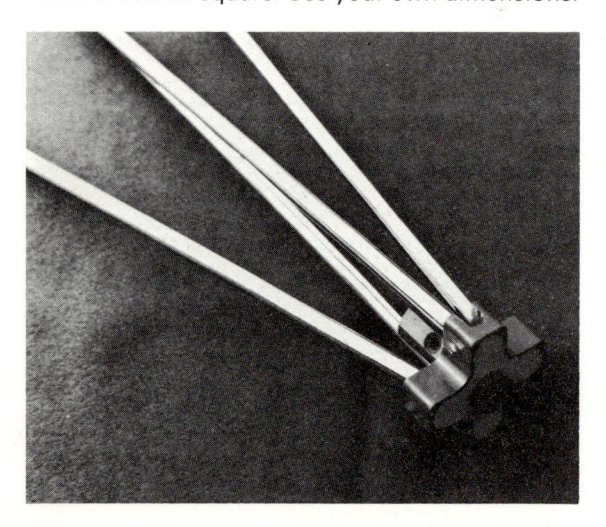

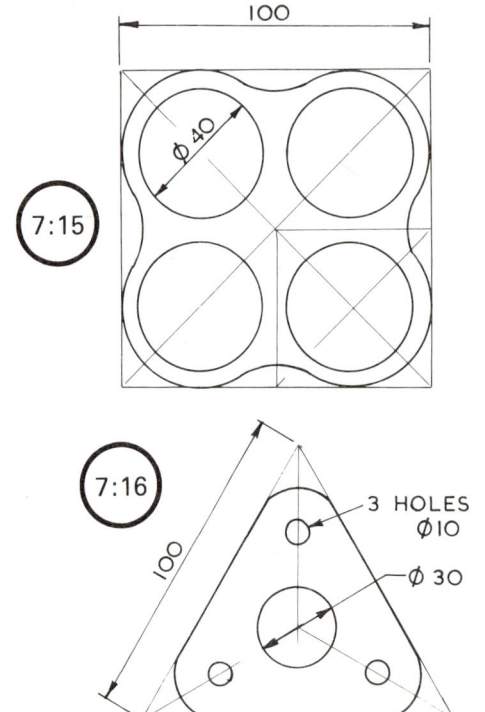

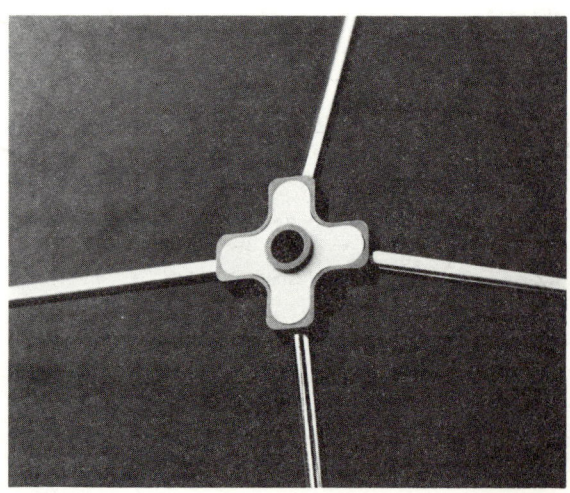

ESCRIBED CIRCLES

An escribed circle is outside the **given** figure but is contained within the sides of the figure **produced**.

Escribing a circle on side BC of a given triangle (Fig. 7:17):
1. Draw a triangle ABC (AB = 65 mm, AC = 70 mm, BC = 40 mm) and extend AB to D and AC to E as required.
2. Bisect the two angles DBC and BCE.
3. The intersection of these bisectors marks the centre of the escribed circle. Sides AB and AC can be similarly treated to produce two more escribed circles.

FURTHER QUESTIONS

Q5 Draw a triangle with sides of 60, 70 and 80 mm respectively and insert a circle to touch all three sides.

Q6 Re-draw the triangle in Q5 and draw a circle passing through its three points.

Q7 Within a circle of 60 mm radius, inscribe three circles of equal diameter touching each other and the given circle.

Q8 Circumscribe an equilateral triangle of 100 mm side and inscribe three equal circles within the triangle to touch each other and the three sides of the triangle.

Q9 Inscribe six equal circles in a regular hexagon of 40 mm side, each circle to touch two others and one side of the hexagon.

Q10 Construct a pentagon within a circle of 60 mm diameter and escribe a circle within two of the pentagon's sides. Measure and write down the diameter of the circle.

Q11 Inscribe five equal circles within a regular pentagon of 100 mm diameter. Each circle should touch two others and one side of the pentagon.

Q12 Figure 7:18 shows a cross-section of a circular pedestrian tunnel on the London Underground. Draw this using 20 mm to represent 1 m.

Q13 Figure 7:19 is the plan of a road junction where it is proposed to substitute a circular roundabout for a triangular island. Draw the largest roundabout that will fit into the site and leave the roads the same width. All roads are 10 m wide. Use 1 mm to represent 1 m.

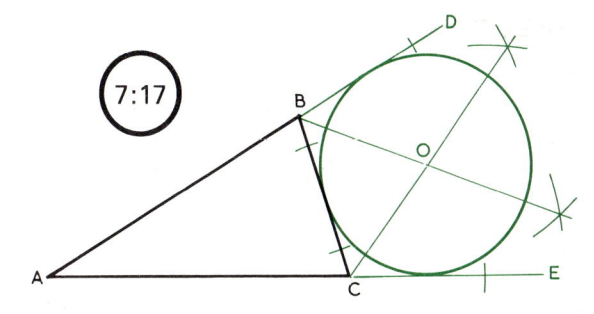

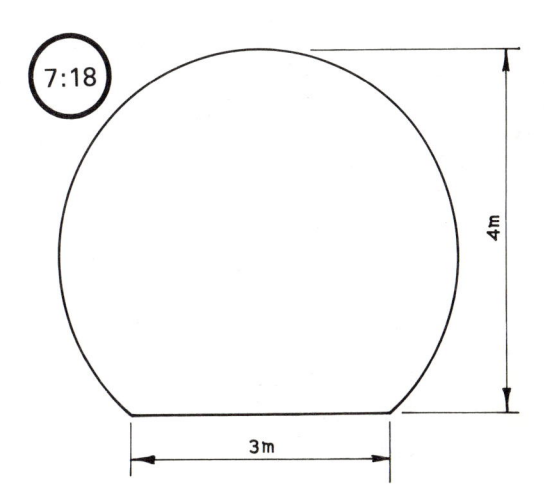

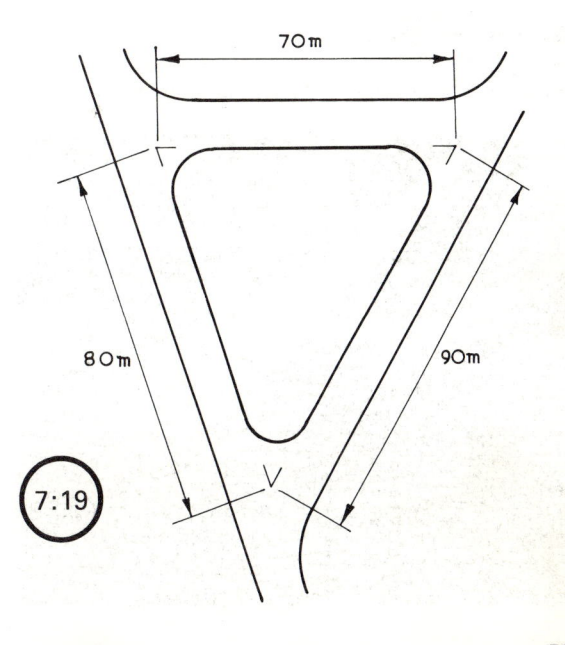

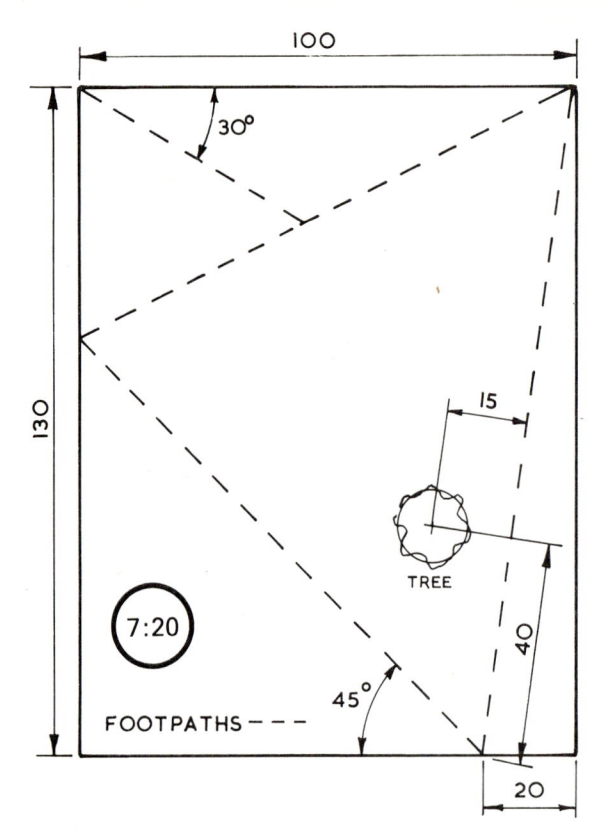

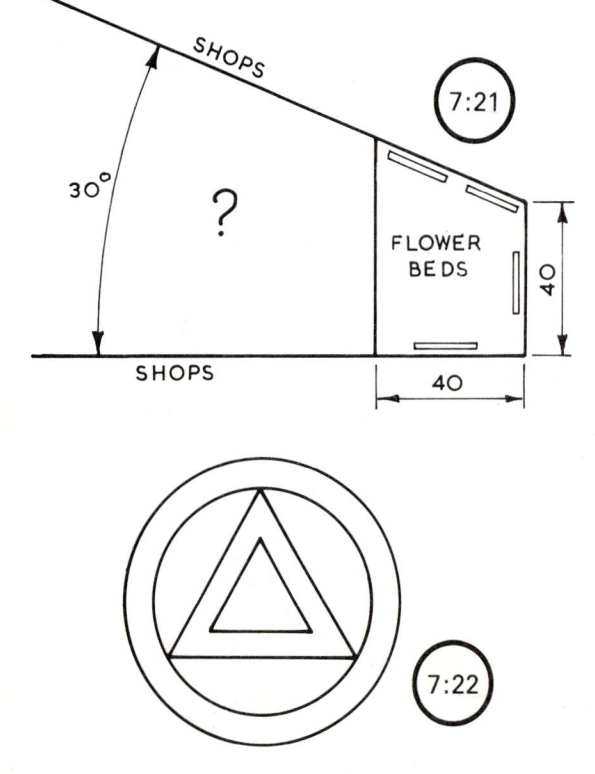

Q14 Figure 7:20 shows a reduced scale drawing of a grassland area crossed by public footpaths. A group of young campers wish to set up camp as far away as possible from the footpaths. (i) Copy the drawing using the dimensions given. (ii) Locate and mark in the centre of the campsite. (iii) Measure and state the distance of the camp from the centre of the tree. 1 mm on the drawing represents 2.5 m on the ground.

Q15 A corner of a new shopping precinct is to include a small garden with four seats to make a rest area for shoppers. An ornamental fountain is to be erected equidistant from the shops and the garden. Copy the outline of the plan (Fig. 7:21) using the dimensions given, and find the centre of the fountain.

Q16 Copy the design for a danger warning sign (Fig. 7:22). Make the outer sides of the triangle 80 mm and all the double lines 10 mm apart.

Q17 Figure 7:23 shows the outline of three meshing gear wheels on a model of a lathe. The distances between their centres are: AB = 45 mm, AC = 36 mm, BC = 40 mm. The three gears are to be protected by a circular guard giving 5 mm clearance over each gear. (i) Copy the drawing using the dimensions given. (ii) Add the circular guard. (iii) Measure and state its diameter.

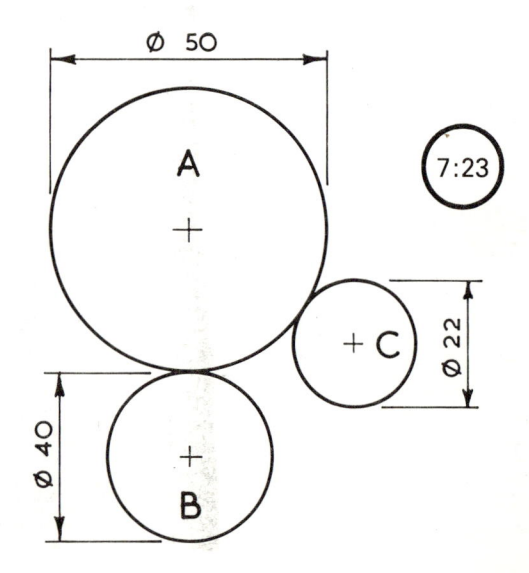

8 The Ellipse

This is a plane figure formed of one complete curve drawn around two points called 'foci', when the sum of the distances from any point on the curve to the foci is constant and equal to the major diameter.

PARTS OF AN ELLIPSE

The **major axis**, or major diameter, is the longest line that can be drawn across the ellipse.

The **minor axis**, or minor diameter, is the perpendicular bisector through the centre of the major axis.

The **foci** are two points (each called a 'focus') situated on the major axis, half its length distant from the outer ends of the minor axis (at C and D below).

The **normal**, or perpendicular, to the curve bisects the angle formed by the two lines drawn from any point on the curve to the **foci**.

The **tangent** is the line perpendicular to the normal at the point where the normal touches the curve.

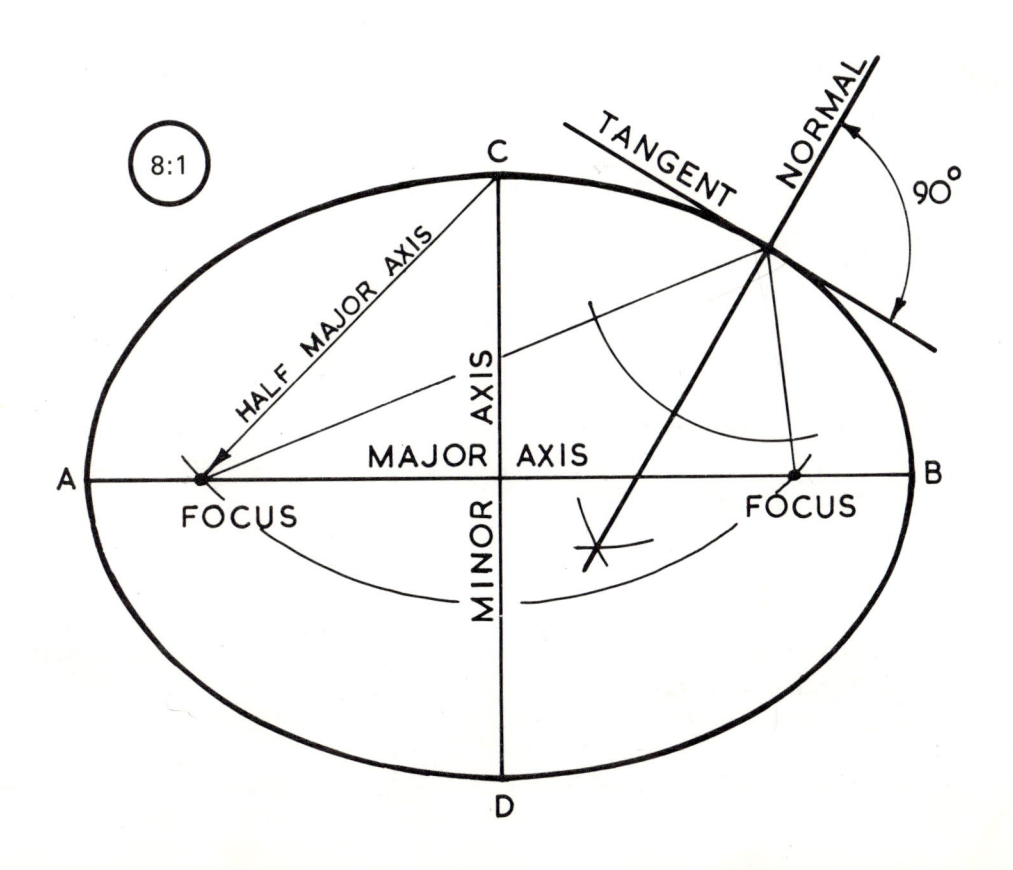

61

DRAWING AN ELLIPSE

The Auxiliary Circle Method
1 Draw the major axis AB (120 mm) and the minor axis CD (80 mm), intersecting at O (Fig. 8:2).
2 Using O as centre and radii of OA and OC respectively, draw the major and minor circles.
3 Divide these into twelve equal sectors using the 60°/30° set square.
4 Draw a series of vertical lines from the points where these sector lines cut the outer circle.
5 Draw a series of horizontal lines from the points where the sector lines cross the inner circle. Then the intersections of the two sets of lines give points on the curve of the ellipse. More intermediate points can be obtained if needed as shown at E.
6 Join all the intersections by a free flowing curve.

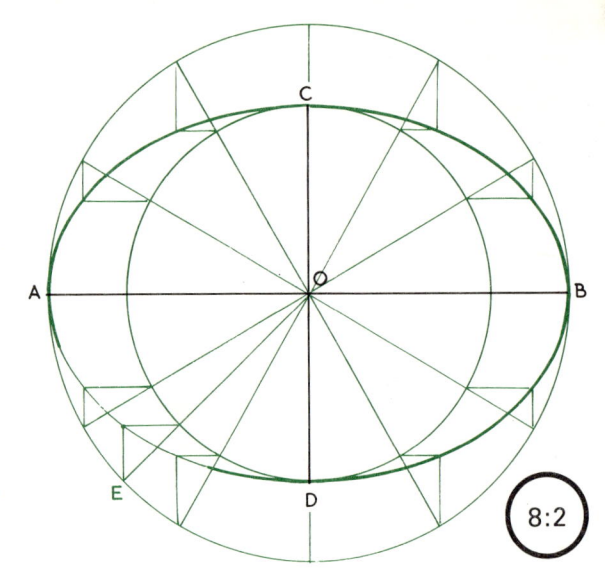

The Trammel Method
This is an easy practical method, the only construction needed being the two axes AB and CD (Fig. 8:3). Only enough points to give easy construction need to be plotted—more at the smaller curved ends and fewer along the flatter parts of the curve.

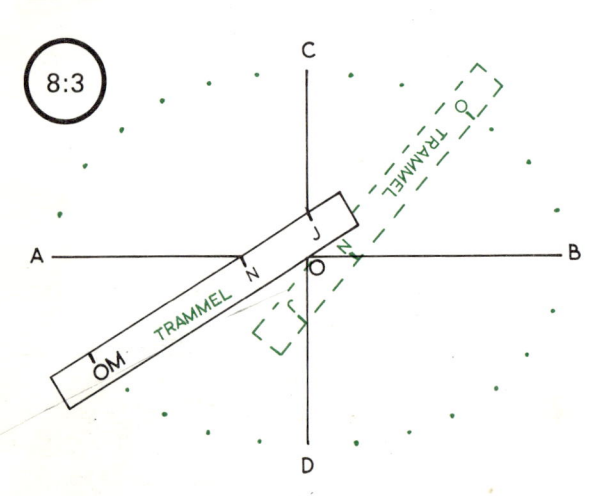

1 Draw the given major and minor axes AB (120 mm) and CD (80 mm).
2 Using a piece of paper with a straight edge, mark off a length OM to N equal to OC, half the minor axis.
3 Mark off a second length OM to J equal to half the major axis, OA.

4 Keeping the marks N and J accurately positioned on their respective axes, move the trammel round and mark off points on the drawing paper to coincide with OM (the outer mark).

Two different positions of the trammel are shown in Fig. 8:3. Complete the drawing.

The Rectangle Method
1 Draw the major and minor axes AB (80 mm) and CD (56 mm). (See Fig. 8:4.)
2 Draw a rectangle about their ends.
3 Divide AB into a convenient number of equal parts and number them from their outer ends.
4 Divide the ends EF and GH into the same number of equal parts numbering these from A and B outwards.
5 Draw lines from D to meet points 3, 2 and 1 on the edge A to F.
6 Draw lines from C to pass through points 1, 2 and 3 on the axis AB. Thes will cut the lines from D at three points on the curve of the ellipse. (Alternatively, instead of drawing these lines right across the figure, mark only the points of intersection.)
7 Repeat in the other half of the rectangle and join the intersections in a smooth curve.

8:4

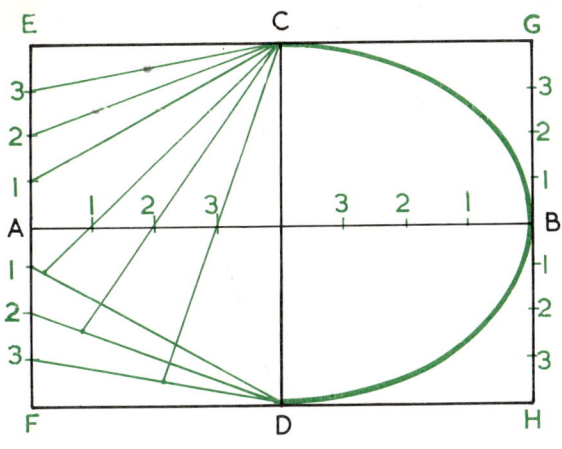

This is a useful construction as it can be applied to both rectangles and parallelograms. In the latter case, where the major and minor axes do not intersect at right angles, they are called **conjugate axes**.

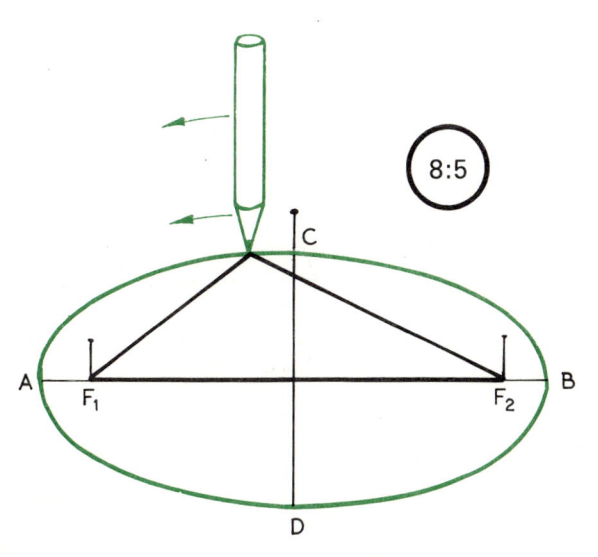

The Pin and String Method

This is a useful practical method for striking an ellipse much used in woodworking for such items as mirror frames and trays. It can be used in much larger work such as marking out elliptical flower beds. See Fig. 8:5.

1. Draw the major and minor axes and insert pins at A, B, C and D (the outer ends of the major and minor axes). Insert two more pins at the focal points F_1 and F_2 (see Fig. 8:1).
2. Tie thin string in a continuous loop round the pins F_1, F_2 and C.
3. Place a pencil inside the loop at C and keeping the loop taut, move the pencil round to mark out the ellipse.

The sum of the distances from the pencil point to the foci is constant at all points on the curve and is equal to the length of the major axis.

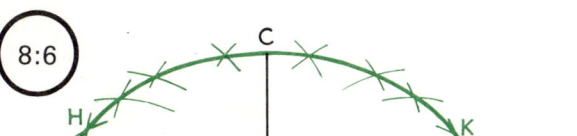

The Foci Method (Fig. 8:6)

1. Draw the major axis (800 mm) and minor axis (500 mm) and mark in the two foci (Fig. 8:1).
2. Divide the distance F_1O into a convenient number of equal parts and number them.
3. Using the distances A1 and B1 as radii and the two foci as centres, cut the four arcs H, J, K, L to obtain four points on the curve of the ellipse.
4. Repeat with radii A2 and B2, and with A3 and B3, and so on. Join all intersections to produce a smooth curve.

This construction depends on the theorem that the sum of the two distances from any point on the curve to the foci is always constant in any given ellipse.

TANGENTS TO ELLIPSES

(a) Drawing a tangent and normal from a point P on the curve, given the ellipse, its axes and its foci (Fig. 8:7):
1. Draw a line from each focus to point P.
2. Bisect the angle so obtained to give line PQ. This is the normal to the curve at point P.
3. Draw a perpendicular to this line at P. This is the tangent to the curve at P.

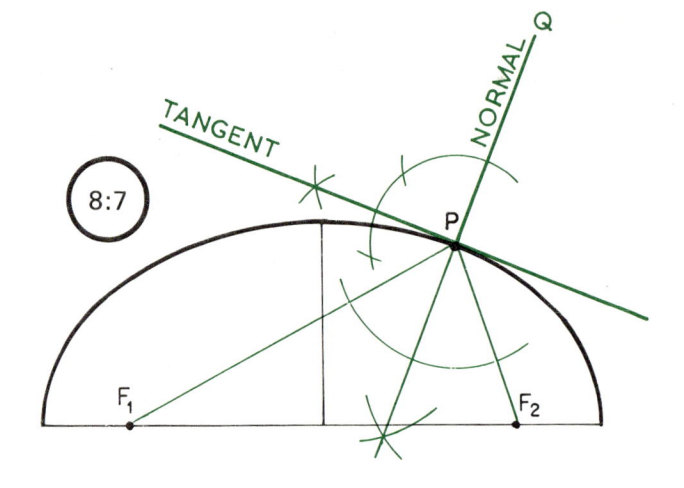

(b) Drawing tangents to an ellipse from a point P outside the ellipse, given the ellipse and its axes (Fig. 8:8):
1. Join P to F_2. Bisect this line to obtain point E.
2. Using E as centre and EP as radius, draw the circle passing through P and F_2.
3. Using O as centre and OB as radius, draw the arc GH cutting the circle at J and K.
4. Draw lines from point P through J and K extending them to touch the curve. These two lines are tangents to the ellipse from point P.

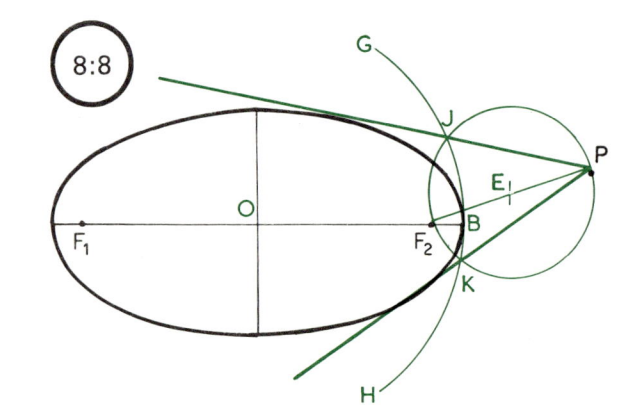

(c) Drawing tangents from an external point P and marking the points of tangency, given the ellipse and its axes (Fig. 8:9):
1. Using P as centre and PF_2 as radius, draw the arc EF.
2. Using F_1 as centre and AB as radius, cut this arc in G and H.
3. Join G and H to F_1. These two lines cut the curve at the points of tangency T_1 and T_2. Lines drawn from P and passing through these points are the required tangents.

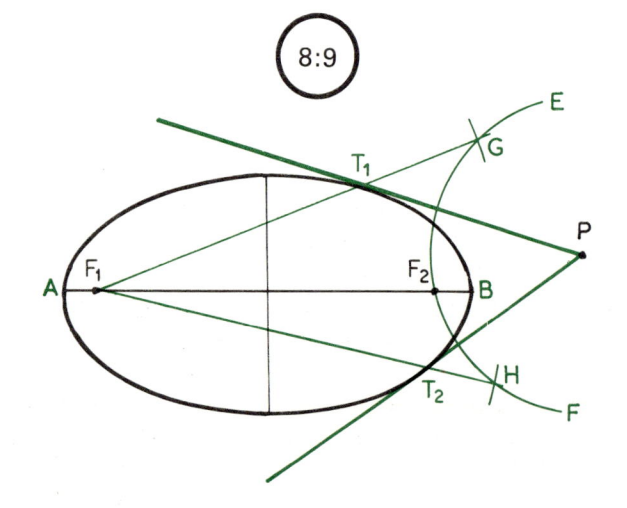

THE AXES OF AN ELLIPSE

Determine and draw the major and minor axes given the ellipse (Fig. 8:10):

1. Draw any two parallel lines across the figure as EF and GH.
2. Bisect them obtaining the points J and K. Draw a line across the ellipse and passing through J and K. This is a diameter and bisecting it will obtain O, the centre of the figure.
3. Using O as centre and any convenient radius, draw an arc to cut the curve at L and M. From these two points draw a bisector to cut the arc at P, a point on the major axis.
4. Draw a line across the ellipse and passing through O and P. This is the major axis.
5 Draw a perpendicular to this from O to obtain the minor axis.

QUESTIONS

Q1 Construct an ellipse on the given major axis AB (Fig. 8:11) using the intersecting arcs method (see Fig. 8:6).

Q2 Draw an ellipse inside the given parallelogram and touching the mid-point of each side (Fig. 8:12).

Q3 Draw the given semi-ellipse (Fig. 8:13). Construct and name the tangent and normal from point P.

Q4 Construct an ellipse within a rectangle measuring 120 mm by 80 mm (Fig. 8:14).

Q5 The foci of an ellipse are 110 mm apart and the minor axis is 60 mm long. Draw the ellipse and one tangent at a point along the curve 40 mm from one focus.

Q6 Construct an ellipse when the length of the major axis is 100 mm and the distance between the foci is 70 mm.

Q7 The minor axis of an ellipse is 80 mm long and the distance between the foci is 110 mm. Find the major axis and draw the ellipse.

Q8 Draw two concentric circles at 60 mm and 110 mm diameter respectively. Using their appropriate diameters as major and minor axes, construct an ellipse.

Q9 The foci of an ellipse are set 80 mm apart. Draw an ellipse around these where the total of the distances of that point from the two foci always adds up to 100 mm.

Q10 Draw an ellipse 120 mm by 60 mm using a different construction for the left-hand half to that used for the right-hand half.

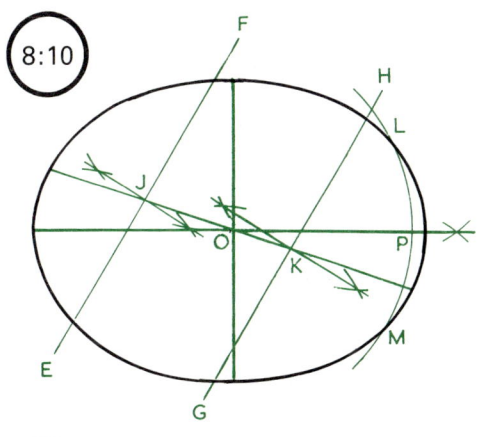

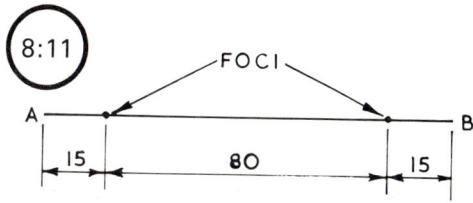

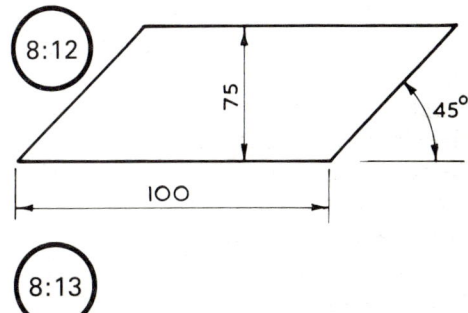

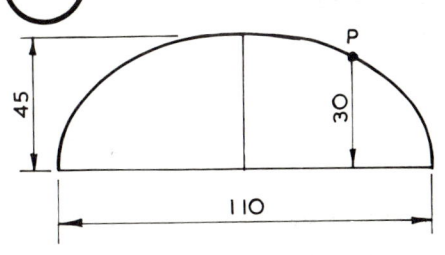

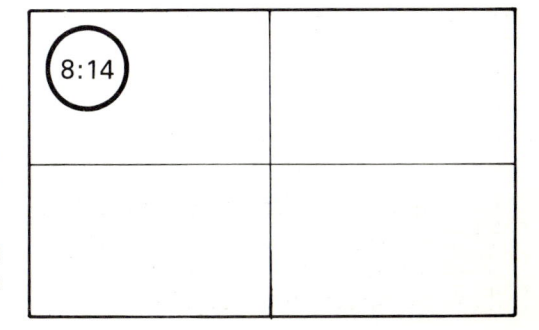

LOGOGRAMS

The drawings on this page, commonly known as **logograms** (or logos), are all based on the letters of the alphabet and are mainly formed from the ellipse and the circle. The logogram is often used as a trade mark for business letter headings, advertising, packaging and display. As a form of Graphic Communication it is the trader's shorthand symbol.

Q11 Draw the following logograms full size from the dimensions given. Note that you need to locate the centre-lines first.

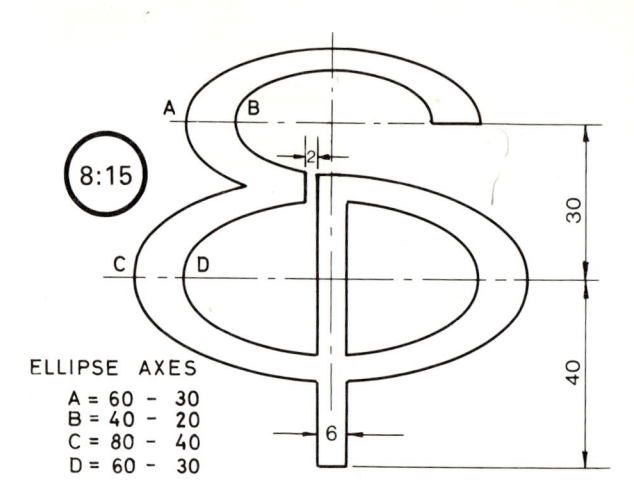

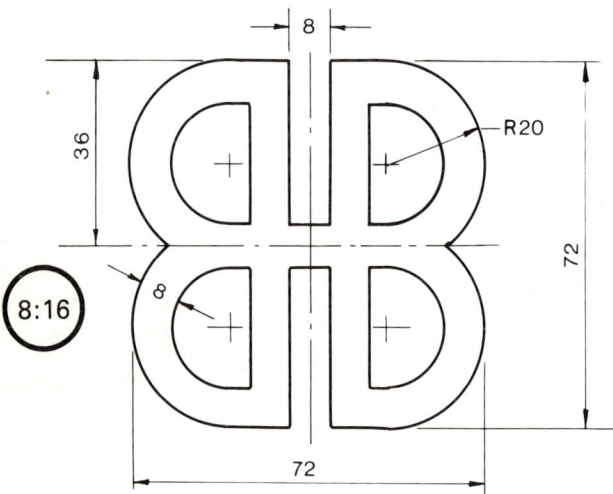

8:15

ELLIPSE AXES
A = 60 - 30
B = 40 - 20
C = 80 - 40
D = 60 - 30

Figure 8:15 is the logo for Ebury Press. It consists of two pairs of ellipses, each pair constructed from the junction of a centre-line. The major and minor axes are given, where the major axis on ellipse A is 60 mm and the minor axis 30 mm. Any suitable method of drawing the ellipse may be used.

8:16

Figure 8:16 is the logo for a manufacturer of bathroom fittings. Draw the logogram to the dimensions given and provide a surrounding border and suitable colouring.

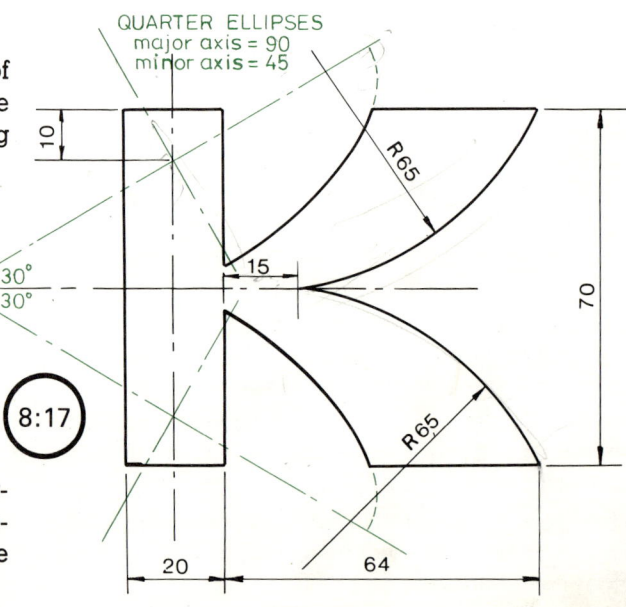

8:17

QUARTER ELLIPSES
major axis = 90
minor axis = 45

Figure 8:17 is the logo for the Kawasaki motor-bike. The vertical and the horizontal centre-lines should be drawn first to locate the centre of the axes for the two quarter-ellipses.

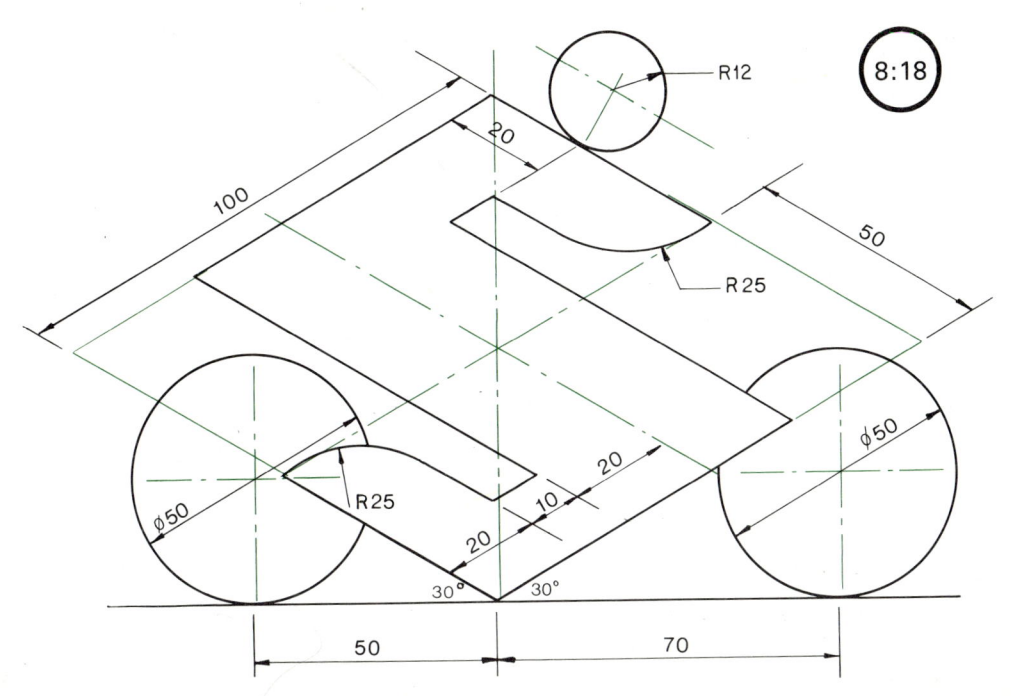

Figure 8:18 is the Suzuki logogram which uses the letter 'S' to indicate a human form. Graphic Communication encourages this use of the imagination in providing stimulating designs for various purposes.

The 30° axes need to be lightly drawn first.

Figure 8:19 is the logogram for the North British Finance Co. The logogram has been cleverly devised using the lower case letters 'n' and 'b' rather than the capital letters normally used for logograms.

The 45° angle should be drawn before the arcs which complete the outline.

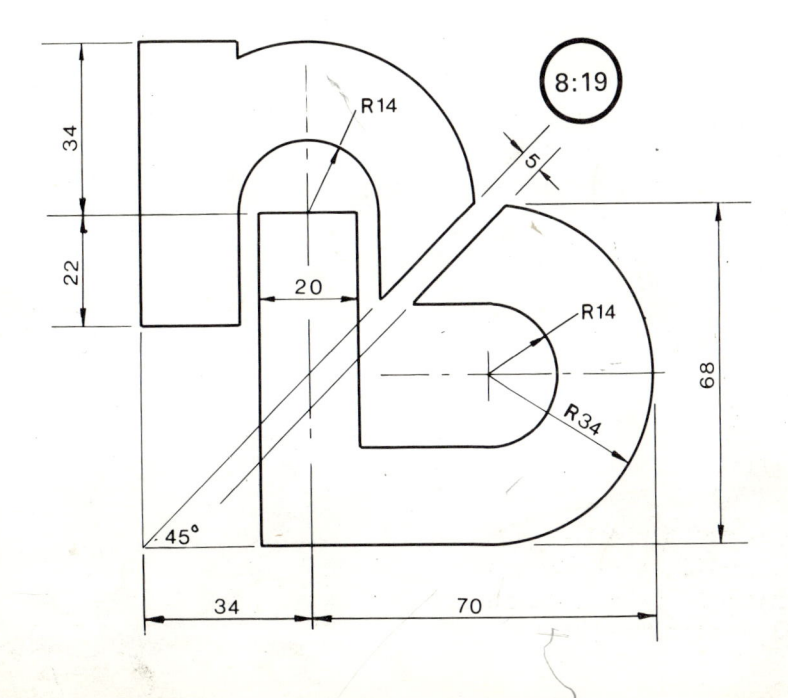

67

9 Loci

A locus (plural = loci) is the path traced by a point or line that moves according to certain given conditions. The study of loci is important as it shows the resulting paths of moving objects, such as space rockets, parts of machines or link mechanisms.

When drawing the locus of a moving point there will always be 'constants' involved such as the stated direction of movement, the fixed distance from a given point, a fixed ratio between two or more points, the fixed length of a rotating crank.

The simplest locus is a straight line made by a pencil point running along the edge of a ruler from say, point P to O (Fig. 9:1).

Figure 9:2 shows the locus of a second point, P_2, which has moved at a constant distance from the first line; thus this second line is parallel to the first.

The definition of a straight line is 'the shortest distance between two points'.

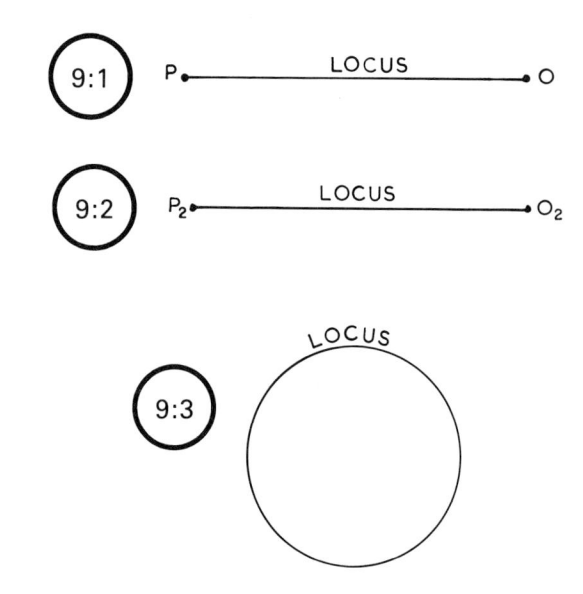

A pencil moving along a line so that it is always a constant distance from a fixed point will trace out a circle (Fig. 9:3). The locus traced by the tip of a watch or clock hand is always a circle.

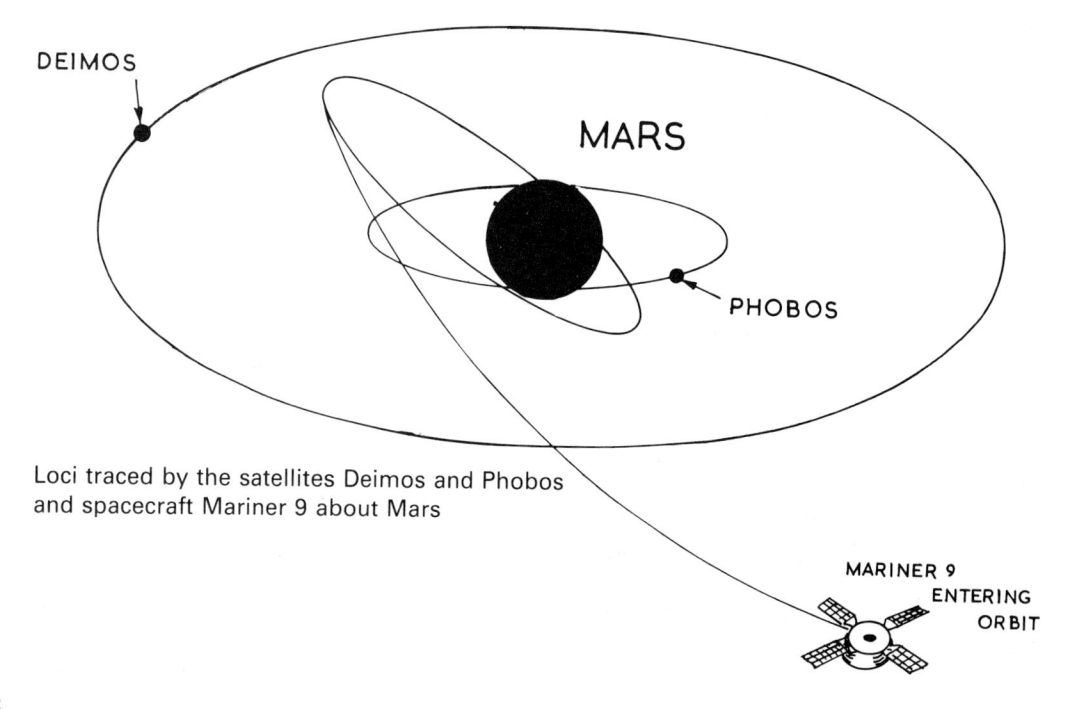

Loci traced by the satellites Deimos and Phobos and spacecraft Mariner 9 about Mars

The right bisector of the two points A and B is the locus of a point moving so as to be equidistant between them (Fig. 9:4).

The locus of a point moving so as to be equidistant between the two arms of a given angle is the bisector of that angle (Fig. 9:5).

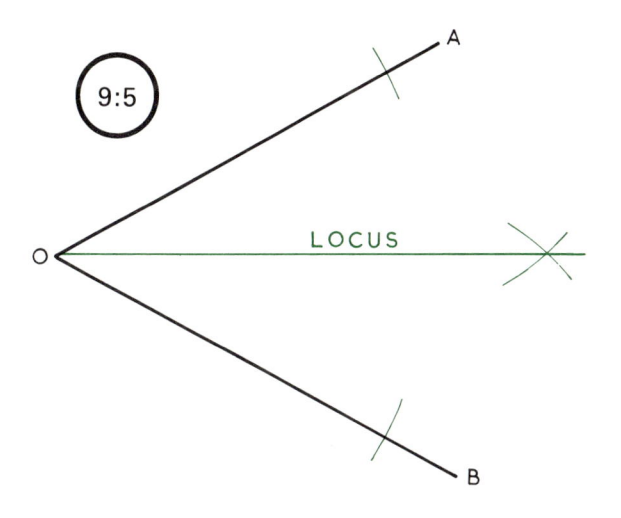

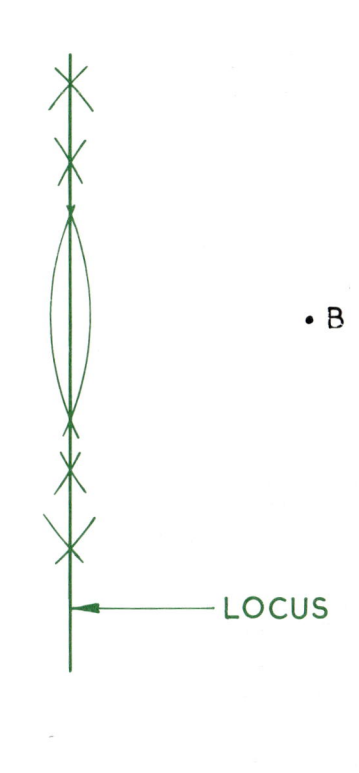

9:4

9:5

DRAWING LOCI

Points to Remember
1 Plot sufficient points to enable you to draw an accurate trace.
2 Mark each new location point with a small dot or a small neat cross and letter or number these in the sequence in which you draw them.
3 Carefully, and with a thin light line, join up all the plotted points in their proper sequence.
4 Make sure that the finished locus is clear, crisp and smooth.

(a) Drawing the locus of a point P moving at equal distances between and from the fixed points A and B (Fig. 9:6):
1 Draw line AB (60 mm in length).
2 Using first A and then B as centres and any suitable radius (say 32 mm), draw the intersecting arcs at P_1.
3 Repeat, using increased radii each time (35 mm, 37 mm, 40 mm), to obtain points P_2, P_3 and P_4 respectively.
4 Join all these points in a smooth line to obtain the locus.

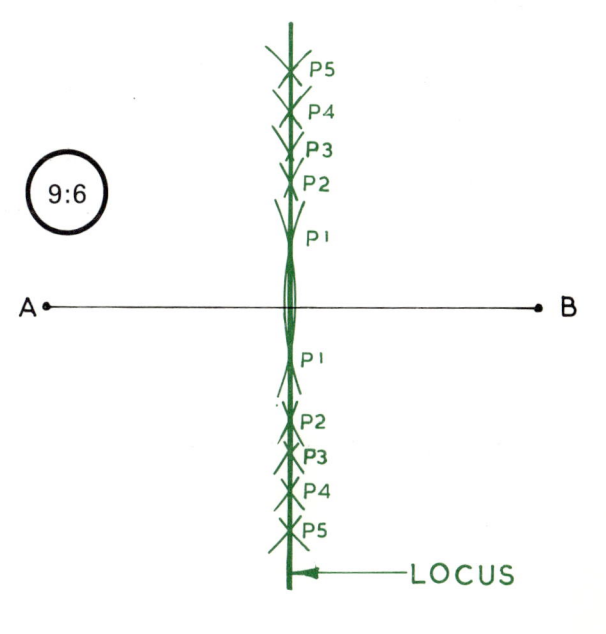

9:6

69

(b) A ladder 8 m in length is leaning with its foot 2 m from the base of a wall. A man is standing 2 m from the top of the ladder. Trace the path followed by his body as the ladder slides down the wall (Fig. 9:7):

Use a scale of 10 mm to 1 m.
1 Draw the ground line AB, the wall AC and the ladder CD. AB will be the ladder length.
2 Divide DB into a number of convenient spaces (say 10 mm) and letter them E, F, G, H and J.
3 Draw 80 mm lines from each of these points to the wall to represent the ladder (to scale) at successive stages in its movement.
4 Mark a fine dot 20 mm from the top of each line and join up the dots by a smooth curve.

The solid green line traces the locus. The dotted line traces the locus which would result if the man had been standing 3 m down the ladder.

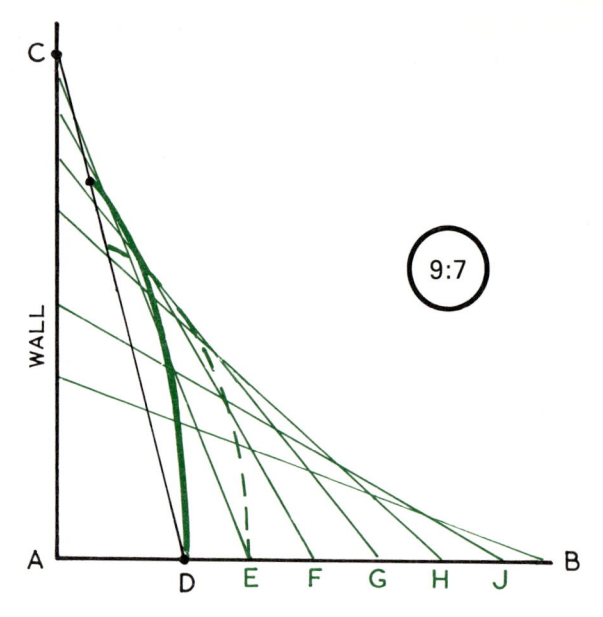

(c) Drawing the locus of point P in a rod which slides with its ends along two fixed tracks, OA and OB (Fig. 9:8):
1 Draw the rod BC in several positions between the tracks.
2 Mark a fine dot on each to indicate the position of P.
3 Join these dots in a smooth curve to obtain the locus.

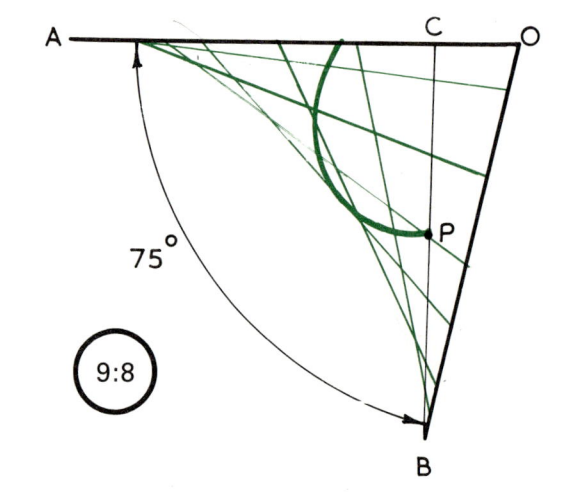

(d) Drawing the locus of a pendulum rod OP (60 mm in length) which swings 30° on either side of vertical (Fig. 9:9):

Use a scale of 1:10.
1 Draw the rod in the two extreme positions OA and OB.
2 Using O as centre and OA as radius, draw the arc AB. This is the required locus.

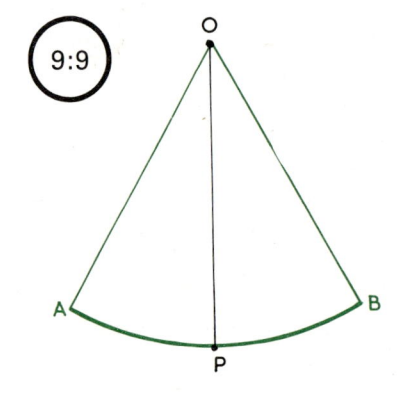

(e) Drawing the locus of a point P on a slider which falls at a uniform rate from O, the top, to the bottom of the pendulum OA during one swing from A to B (Fig. 9:10):
1. Draw the pendulum at the start and finish of the swing OA and OB.
2. Bisect the angle AOB to obtain OC and bisect the two angles so obtained to find points D and E. Join these to O.
3. When the pendulum has swung over a quarter of its arc from OA to OE the slider will have moved down the rod a quarter of its length from O to P_1, and so on through P_2 and P_3 to finish at B. Draw a smooth curve through the five points as shown.

(f) Drawing the locus of a point P moving between the fixed points A and B and at a given ratio of distance from each (Fig. 9:11):
1. Draw AB, 50 mm. (This is a convenient length to divide into the given ratio.)
2. Mark P on this line at 30 mm from A and 20 mm from B (ratio 3:2).
3. Using B as centre and 24 mm as radius mark in arcs at P_1. The radius AP_1 must compare with the radius BP_1 (24 mm) as 3:2, so $24 \div 2 = 12$; $12 \times 3 = 36$, which is the radius for AP_1.
4. The remaining arcs will be found using the following pairs of radii.
    P_2 to B = 28 mm, to A = 42 mm.
    P_3 to B = 32 mm, to A = 48 mm and so on.
5. Join all these intersecting arcs with a smooth curve.

(g) Drawing the locus of a point which moves equidistant from a straight line AB and the circumference of a given circle (Fig. 9:12):
1. Draw OC perpendicular to AB, cutting the circle at D.
2. Bisect CD at P (the mid-point of the locus).
3. Divide CP into a number of equal parts and divide PD into the same number of equal parts.
4. Draw a series of lines through these points (X, Y, Z) parallel to AB.
5. Using O as centre and radius O1, draw an arc to cut the line X. These are two further points on the locus.
6. Repeat using O2 as radius and to cut the line Y, and with O3 as radius to cut the line Z.
7. Join all these points in a smooth curve to obtain the locus.

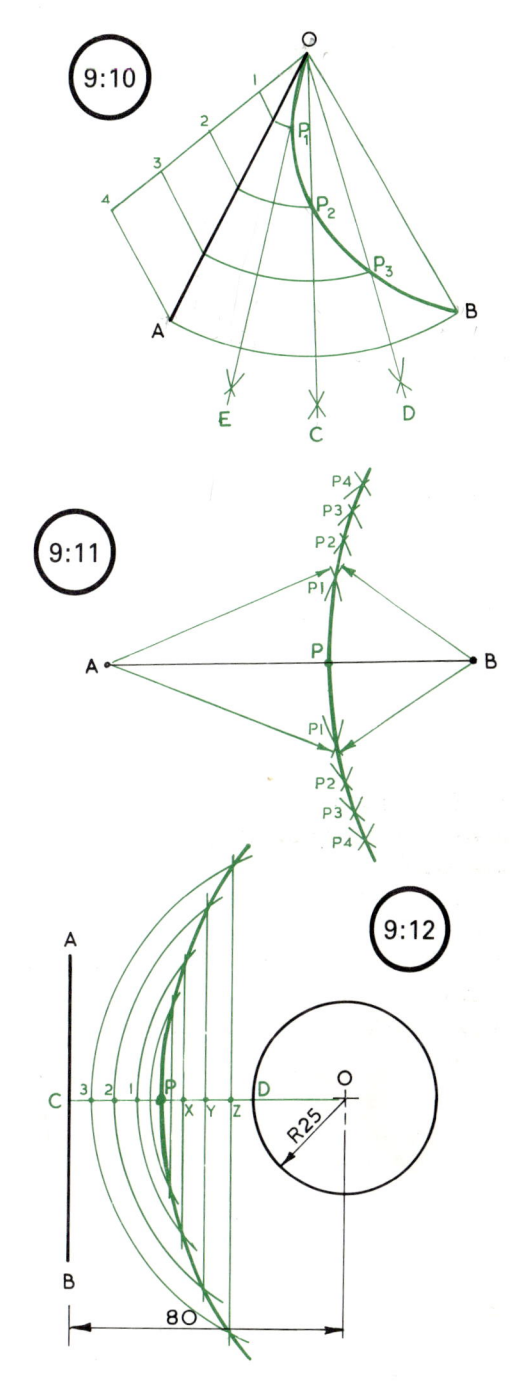

When a large gap is left between any two plotted points along the locus as between 1 and P in Fig. 9:12, intermediate points can easily be obtained by bisecting the gaps and inserting another pair of lines to gain two more intersections as shown.

(h) Drawing the locus of a point which moves equidistant between two given circles of differing diameters (Fig. 9:13):

Use 20 mm and 50 mm diameters with centres 55 mm apart.
1 Draw the line AB and the two circles.
2 Mark in the point P which is mid-way between the points where the circumferences of the two circles cut AB.
3 Using A as centre and AP plus 4 m as radius; and using B as centre and BP plus 4 mm as radius, draw the intersecting arcs at P'.
4 Repeat this process adding increments of 4 mm each time to obtain the remaining arcs.
5 Join all these intersections in a smooth curve to obtain the required locus.

Wherever parts move in a machine, a clear understanding of loci is of the greatest importance. Room has to be made for the moving parts to be able to work and—most important—to prevent accidents, they must be protected by guards, each of which is designed from loci.

One of the most commonly used mechanisms is the crank and wheel linkage as found in bicycles, car and motor cycle engines, pumps, compressors and steam engines.

(i) Drawing the locus of a point P halfway along a connecting rod AB which has one end hinged to the crank BO revolving about O, and the other end sliding along a trunnion bearing on the centre-line OX (Fig. 9:15):

1 Draw the centre-line OX and the circle radius OB (40 mm).
2 Divide the circle into 12 equal parts and number each part.
3 From number 1 mark the length AB (90 mm) onto the centre-line OX.
4 Mark the mid-point of the line to find point P. Figure 9:14 shows numbers 4 and 7 located.
5 Repeat this for each numbered division finding the centre of each line in turn. Twelve divisions = one complete revolution of OB.
6 Join the 12 positions of point P together to obtain a smooth curve showing the path of point P (Fig. 9:15).

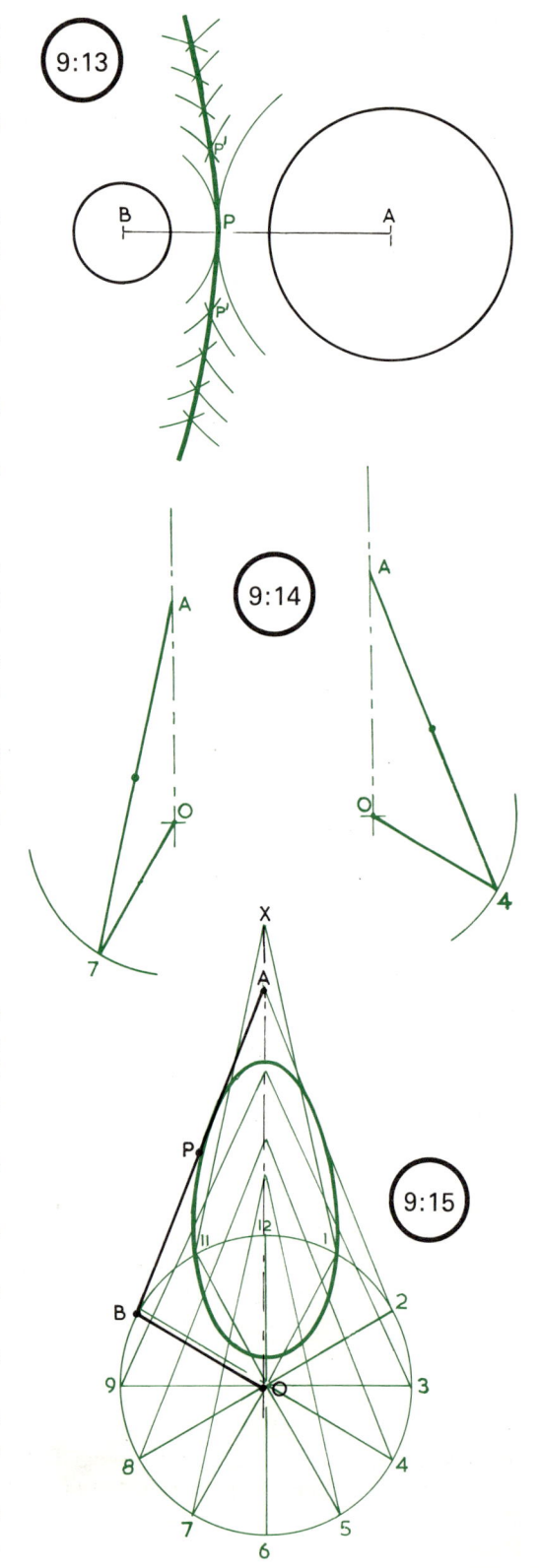

72

QUESTIONS

Q1 Draw the two circles given in Fig. 9:16 and trace the path followed by point P which moves between and at an equal distance from each of the two circumferences.

Q2 Copy the schematic drawing (Fig. 9:17) of a crank arm and its connecting rod. Trace the path of the point P when the crank turns through one complete revolution and the end of the rod slides along the centre-line at C.

Q3 A point moves from A to B as the line AB pivots on B and swings over from A to C. (Fig. 9:18.) Trace the path of the point when both point and line move at a uniform speed.

Q4 Figure 9:19 is a line drawing of an 'up and over' door fitted to a toy garage. AB shows the door closed and CD shows the door when it is raised. To move from *closed* to *open* A moves to D and B moves to C. Trace the path followed by point A while the door is being opened.

Q5 Figure 9:20 is a line drawing of a toy playground swing. The point P represents the head of a toy child seated mid-way along the seat bar. The arc AB shows the swing moving through 60°. Plot the path of P when it swings through 45° on either side of vertical.

Q6 A point moves so that the sum of its distances from two fixed points which are placed 80 mm apart is always 100 mm. Trace the path followed by the point and name the curve so obtained.

Q7 A ladder 12 m long leans against a house, the ladder bottom being 4 m from the wall. A man is standing 2 m down from the top of the ladder. Make a reduced size drawing showing the ladder 120 mm long, the base set 40 mm from the wall and the man 20 mm from the top. Draw the path of his falling body as the ladder base slips out from the wall.

Q8 A pendulum 120 mm in length swings through 60°. A slider moves from the top to the bottom of the pendulum at a uniform rate during one swing. Trace its path.

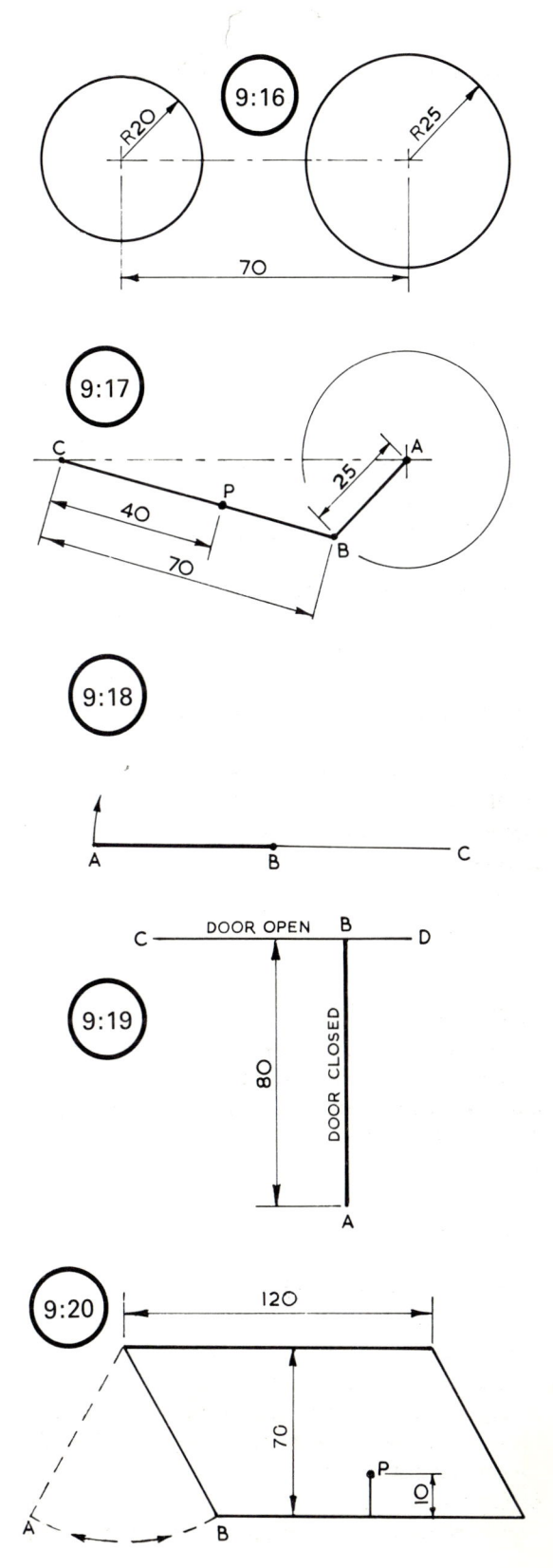

10 Scale Drawing

If a drawing can be made the same size as the finished object it will give a clear picture of its size, proportions and shape. This 'true size' drawing will then be called a **full scale** drawing, or **to a ratio of 1:1**.

There are many times when the object cannot be drawn full scale, as for example a block of flats, or a giant oil tanker. In these cases the drawing is made much smaller than the object. Such a drawing is called a **reduced scale** drawing. On the other hand, small items such as the parts for a tiny watch need to be drawn much larger than true size. These latter are called **increased scale** drawings. Thus there are two situations when the actual full size outlines cannot be drawn and scale drawings must be made:

(i) When the object is too large to fit on the paper and has to be decreased in drawing size.
(ii) When the object is too small to result in a readable drawing and has to be increased in drawing size.

Many problems would arise when making these increased or decreased drawings if every single measurement had to be multiplied or divided proportionately. Using a converting scale avoids all these calculations and thus makes scale drawing both easier and simpler. A scale is simply a straight line that is divided into equal lengths that may be less or greater than, or equal to, the original size of the object. This scale is then used to reproduce the dimensions of the object on a drawing which, in turn, may be full scale, or reduced or enlarged in some larger proportion. The choice of scale depends on the comparative sizes of the object and the drawing paper.

Figure 10:1 shows a 50-pence coin drawn twice full size, or to a ratio of 2:1 (2 mm on the drawing represents 1 mm on the coin).

Figure 10:2 shows the same coin drawn full size.

Figure 10:3 shows the coin drawn half size (1 mm on the drawing represents 2 mm on the coin).

SCALE REDUCING

Making a reducing scale for drawing a plan of a football pitch (Fig. 10:8):

Depending on its use, a reasonable drawing size for a pitch 120 m × 80 m would be 240 mm in length. To find the reducing ratio divide the longest measurement of the object by the longest drawn line. In this case it is 120 m ÷ 240 mm. Simplify this to give 120 000 mm ÷ 240 mm = 500. Therefore the reducing ratio is 1:500. (1 mm on the drawing represents 500 mm on the pitch.)

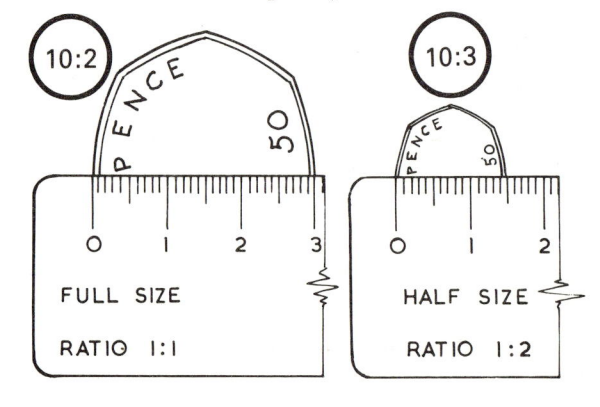

1 Draw a line to represent the longest dimension, in this case 240 mm, representing 120 metres on the pitch (Fig. 10:4).
2 Divide this line into any convenient number of equal parts, in this case 12. Each of these represents 10 m on the pitch (Fig. 10:5).
3 The shortest distance we need to show at the moment is the width of the goal mouth, which is 7.5 m (Fig. 10:6). This will appear as 15 mm on the drawing, so divide the first of the equal spaces into a convenient number of equal parts to accommodate this dimension. Those shown here represent 2 mm spaces, each representing 1 m on the pitch.

The finished scale should then be numbered as shown and can be left as a straight-line scale (Fig. 10:6), or made into a block scale as in Fig. 10:7.

The zero or figure 0 is always placed at the first major graduation line. This makes it easier to read off small measurements which use the subdivisions. For example, to read off 33 m, place one point of the dividers on the graduation marked 30. Open them out and place the other point on the third graduation to the left of the 0 mark. Thus the dividers are opened to a distance of 3 large spaces (30 m) plus 3 small spaces (3 m) thus totalling 33 metres. This distance can then be pricked off on the drawing.

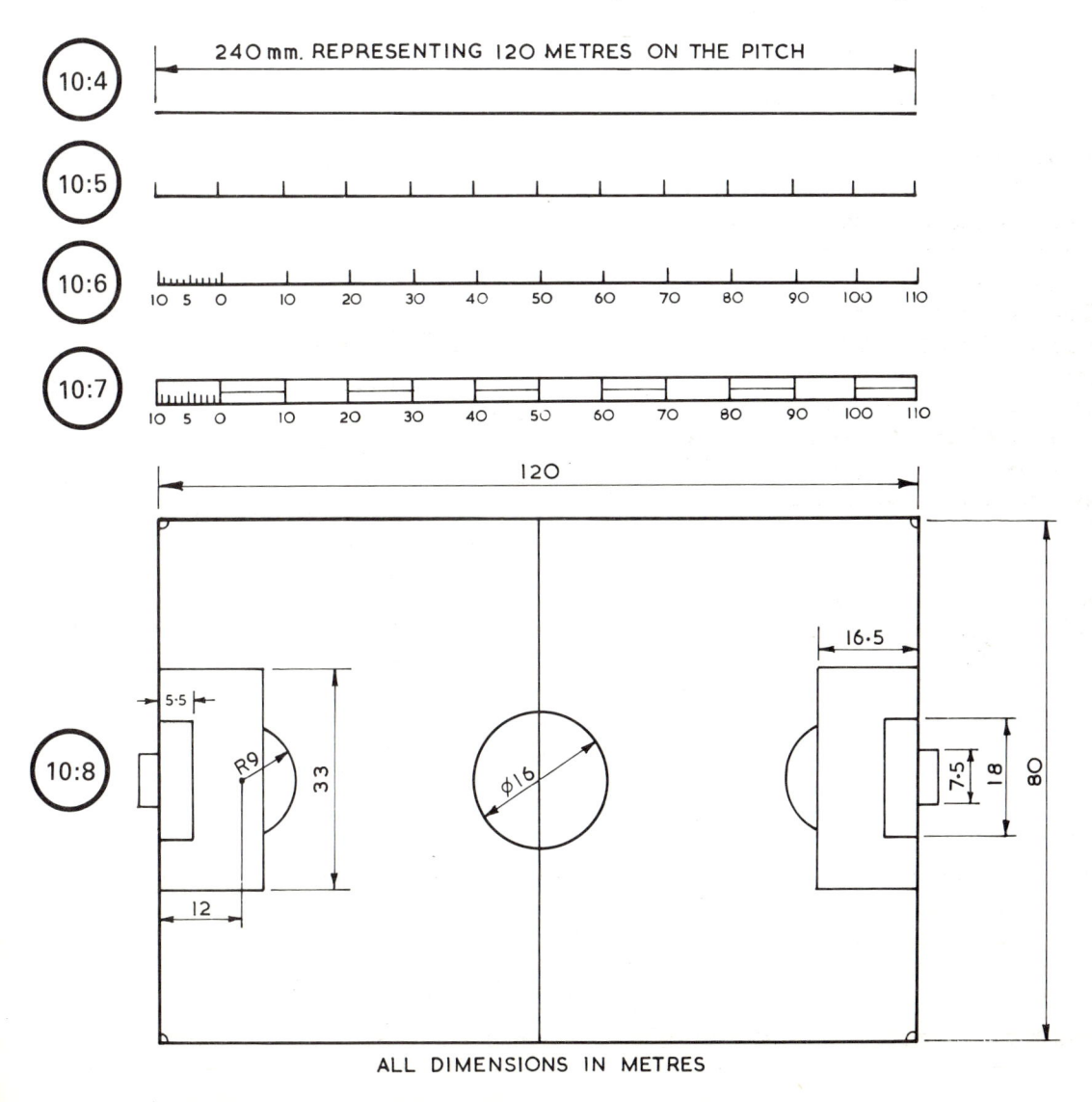

10:4 — 240 mm. REPRESENTING 120 METRES ON THE PITCH

10:5

10:6 — 10 5 0 10 20 30 40 50 60 70 80 90 100 110

10:7 — 10 5 0 10 20 30 40 50 60 70 80 90 100 110

10:8

ALL DIMENSIONS IN METRES

75

SCALE ENLARGING

Making an enlarging scale to use in drawing a wrist watch balance staff (Figs 10:9 and 10:10): A sensibly sized drawing that will give a workman a clear picture of the required object needs to be about 20 times full size.
1. Multiply the longest dimension by 20 (5 mm × 20 = 100 mm).
2. Draw a line this length and divide it into 5 equal spaces.
3. Divide the first space into 10 equal spaces to represent tenths of a millimetre.
4. The complete scale is shown in Fig. 10:10.

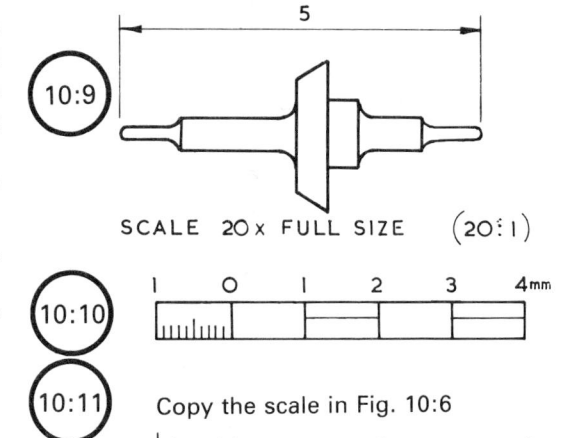

DIAGONAL SCALES

Sometimes it is necessary to measure very small dimensions, such as the corner flag quadrants on the drawing of the football pitch (Fig. 10:8). In cases such as this, where very tiny divisions need to be shown, we use diagonal scales.

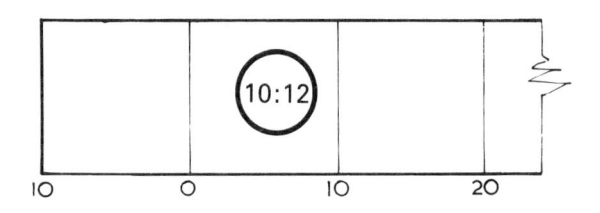

Making a Diagonal Scale

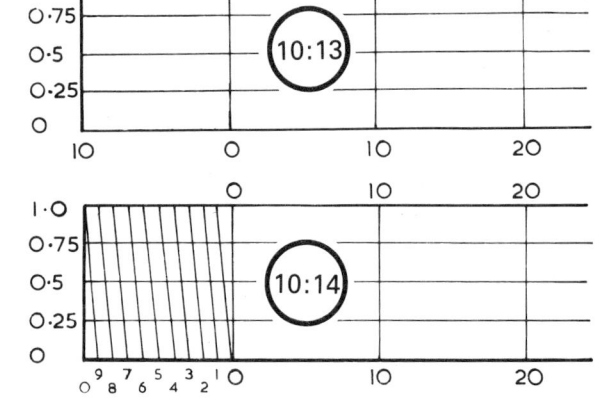

To make a scale to read quarter-metres (0.25 m) **for use with the scale drawing** (Fig. 10:8, Figs 10:11–10:15):
1. (Fig. 10:11.) Draw the scale exactly as shown in Fig. 10:6. Each of the tiny divisions 0 to 10 on the left need to be further sub-divided by 4 to show quarter-metres.
2. Draw a parallel line 20 mm above the scale base-line and erect perpendiculars to it from every major graduation from 10 through 0 to 110 (Fig. 10:12).
3. Divide the first vertical line into 4 equal spaces and draw parallel horizontal lines from these across the scale, numbering them as shown (Fig. 10:13).
4. Divide the top line to the left of the 0 into 10 equal spaces and join these graduations to those on the base-line by inclined lines (Fig. 10:14).
5. Number all the graduations as shown.

You can now see that each sloping line travels one quarter (0.25) of a metre to the left as it crosses each horizontal division when rising from the base-line.

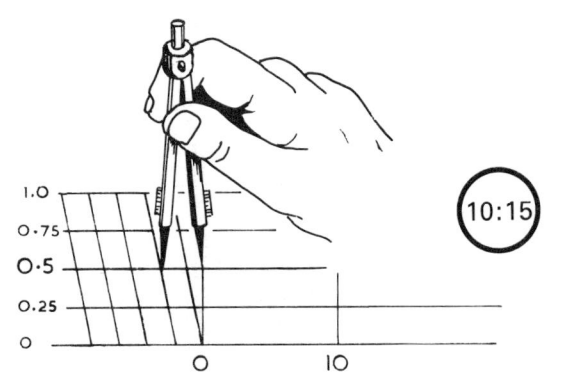

The number on the extreme left perpendicular gives the increase in length of the lines measured along successive horizontals. Figure 10:15 shows the dividers measuring off 1.5 m, the radius of the quadrant mentioned above.

Always think of each division as full size regardless of the scale used, because the dimensions you print on your drawing must be the full size measurements of the object.

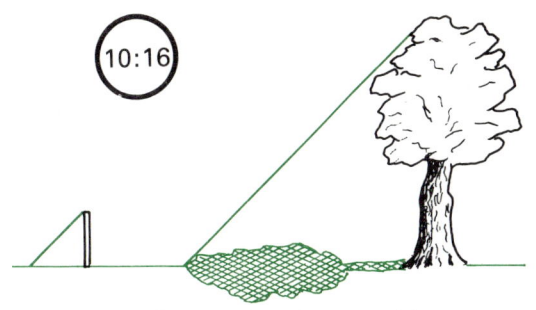

10:16

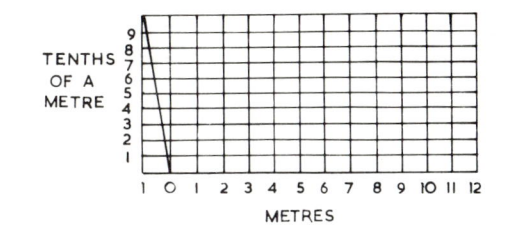

Diagonal scale to read in metres and tenths of a metre

DETERMINATION OF HEIGHTS

Scale drawing provides an easy method for civil engineers and surveyors when determining the heights of inaccessible objects, such as tall buildings.

(a) Finding the height of a tree from the length of its shadow (Fig. 10:16):
1 Set up a suitable rod (2 m); measure its length, the length of its shadow and the length of the tree's shadow.
2 Construct a suitable scale similar to the one shown.
3 Use this scale to draw the two similar triangles (Fig. 10:17).
4 Read off the height of the tree to scale.

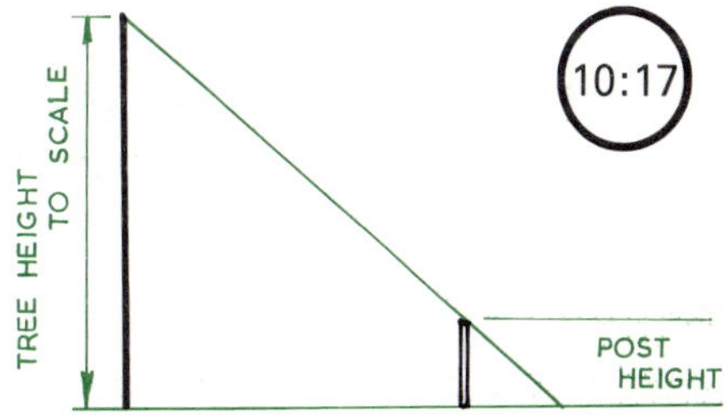

(b) Finding the height of a building using a sight pole (Fig 10:18):
1 Holding a suitable sight pole as shown, move it until its top, the top of the building and your eye are all in line.
2 Write down all the relevant measurements and, using the scale (Fig. 10:17), draw the two similar triangles (Fig. 10:19). AB is your height, CD the pole and AE the distance from yourself to the building. FE then becomes the scale height of the building.

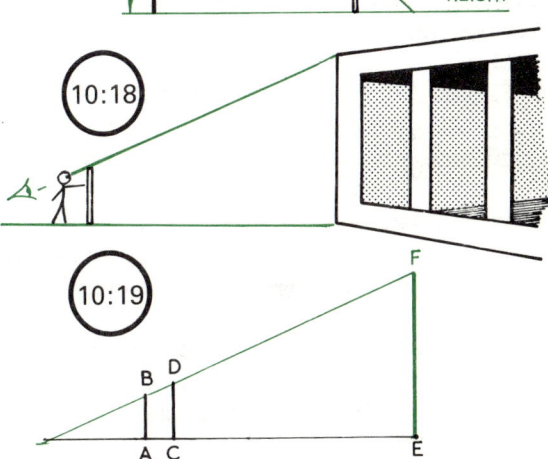

10:17

10:18

10:19

QUESTIONS

Q1 By scale drawing find the length of a ladder required to reach the top of a building 16 m high, if the angle at the base of the ladder to the ground is 80°.

Q2 The plan of a room 30 m by 12 m is to be drawn on a sheet of paper 420 mm by 300 mm, leaving 15 mm all round for a border. Construct a suitable scale.

Q3 Construct a suitable scale and draw a plan of the room you are occupying. Show the position of the windows, door and furniture.

Q4 Construct a diagonal scale to measure to a maximum of 5 km and a minimim of 10 m. Use this to plot the relative positions of three points: A is 3.55 km due north of B, C is 4.2 km east of B and 5.25 km south-east of A. Link all three points by a circle.

Q5 Draw a scale view of the front of your home. State the scale used.

Q6 Copy the house plans given in Figs 10:20, 10:21 and 10:22. Take measurements direct from the drawing with your dividers as in Fig. 10:15. Then draw the appropriate line double that length.

HOUSE PLANS

10:20

DETACHED THREE BEDROOM HOUSE

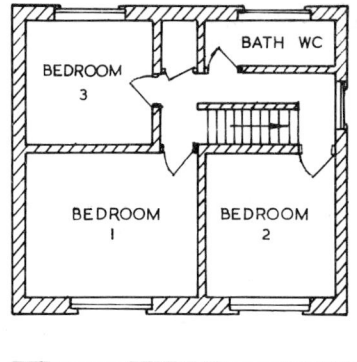

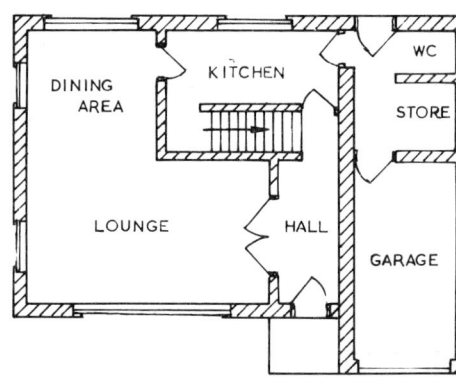

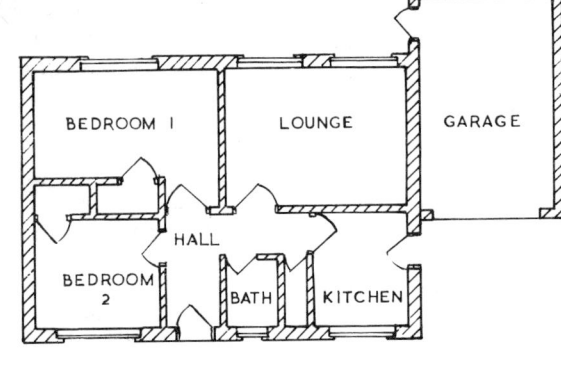

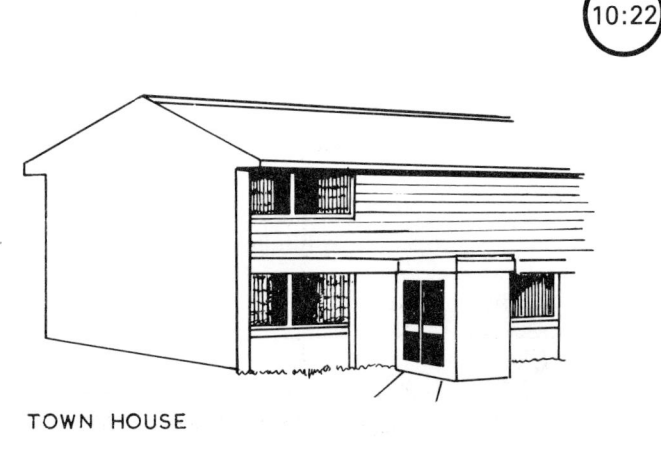

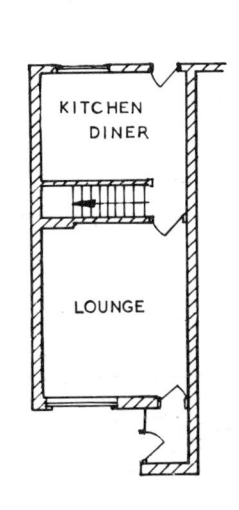

10:21

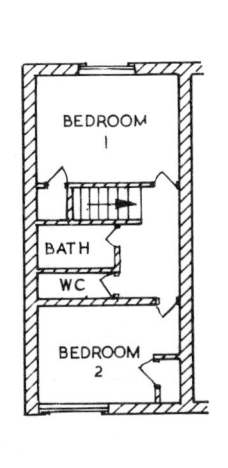

DETACHED TWO BEDROOM BUNGALOW

10:22

TOWN HOUSE

78

11 Areas

Good draughtsmen must be able to design objects as well as just copy drawings of them. A most important part of this designing lies in getting the proportions right. To do this a draughtsman must be able to calculate the areas of figures and then draw similar shapes in fixed ratios of enlargement or reduction of either the area or the lengths of the sides.

The area of a plane figure is the amount of surface that is surrounded by its boundary line or lines. This area is always stated by the number of squares or fractions of a square that will cover it exactly.

QUADRILATERALS

Figure 11:1 shows a square of 10 mm side. The area of this is the length multiplied by the height, 10 mm × 10 mm = 100 square millimetres. This is written as 100 mm². As 10 mm equals 1 cm, the area could also be described as one square centimetre or 1 cm².

Figure 11:2 shows a rectangle 40 mm × 20 mm (4 cm × 2 cm). The area is found by multiplying length and height as before: 40 mm × 20 mm = 800 mm².

Figure 11:3 shows a parallelogram drawn on the same size base-line and between identical parallels as the rectangle in Fig. 11:2. Counting the dotted squares, or better still, cutting out the triangle BEF and laying it on the space ACD will prove that:

Parallelograms on the same base and between the same parallels are equal in area.

Figure 11:4 shows three different parallelograms all of the same area. This is because they all have the same base and fit between the same parallel lines.

AREA OF SQUARE = BASE × HEIGHT
10 × 10 = 100 mm² (or 1 × 1 = 1 cm²)

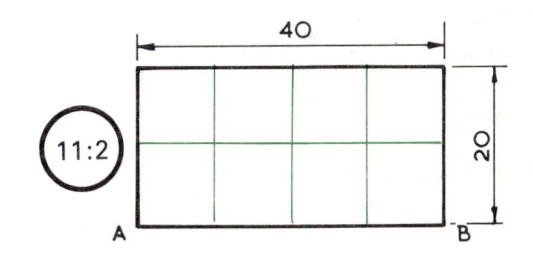

AREA OF RECTANGLE = BASE × HEIGHT
40 × 20 = 800 mm² (or 8 cm²)

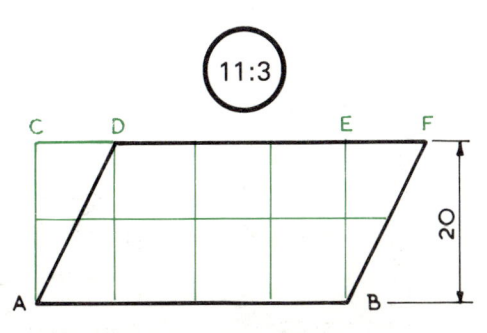

AREA OF PARALLELOGRAM =
BASE × PERPENDICULAR HEIGHT
40 × 20 = 800 mm² (or 8 cm²)

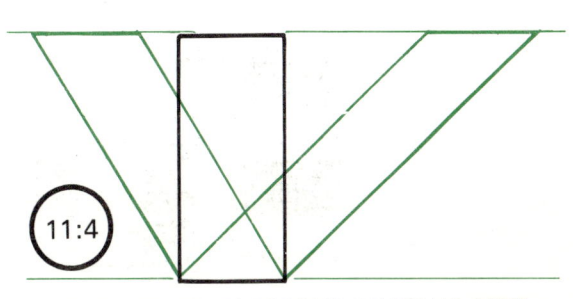

THREE PARALLELOGRAMS OF EQUAL AREA

TRIANGLES

Figure 11:5 shows a rectangle and a parallelogram each cut by a diagonal. From these it can be seen that the diagonal cuts each figure into two equally sized triangles.

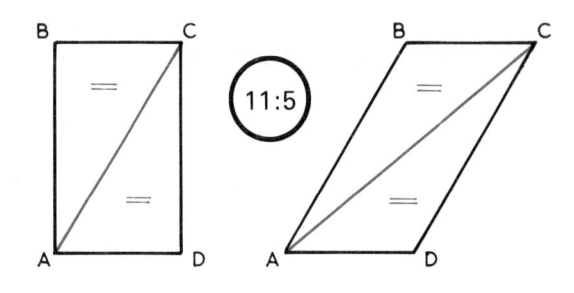

A triangle has half the area of a rectangle or parallelogram when drawn on the same base and between the same parallels.

Figure 11:6 shows the same two shapes cut horizontally into halves. From these it can be seen that in the rectangle, the triangle ABC is exactly the same size as the triangle EDC; similarly, in the parallelogram, the triangle FGH is equal in area and shape to the triangle KJH. The truth of this can be tested and proved by cutting one triangle out and laying it on top of its companion.

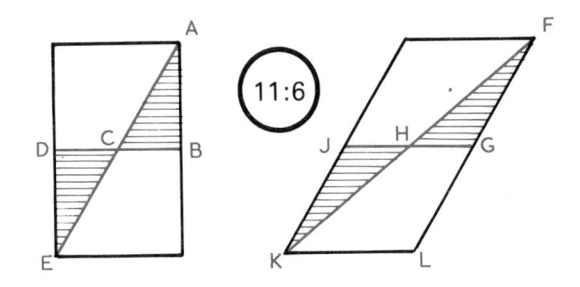

The area of any triangle is the base multiplied by half the perpendicular height.

Figure 11:7 shows the parallelogram laid over on its side and divided in the same way as Fig. 11:6. If we consider only triangle FLK it will be seen that triangle FGH can be moved over to KJH, thus converting the triangle to a parallelogram equal in area to the triangle FLK; so an alternative way of stating the theorem is:

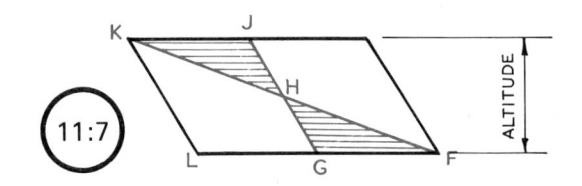

The area of any triangle is half the base multiplied by the perpendicular height.

Figure 11:8 repeats the rectangle and parallelogram from Fig. 11:6 above, but this time they include an isosceles triangle. From these two drawings it can be seen that:

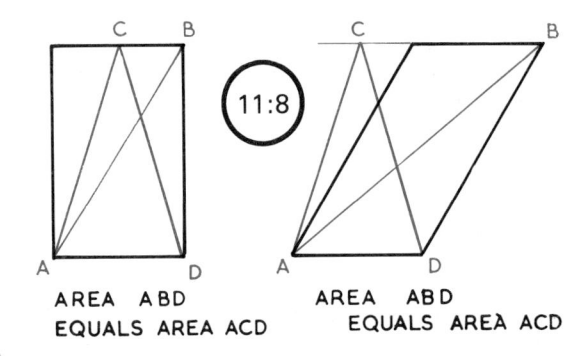

Triangles on the same base and between the same parallels are equal in area.

(a) Drawing an isosceles triangle equal in area to a given scalene triangle (ABC) (Fig. 11:9):
Given AC = 70 mm, AB = 90 mm, BC = 50 mm:
1 Draw a line from B parallel to the given baseline.
2 Erect a perpendicular bisector on AC to cut this line at D.
3 Join D to A and C to obtain the required triangle.

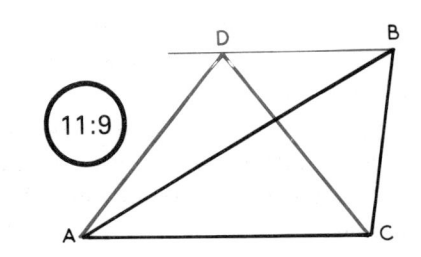

AREA ABC = AREA ACD

AREA ABD EQUALS AREA ACD

AREA ABD EQUALS AREA ACD

80

(b) Drawing a rectangle equal in area to a given triangle (ABC) (Fig. 11:10):
Given AC = 40 mm, AB = 70 mm, BC = 50 mm:
1 Erect a perpendicular from the base-line to obtain the altitude.
2 Draw the bisector of this perpendicular (parallel to the base).
3 Erect perpendiculars from A and C to meet this bisector, thus using the base of the triangle and half its perpendicular height to obtain the rectangle of equal area.

(c) To demonstrate that a rectangle drawn on the same base as a triangle and having half its perpendicular height is of equal area (ABCD = CDE) (Fig. 11:11):
Given CD = 60 mm, DE = 65 mm, CE = 50 mm:
Erect a perpendicular from DC to cut the apex in E. Then the height JH equals HE.

From this it should be seen that the triangles ADF and FEH are equal in area. Furthermore, the triangles EHG and GBC are equal in area and are contained in the new triangle DEC. Area of triangle DEC = base DC × half height JE. Area of rectangle ABCD = base DC × height AD.

POLYGONS

All regular polygons can be divided up into the same number of equally-sized isosceles triangles as the polygon has sides. This property can be used when drawing a triangle equal in area to any regular polygon as shown in Fig. 11:12, where the five sides of the pentagon are laid out straight on a base-line, from A round to A.

All five triangles are of equal area by virtue of the theorem already proven, that triangles on the same base and between the same parallels (the same perpendicular height) are equal in area.

Reducing Polygons to Triangles of Equal Area
Both regular and irregular polygons can be readily reduced to triangles of equal area, thus simplifying the determination of their areas. Draw the irregular polygons to your own dimensions for the following examples.

(a) Reducing a given irregular quadrilateral (ABCD) to a triangle of equal area (Fig. 11:13):
1 Join AC thus cutting off one corner (B) of the quadrilateral.
2 Extend the base-line AD to the left. Draw a line from B parallel to AC and cutting the base-line produced at E.
3 Join EC to give the required triangle ECD, which is equal in area to the quadrilateral ABCD.

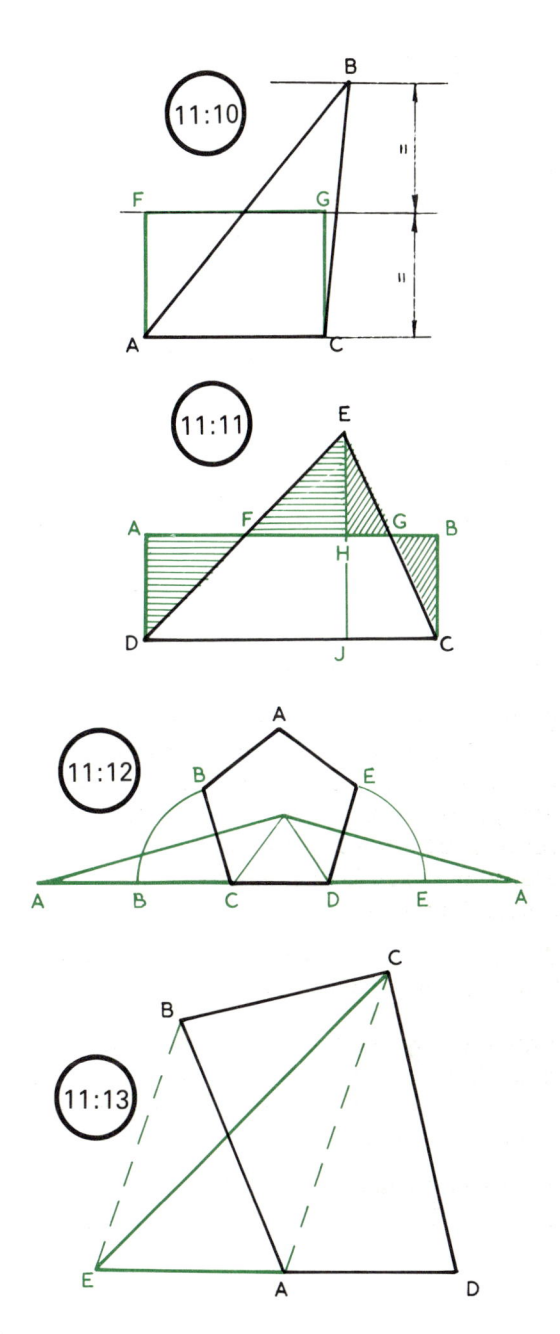

The quadrilateral is reduced to a triangle by the removal of one corner.

81

(b) Reducing a given irregular pentagon (ABCDE) to a triangle of equal area (Fig. 11:14):
1. Join A and E to C thus cutting off two corners, B and D.
2. Extend the base-line in both directions.
3. Draw a line from B parallel to AC and cutting the base at F.
4. Draw a line from D parallel to CE and cutting the base at G.
5. Join F and G to C to produce the triangle CFG, which is equal in area to the pentagon ABCDE.

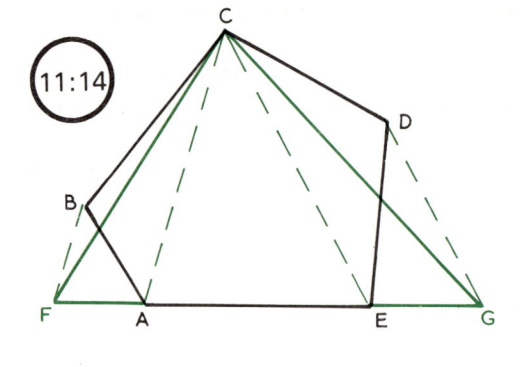

(c) Reducing a quadrilateral (ABCD) having a re-entrant angle to a triangle of equal area (Fig. 11:15):
(ABC is the re-entrant angle.)
1. Join A to C, thus cutting off corner B.
2. Draw a line from B parallel to CA cutting the base at E.
3. Join E to C to obtain the required triangle.

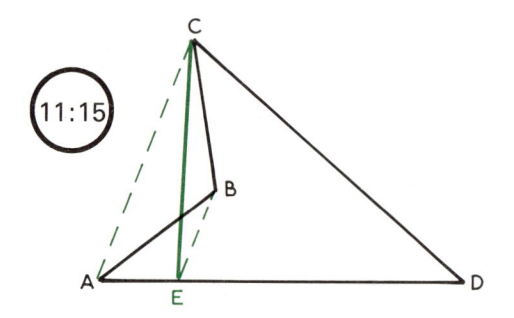

(d) Reducing an irregular heptagon to a triangle of equal area (Fig. 11:16):
This is completed by removing corners in succession by the method detailed above.
1. Remove the corners B and F to obtain the irregular pentagon HCDEJ.
2. Remove the corners C and E to obtain the required triangle.

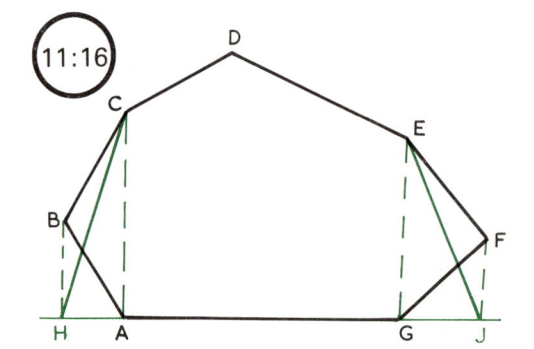

Figures of Equal Area

Drawing a square equal in area to a given rectangle (ABCD) (Fig. 11:17):
Given AB = 70 mm, BC = 40 mm:
1. Using B as centre and BC as radius, swing the end BC over to the base-line produced at X.
2. Bisect AX and draw a semi-circle using the point of bisection as centre.
3. Extend line BC to cut the semi-circle at M; then BM is the first side of the required square.

The line BM is called the **mean proportional** of AB and BC and produces the side of a square equal in area to the rectangle.

82

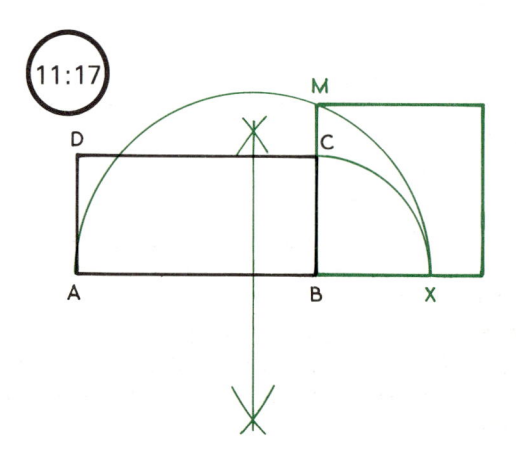

Drawing a square equal in area to an irregular polygon (ABCDE) (Fig. 11:18):
1. Follow the sequence detailed in Fig. 11:14, thus reducing the polygon to a triangle of equal area (FDH).
2. Reduce the triangle to a rectangle of equal area, as in Fig. 11:10 (RHJK).
3. Reduce the rectangle to a square of equal area as above.
4. FL is the first side of this square.

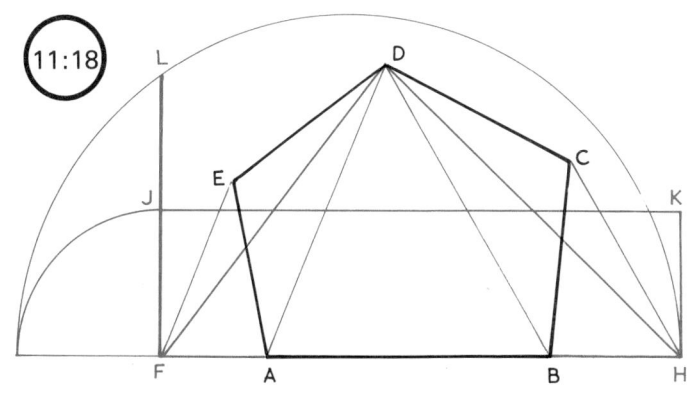

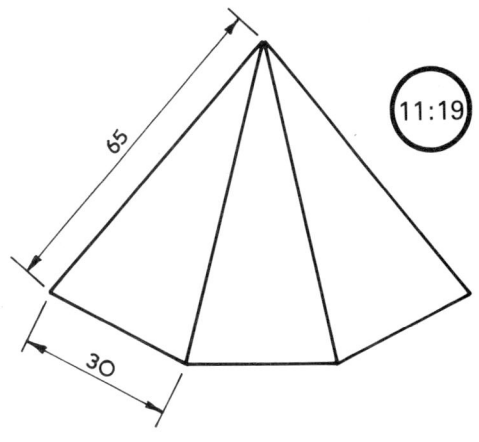

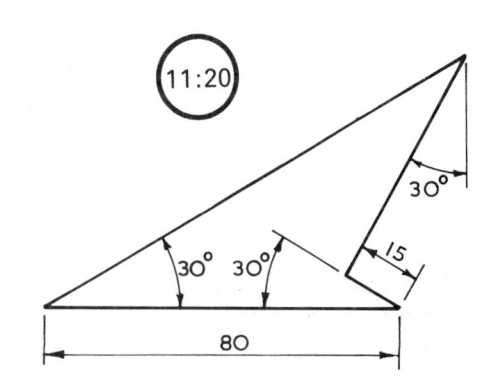

QUESTIONS

Q1 Given a rectangle with sides of 30 mm and 50 mm, draw a parallelogram equal in area and with one base angle of 40°.

Q2 A right-angled triangle has adjacent sides of 40 mm and 55 mm. Draw a rectangle equal in area.

Q3 Draw a triangle ABC having sides AB = 60 mm, BC = 55 mm, AC = 45 mm. Draw an isosceles triangle equal in area.

Q4 The area of a rectangle is 500 mm² (5 cm²). Draw a triangle equal in area.

Q5 A regular hexagon has a distance across corners of 80 mm. Reduce the hexagon to a triangle equal in area.

Q6 A triangle ABC has a base of 70 mm, a base angle of 50° and an altitude of 80 mm. Draw a triangle RST equal in area, but having an altitude of 65 mm.

Q7 A parallelogram has an altitude of 50 mm, a base side of 70 mm and a base angle of 45°. (i) Copy the parallelogram and draw a triangle equal in area. (ii) Draw a triangle equal in area to the first but with a base length 15 mm longer.

Q8 Adjacent sides of a parallelogram are 110 mm and 60 mm long and include an angle of 50°. Draw this parallelogram and reduce it to a square equal in area. Measure and write down the length of the side of the square.

Q9 The frame of a kite is shown in Fig. 11:19, and is formed by three triangles. Copy this figure and reduce the kite to a quadrilateral. Measure and state this area.

Q10 A re-entrant quadrilateral is shown in Fig. 11:20. Construct a triangle equal in area. State the area of the triangle.

CALCULATING AREAS BY GRAPHIC MEANS

Grid Method

Figure 11:21 shows a mass-produced name disc. The area is found by drawing one-centimetre squares over the drawn shape, counting the whole squares and approximating the total of the remaining squares.

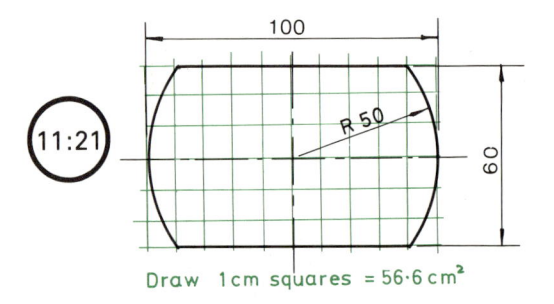

Draw 1 cm squares = 56·6 cm²

Figure 11:22 uses the same method but employs the use of 5 mm squares to obtain an area in mm².

Q11 Find the areas of Figs 11:22 and 11:23.

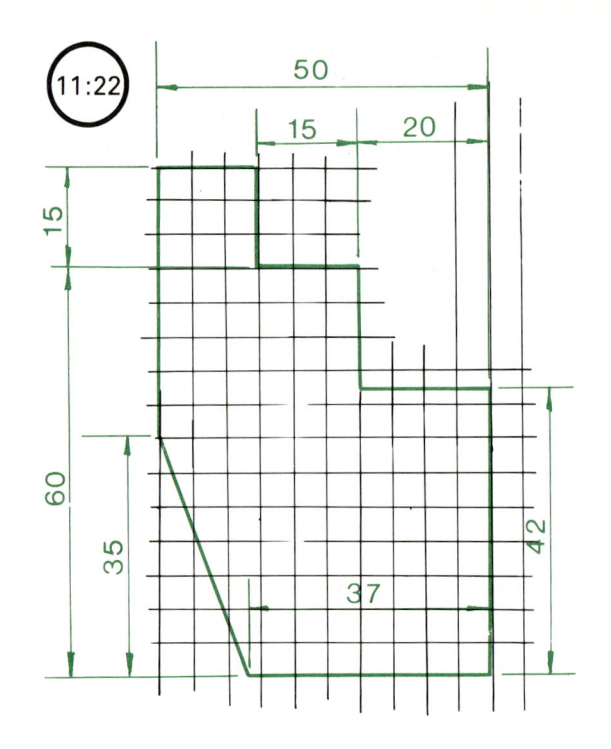

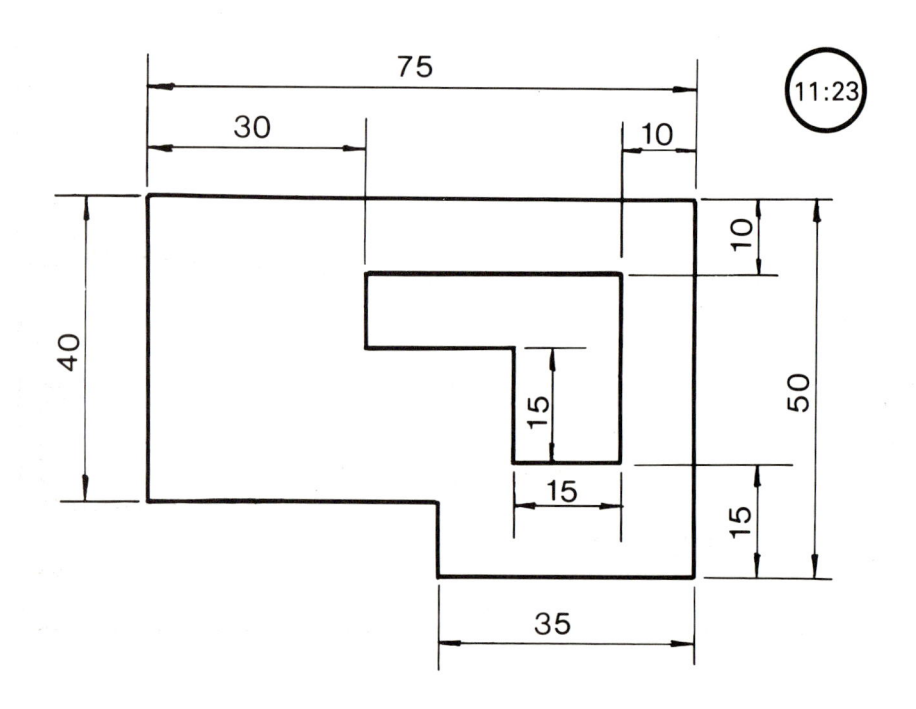

Mid-ordinate Method

Figure 11:24 shows the name disc divided on its central axis into 10 mm divisions. The mid-point of each division is then found and measured in length as centimetres. As each division is one centimetre wide the length in centimetres multiplied by 1 cm equals the area. The ten areas are then added to give a total area.

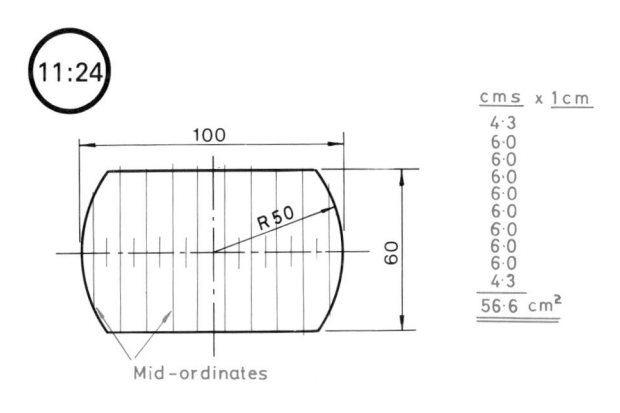

cms	x 1cm
4·3	
6·0	
6·0	
6·0	
6·0	
6·0	
6·0	
6·0	
6·0	
4·3	
56·6 cm²	

Q12 Calculate the areas of Figs 11:25 and 11:26.

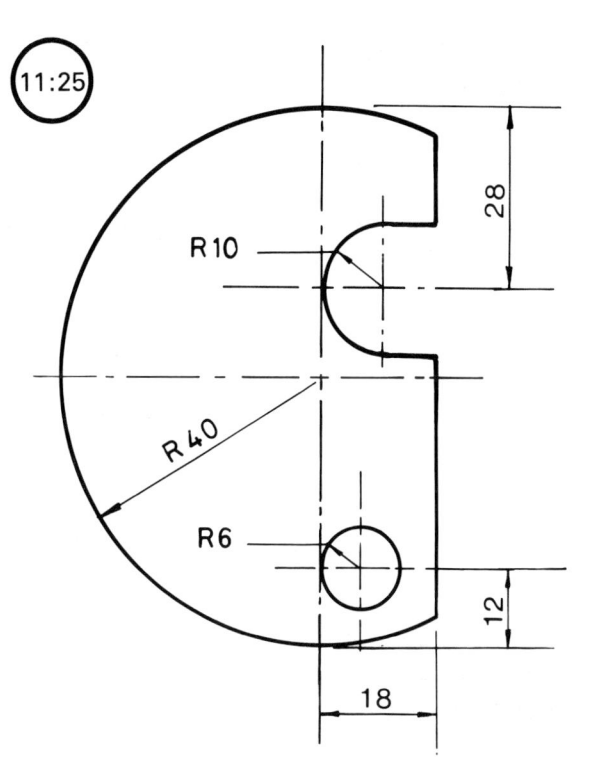

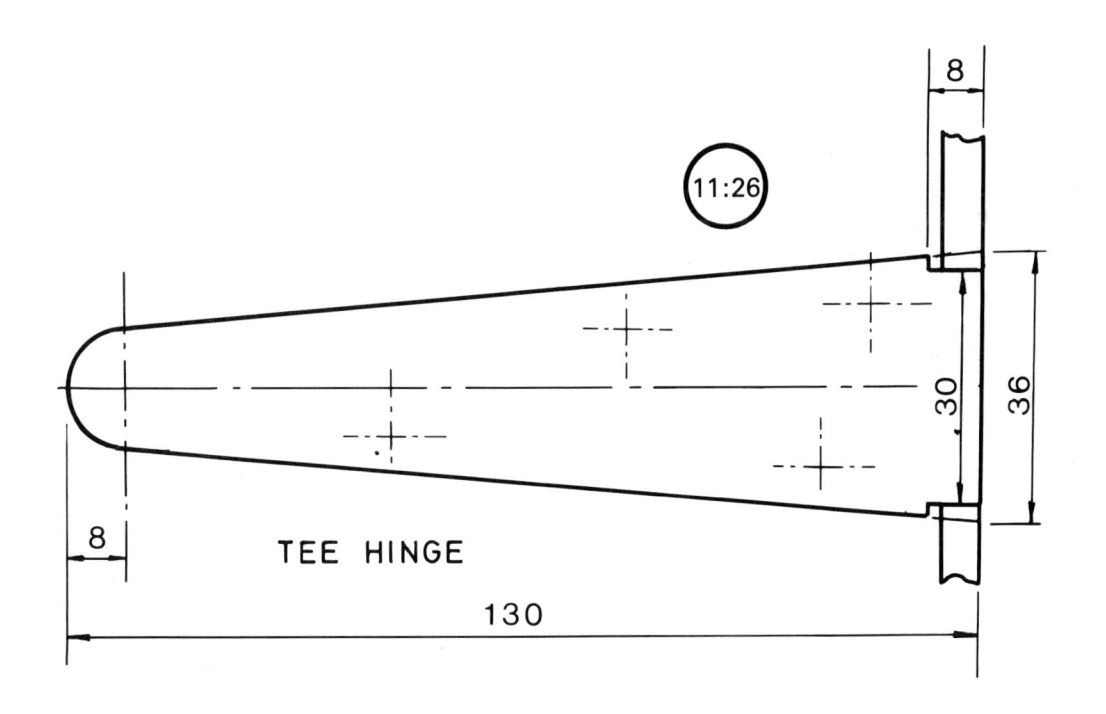

85

12 Enlargement and Reduction

Designers often have to alter the size of a figure proportionally, either by area or by the length of side. The easiest way to do this is by the construction of similar triangles, all drawn from one point (the **pole**) and passing through the corners of the figure.

The pole O may be set in any convenient position as shown in the three different solutions to the same problem in Figs 12:1, 12:2 and 12:3.

Drawing a polygon similar in shape to but having sides twice the length of those in a given polygon (ABCDE) (Fig. 12:4):
1. Using the corner A as a pole, draw radiating lines to pass through the corners BCDE.
2. Using dividers, step off the distance AE from E to establish point K.
3. Draw a line from K to J parallel to ED.
4. Similarly, draw lines from J to H parallel to DC and from H to G parallel to CB.
5. Join G to A to complete the enlarged polygon.

Drawing a polygon similar in shape to but having sides two-thirds of the length of a given polygon (ABCDEF) (Fig. 12:5):
1. Divide AF into three equal parts establishing AG as two-thirds the length of AF.
2. Complete as given in numbers 3, 4 and 5 above.

Reducing or enlarging figures using an external pole (Fig. 12:6):
1. Copy the given figure (ABCDE) and select a suitable site for the pole O.
2. Draw radiating lines from the pole passing through each corner ABCDE.
3. Produce DC to F making the ratio FC:CD equal to the ratio of enlargement or reduction required.
4. Draw FC parallel to OB and to cut line OC at C', the first corner of the new figure.
5. Draw C' to D' parallel to CD, thus obtaining the second corner.
6. Repeat the process round the radiating lines to complete the figure.

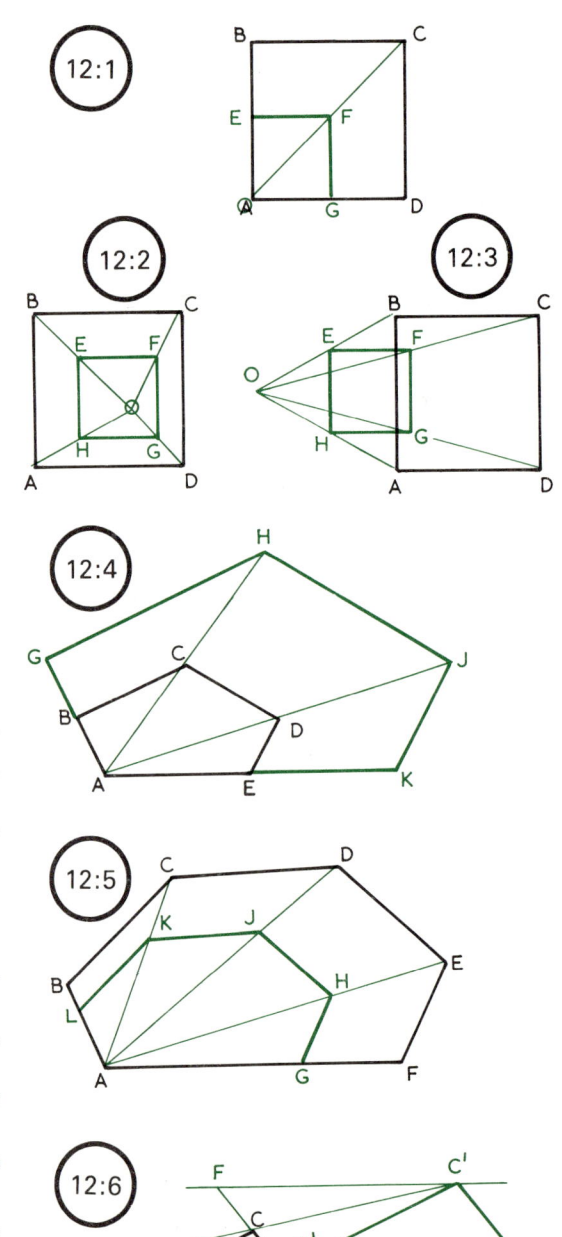

THEOREM OF PYTHAGORAS

Problems in areas can be solved by a graphic use of the theorem of Pythagoras combined with the mean proportional (see Fig. 11:17).

The theorem of Pythagoras states:

The square on the hypotenuse of a right-angled triangle is equal to the sum of the squares on the two opposite sides.

A ready way to establish the proof of this is to draw a right-angled triangle having sides of 3, 4 and 5 cm respectively. Draw the squares on each of the three sides and mark them out in centimetre squares as shown in Fig. 12:7. Counting the small squares proves that $AB^2 + AC^2 = BC^2$.

An interesting alternative method of proof is to dissect the largest square in such a way that it will fit exactly over the two smaller squares. Three different dissections are shown:

(1) In Fig. 12:8 the two enveloping outer squares are equal in area and the triangles A, B, C and D in both squares are equal to each other. Therefore, the square X (the square on the hypotenuse) in the left-hand figure is equal to the sum of the two squares Y and Z in the right-hand figure.

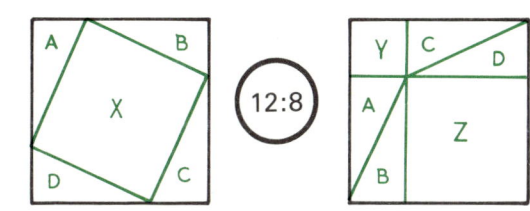

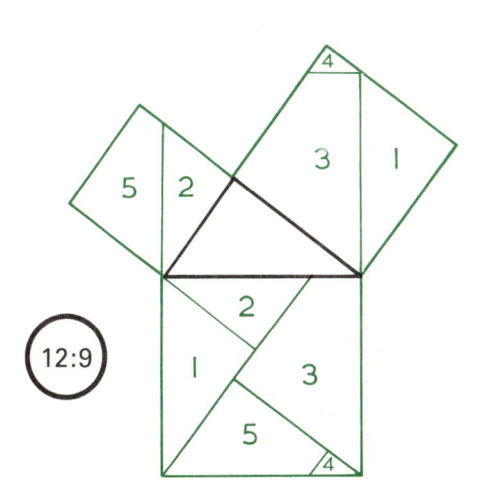

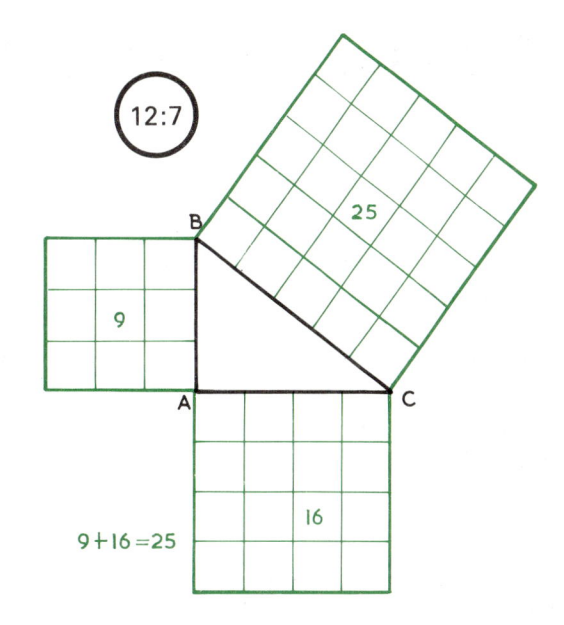

(2) Figure 12:9 shows a well known dissection. The parts number 1, 2, 3, 4 and 5 in the two upper squares fit perfectly into the lower square (the square on the hypotenuse).

(3) Figure 12:10 shows a simplified version of Fig. 12:9. Draw the two smaller squares side by side as shown. Transfer X, the length of side of the larger of the two squares, to the base-line to obtain point P. Join P to the two upper outside corners. The three parts A, B and C will then exactly cover the third and largest square.

The theorem of Pythagoras (Fig. 12:7) also applies to all other regular figures which may be drawn on the sides of a right-angled triangle.

Examples are given overleaf.

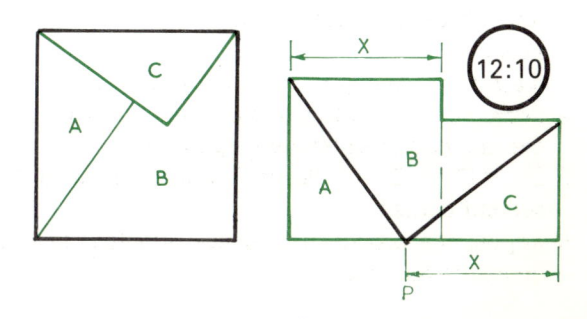

87

Drawing a circle equal in area to the sum of the areas of two given circles (Fig. 12:11):
1 Draw AC (45 mm) at right angles to AB (65 mm).
2 Join B to C and bisect this line, drawing a circle to pass through C and B.

This circle of diameter BC is equal in area to the sum of the areas of the two circles diameters AB and AC.

This is a useful construction for civil engineering draughtsmen as it greatly simplifies the designing of major water pipes and main sewers where the minimum bore diameters are required.

Drawing a regular hexagon equal in area to two given regular hexagons (Fig. 12:12):
1 Draw the base DE (50 mm), and at right angles to it, draw EF (30 mm) as shown. These are sides of the regular hexagons A and B.
2 Join D to F, and from this line construct hexagon C (see Fig. 5:17 for method).

Hexagon C is equal in area to the sum of the areas of the two hexagons A and B.

Subtraction of Polygons

Drawing a hexagon equal in area to the difference between two given regular hexagons (Fig. 12:13):
The two sides AB and AC are sides of the given regular hexagons.
1 Draw AB (80 mm); bisect it and draw the semicircle.
2 Using A as centre and AC (30 mm) as radius, cut the semicircle at C. Join AC.
3 Join CB to form a right angle in the semicircle: CB is the first side of the required hexagon.

Drawing an irregular pentagon of similar outline but having twice the area of a given pentagon (ABCDE) (Fig. 12:14):
1 Using A as centre and AE radius, draw an arc cutting the perpendicular from A at F.
2 Using E as centre and EF as radius, draw the arc cutting EA produced at A'.
3 Draw radiating lines from E through all the corners.
4 Draw a line from A' parallel to AB to establish point B'.
5 Draw a line from B' parallel to BC to establish point C' and similarly from C' parallel to CD to establish D', thus completing the figure.

AE = 25
AB = 22
ED = 20
CD = 26
BC = 30
EAB = 135°
AED = 105°

Because EF is the hypotenuse of a right-angled triangle, the solution depends on the theorem of Pythagoras and $AE^2 + AF^2 = EF^2$.

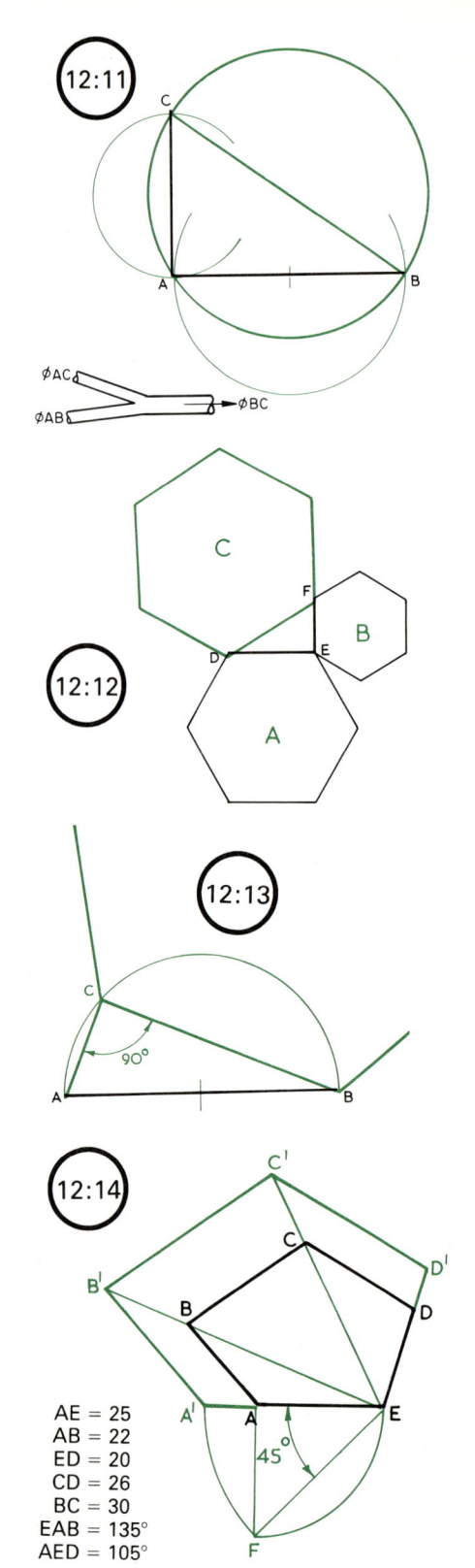

Reducing a given irregular pentagon (ABCDE) to a similar shape having only half its area (Fig. 12:15):
1. Draw radiating lines from E through all the corners.
2. Bisect AE at F and from this point drop a perpendicular making FG equal to FE.
3. Using E as centre and EG as radius, draw the arc cutting AE at A'.
4. Proceed to draw the parallels A' to B', B' to C' and C' to D' thus completing the figure.

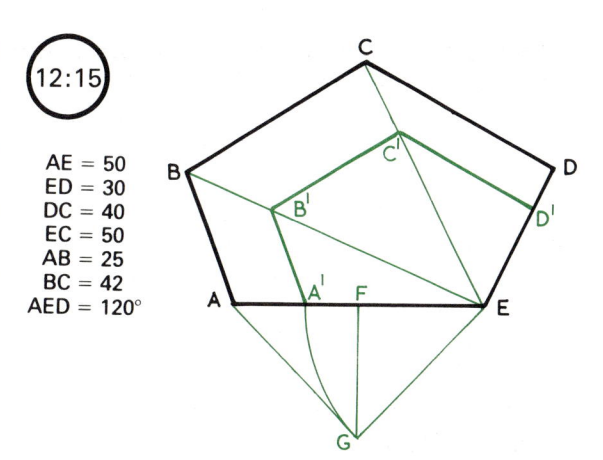

AE = 50
ED = 30
DC = 40
EC = 50
AB = 25
BC = 42
AED = 120°

Reducing a given irregular pentagon (ABCDE) to a similar shape and having an area in the ratio of 3:5 (Fig. 12:16):
1. Extend EA and from A step off 5 equal spaces of any convenient length and number them.
2. Bisect 5E and draw the larger semicircle. The centre for this semicircle does not necessarily fall at A.
3. Bisect 3E and draw the smaller semicircle.
4. Draw a perpendicular from A cutting the two semicircles in 3' and 5' respectively.
5. Draw a line from 5' to E, and a second from 3' parallel to this obtaining point E'.
6. Draw lines parallel to the sides of the original figures from E' to D', D' to C' and C' to B' to complete the figure.

AE = 35
AB = 25
AC = 62
BC = 60
ED = 45
CD = 23
EAB = 120°

Increasing the area of a given figure (ABCDE) in the ratio of 5:3 (Fig. 12:17):
The method of construction is similar to that in Fig. 12:16 except that in this case, the first diagonal is drawn from 3' to A and the proportionately increasing parallel is drawn from 5' to establish the first corner in A'.

Because a mean proportional is the square of two measurements, it is here combined with the right-angled triangle to solve the two problems.

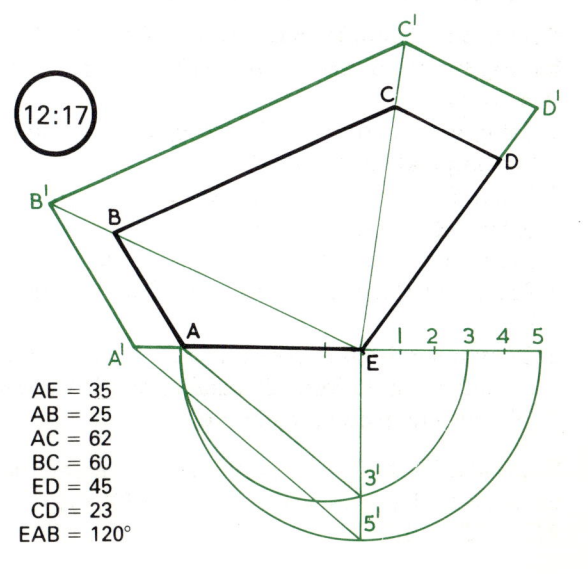

AE = 35
AB = 25
AC = 62
BC = 60
ED = 45
CD = 23
EAB = 120°

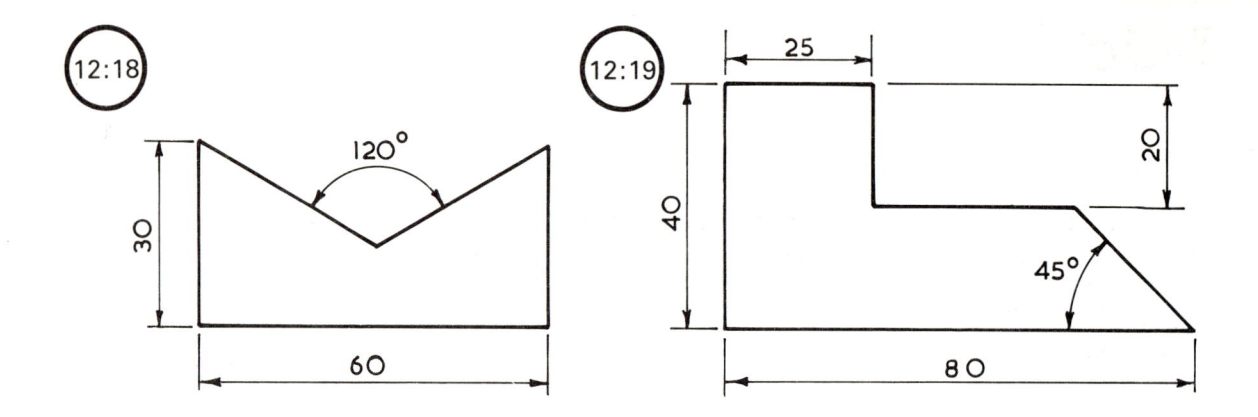

QUESTIONS

Q1 A polygon ABCDE has a base AB = 32 mm; BC = 46 mm, angle ABC = 120°; angle BAE = 120°, AE = 52 mm; angle BCD = 90°, CD = 72 mm. Construct a polygon similar in shape but having sides in the ratio three-quarters the length of the given polygon.

Q2 Copy the vee block (Fig. 12:18). Enlarge this proportionally to increase the base to 80 mm.

Q3 A ventilation shaft has two pipes of diameter 70 mm and 90 mm. These are to be replaced by one shaft that must have the same volume. Draw the two pipes and, by construction, the third pipe that is to replace them.

Q4 Given a regular hexagon of side 40 mm, draw a similar regular hexagon which has an area in the ratio of 3:2.

Q5 Draw a triangle ABC having sides of AB = 65 mm, BC = 70 mm, AC = 50 mm. Divide the triangle into two equal areas by a line parallel to AC.

Q6 Copy the wedge block (Fig. 12:19) and enlarge it to twice its area.

Q7 Given a triangle of sides 85 mm, 70 mm and 60 mm, reduce its area by two fifths.

Q8 Adjacent sides of a parallelogram are 100 mm and 60 mm long and include an angle of 60°.
(i) Draw this parallelogram and reduce it to a parallelogram in the ratio of three quarters, 3:4.
(ii) Divide the longest diagonal into two parts in the ratio 5:2. Measure and write down these lengths.

Index

Angles, 18, 21, 22
Arcs, 18, 46, 51
  blending, 51
  tangential, 50, 52
Areas, 79–83
  calculation of,
    grid method, 84
    mid-ordinate method, 85
Arrows, 14
Axes of ellipse, 61, 65

Bisecting lines, 19
  angles, 22
Blending arcs, 51

Centre-line, 8
Circles, 45, 46
  escribed, 59
  inscribing, 55
  properties, 46
  tangential, 50
Circumference, 46
Circumscribing figures, 57
Colour, 4, 13
Construction lines, 8

Deltoid, 37
Diameter, 46

Ellipse, 61
  drawing methods, 62, 63
  parts of, 61
  tangents to, 64
Enlargement, 76
  grid method of, 15
  of polygons, 86

Flow diagrams, introduction, 17
Foci of ellipse, 61

Graphics, introduction, 12
Grid, for calculation of area, 84
  for enlargement, 15

Hexagon, 40, 44, 56
House plans, introduction, 78

Inscribed figures, 55–7
Instruments, 1

Lettering, 7
Lines, 8
Loci, 68–73
Logograms, 66–7

Measuring, 5
Motion, 14

Normal, 46, 61

Octagon, 41
Ordinates, 85
Outlines, 8

Paper, 4
Parallel lines, 18, 20
Parallelograms, 35, 36
Pencils, 1, 2
Pens, 2
Pentagon, 42, 81, 82
Perpendicular, 18, 19
Pictograms, 13, 17
Polygons, 35, 38
  areas of, 79
Presentation of work, 6
Pythagorus, 87

Quadrilateral, 35, 37, 82
  areas of, 79

Radius, 46
Reduction, of polygons, 86
Rectangles, 36
Reducing, 86–9
Right-angled triangle, 27, 30
Rhombus, 37

Scale drawing, 74
Scales, 74–8
  diagonal, 76
  enlarging, 76
  reducing, 75
  surveying, 77
Set squares, 1
  angles, 23
Setting out, 6
Similar shapes, 88–9
  triangles, 30

Tangential circles and arcs, 50, 52
Tangents, 46, 48, 61
  common, 48
  external, 48
  internal, 49
  to ellipses, 64
Title block, 6
Triangles, 26–8, 56
  areas, 80–1
  construction, 28, 31
  properties, 28
  right-angled, 30
  types, 27
Trapezium, 37
Trapezoid, 37